PRAISE FOR A BURNING HOUSE

Prophetic truth is hard truth. It demands that we see what we would rather ignore and do what we would rather neglect. But prophetic truth is also hopeful truth, for it points us to One who redeems all things. This book speaks prophetic truth, in equal measure hard and hopeful. It calls us to look at our history and our present honestly, to see our place in both, to grieve, and to repent. And then it lifts our gaze to a vision of gospel-centered redemption that inspires and commands. Evangelicals need this book. Even more they need to heed its voice.

—**MARK YOUNG,** PhD, president, Denver Seminary

A Burning House falls in a category of its own when it comes to today's Christian literature. By joining biblical faith with sound reasoning, Pastor Brandon Washington tackles a number of sensitive topics such as race, history, culture, and the church. His presentation incorporates personal accounts with hard data to offer thought-provoking arguments pertaining to American evangelicalism. This book is real, relevant, and right on time for believers who desire to see God's kingdom come and his will be done, on earth as it is in heaven.

—**PASTOR JOHN K. JENKINS SR.,** senior pastor,
First Baptist Church of Glenarden

Brandon Washington has emerged as a much-needed prophetic voice for such a time as this. When many "*ex*vangelicals" are publicly disavowing American evangelicalism and leaving the church, he affirms his commitment to evangelicalism as he not only diagnoses what has gone wrong but offers a cogent way forward. He passionately calls us to restore American evangelicalism by a return to our roots by bringing the gospel to bear on sins such as injustice, racism, classism, and sexism. He deals with historical, cultural, and theological complexity in a way that is engaging and accessible.

—**CYNTHIA LONG WESTFALL,** PhD, associate
professor, McMaster Divinity College

Virtuous deconstruction is what Washington calls this exposé of racism in the history of the United States and the American church. This book is truly virtuous: it is honest while gracious, courageous, and informed. It is a timely call by an evangelical African American pastor-theologian to a compromised evangelicalism to rediscover its authenticity and commit itself to an authentic gospel and kingdom ethic. Direct, passionate, and constructive . . . a necessary word!

—M. DANIEL CARROLL R. (RODAS), PhD, professor of biblical
studies and pedagogy, Wheaton College and Graduate School

It is impossible to convey the content of the gospel without attaching cultural fingerprints. Such is the case with what my friend Brandon Washington repeatedly references as "American evangelicalism." Because of this we are in need of a "virtuous deconstruction," where the content of the gospel has been emancipated from its cultural captivity. *A Burning House* is a timely, prophetic forensic into this much-needed process.

—BRYAN LORITTS, PhD, author, *Insider/Outsider*

"Friendly fire" is a strange expression: How can accidental killing ever be "friendly," no matter who pulled the trigger? The expression should be reserved for warning shots fired to alert one to clear and present danger! In this book Brandon Washington, an African American evangelical pastor and scholar, provides us with "friendly fire" of this second kind. Rev. Washington is one of the friendliest and most committed Christians I know, but he has learned, seen, and experienced things in his life that many white evangelicals never have. Hopefully, we can work together to put out this fire and save the church.

—CRAIG L. BLOMBERG, distinguished professor
emeritus of New Testament, Denver Seminary

A
BURNING
HOUSE

A
BURNING
HOUSE

Redeeming American
Evangelicalism by Examining Its
History, Mission, and Message

BRANDON WASHINGTON

ZONDERVAN REFLECTIVE

A Burning House
Copyright © 2023 by Brandon Washington

Requests for information should be addressed to:
Zondervan, *3900 Sparks Dr. SE, Grand Rapids, Michigan 49546*

Zondervan titles may be purchased in bulk for educational, business, fundraising, or sales promotional use. For information, please email SpecialMarkets@ Zondervan.com.

ISBN 978-0-310-13939-3 (hardcover)
ISBN 978-0-310-13928-7 (audio)
ISBN 978-0-310-13927-0 (ebook)

Published in association with the literary agency of Wolgemuth & Associates, Inc.

Cover design: Brock Book Design Co.
Cover photo: © Photitos2016 / Getty Images
Interior design: Sara Colley

Printed in the United States of America

23 24 25 26 27 LBC 5 4 3 2 1

To
Cheri, the beloved wife of my youth (Prov. 31:10),
Reese, my sweetest daughter (Ps. 144:12),
and *Ellis*, my favorite son (Ps. 127:3–5)

CONTENTS

PART 4: REPENTANCE AND RESURGENCE

FOREWORD

IN ANY RELATIONSHIP, THERE WILL BE ARGUMENTS AND ANGER. TRUTH WILL cause sparks to fly. My best relationships are the ones that survive the sparks. One of my best friends in the world and I have had our share of spats. In the more intense disagreements, we don't speak for a week or so. However, we end up talking again and moving on despite the lack of agreement. With others, truth and disagreement can reveal the relationship's expiration date.

We have experienced, in our day, a schism of sorts in Western Christianity. It's not an overtly public schism (although there have been public fights), but in the eleven years since the fatal killing of Trayvon Martin and other police-related shootings of unarmed black men and women, there has developed a divide in the American church so deep that it defines fellowship. On one side are those who acknowledge systemic injustice and racism, and on the other are those who believe they are myths. The first group desires to get a full-bodied picture of our historical past involving racism to do an autopsy on our pending missiological death. The other views the past as moot and not requiring further study.

As a pastor, when I enter a counseling session with someone, I want to know three things: if and when they met Jesus, what they need, and what their family history looks like. People are always a product of sociological, emotional, psychological, and spiritual upbringings under which they were raised. That rearing environment is the stew that brewed them. To ignore their past would be a great misstep; it can inform me of the issues and story that produced their needs. The same is true of our broader culture.

It is critical that we visit the formation of the social construct of race. It has been weaponized to affirm one group and disparage others. Many within the evangelical movement seek to sweep the past under the rug and classify any talk of race as "Critical Race Theory." Once it has been tagged as "CRT" in those circles, it can be vilified and ignored. Massive damage has been done by attributing biblical assessment of partiality in America and the church to CRT, making it nearly impossible to find common ground to deal with the overt and covert challenges of race in our world.

Our familial past plays a role in our familial present as believers and humans. It is impossible to ignore the effects of chattel slavery. Its impact is still felt in how blacks are viewed and how we view ourselves. You cannot ignore black codes that were put in place to stifle the progress of the descendants of African slaves in America. How can we forget Jim Crow, which attempted to govern the access blacks had to human equality in states that enforced these laws? From redlining to the so-called war on drugs, descendants of African slaves have experienced a great deal of challenges in being valued as fully functioning citizens in this country.

At every phase of our country, many white Christians have played a role in both promoting racism and suppressing its systemic reality. During slavery many said, "Where in the Bible did slaves seek to be free? The Bible never makes that move." At the same time, they supported the American Revolution and the Declaration of Independence. During segregation others said, "Protesting isn't biblical. We must honor government." Yet they stood outside of abortion clinics with pictures of unborn fetuses to communicate the importance of a pro-life ethic—not just from a spiritual standpoint but from a socio-political standpoint as well. And more recently, when blacks fought for social reforms to counter decades of entrenched, systemic racism, many evangelical pastors said, "Politics don't belong in the pulpit" (although politics appear all through the pages of the Bible). Yet these same people used their pulpits to encourage their congregations to vote for Donald Trump.

Our country has seen a lot of hypocrisy come from the ranks of what many would call conservative evangelicalism. This has played a role in a generation becoming disillusioned with the faith. At the same time, another group calling themselves evangelicals sought to rebrand Christianity in America from a coconspirator with oppression to something full of grace and truth like the savior in whom we trust.

In 2020, Brandon Washington wrote a piece in *Christianity Today*, and it is one of the best written articles on the subject of racism and justice. I have recommended it to many people looking to get a grasp on this important conversation. Prior to being accused of CRT, I had never heard of it! Brandon has been a great help to me in this culture of conflict.

That is why this book by my dear friend and brother Brandon is enormously important in our time. Many skim an idea and then respond to it. Brandon isn't that way. Over the past two-and-a-half decades I've known him, he has taken a studious and thoughtful approach to any issue he takes on. His work in *A Burning House* is no different. It is a labor of love to help us get through the mire of information out there and to synthesize material that would overwhelm most.

Although this resource deals with history, sociology,

politics, and ethics, it is deeply theological as well. Brandon shows us it isn't enough to know what the gospel is; one must also know what the gospel does. Too much of evangelicalism has focused on the content of the gospel while neglecting and even denying its scope: applying the glorious incarnation, life, death, resurrection, and ascension of our Lord to the issues in our culture. With this volume, Brandon reminds us why Jesus told the Pharisees, "Woe to you, scribes and Pharisees, hypocrites! For you tithe mint and dill and cumin, and have neglected the weightier provisions of the Law: justice and mercy and faithfulness; but these are the things you should have done without neglecting the others" (Matt. 23:23 NASB).

Brandon has given us a seminal tome for reflecting on the racial-justice issues of our day in a balanced, honest, healthy way and engaging them with godliness, grace, and scholarship.

ERIC MASON

INTRODUCTION

Here is no unanchored liberalism—freedom to think
without commitment. Here is no encrusted dogmatism—
commitment without freedom to think. Here is a
vibrant evangelicalism—commitment with freedom
to think within the limits laid down in Scripture.
—VERNON C. GROUNDS[1]

SINCE MY CONVERSION, I'VE THOUGHT AMERICAN EVANGELICALISM WAS
mine—not possessively but relationally, as my wife and children are mine. But I've long since realized I am not hers. I'm
bothered by American evangelicalism's indifference toward
and participation in social brokenness. After years of consciously vying for the movement's racial integration, I wrestle
with the prospect that I've ushered dear people into a doltish,
in-house schism. It has resulted in a years-long night of depression that, if unaddressed, will descend into an unholy rage that
will consume me.

This book is my historical and theological appraisal of
American evangelicalism; writing it was cathartic obedience.
If readers can empathize, we may avoid dumping the favor-
able qualities of the movement into a trash heap with the

unfavorable. The adage "Don't throw the baby out with the bathwater" comes to mind. American evangelicalism is stymied by myopic political tribalism, so the line between the baby and the filthy water is not quickly discerned and our public dysfunction has provoked a public exodus *en masse*.[2] I do not affirm the exodus, but, frankly, I understand it. Dear friends bid me out of the evangelical house, and in recurring moments of disappointment and heartache, their voices are sirens' songs. But I will stand firm and seek redemption; doing so is, for me, compulsory (1 Cor. 15:58).

RACE

In America, we tend to treat *ethnicity* and *race* as synonyms. They are not. *Ethnicity* and *culture* have merit; they are deliberate and can be objective means of identifying people groups. But *race* is a somewhat new "social construct" born of depraved intent—a byproduct of an artificial human hierarchy.[3] Jarvis Williams sums it up best:

> The English term *race* first referenced human beings as a term of classification in the sixteenth century. In the eighteenth century, the term *race* was broadly applied to the diverse populations of native Americans, Africans, and Europeans in England's American colonies. In this historical context the term *race* developed to reference a hierarchal ranking system, which reflected English attitudes toward diverse groups of people.[4]

To be white was to be inherently superior; to be non-white was to be innately inferior.

Pejorative notions of race were not limited to bigoted

cliques like the Ku Klux Klan. The ethnic hierarchy was a mechanical value that permeated society. For instance, upon the death of Frederick Douglass, a premier American intellectual and abolitionist, the *New York Times* published a glowing obituary. Bizarrely, it conceded the American tendency to credit Douglass's intellectual acumen to his unidentified white father. It reads, "Every step that [Douglass] makes in advance of the inferior race from which he derives part of his ancestry is credited by whites to his white blood, and indeed there is no conspicuous instance of such steps being taken by a full-blooded African."[5] Superior intellect was treated as evidence of whiteness.

Even some black intellectuals defended the racial caste system. William Hannibal Thomas, a free-born black man, published *The American Negro*, a scathing critique of black Americans. In it he asserted, "There is, of course, broadly speaking, a common agreement in the public mind that the negro represents an accentuated type of human degradation."[6] His notions of black people were common. In America, the ideology of white supremacy was prevalent and fed the desire to insolently distinguish between "black" and "white" people. Even now, it plagues us. It resulted in the phenomenon known as "race."

THE INITIAL MOTIVES OF RACE

Race is a biological fiction ensuing from erroneous notions of human beings.[7] Historically, race classified individuals "as superior or inferior because they are believed to share imagined physical, mental, and moral attributes with the group to which they are deemed to belong."[8] True to form, journalist Ta-Nehisi Coates turns a gripping phrase to express this: "Race is the child of racism, not the father."[9]

The motives behind racialized categories were never veiled.

While serving as Senator of Mississippi, Jefferson Davis laid race bare by declaring, "White men have an equality resulting from a presence of a lower caste, which could not exist where white men fill the position here occupied by the servile race."[10] Following Davis's logic, his presumptuous rank as a "white" man necessitated stationing some people at the bottom. Davis did not devise this idea. Long before him, the American populace decided that blackness amounted to "servile," and whiteness connoted non-blackness.[11] In the nineteenth century, the Confederacy elected Davis Provisional President, and the pompous need to spread the notion of a black "servile race" was pivotal kindling for the American Civil War.[12]

Whiteness, as used by Davis and the likeminded, was not a thing; it was the denial of a thing. A seat at the top came with being coronated as "white," that is to say, nonblack. Blackness was a contrived cudgel of a racial caste system. In response, enslaved Africans and their progeny gradually and vigilantly refashioned blackness into a culture. It was a laudable act of resilience when they were far removed from Africa, but were not yet American. It is a prized culture conceived on the Atlantic in the cargo holds of slave ships and refined through and despite bondage, black codes, and Jim Crow.[13] I am able, with no reservations, to be a proud descendent of enslaved people who were cultural architects. And I am indignant toward those who diminish their formative story.

THE FLUIDITY OF RACE

After emancipation and Reconstruction, the intent behind *race* was tuned to the new circumstances. W. E. B. Du Bois called whiteness a "public and psychological wage" for "poor whites."[14] It was a consolation prize for white citizens who, though they may be relegated to the financial lower *class*, could take solace in being the racial upper *caste*. Dr. Du Bois maintained that *race* offered "poor whites in the nineteenth and early twentieth century a valuable social status bound to their categorization as not-black."[15]

The convenient fluidity of *race* demonstrates its artificiality.[16] For instance, in the nineteenth century, Italian Americans were provisionally white.[17] Historian Matthew Jacobson notes that they held a "racial middle-ground within the otherwise unforgiving, binary caste system of white-over-black."[18] Society acknowledged their racial ambiguity through mingled racist jabs like "white nigger."[19] The Jim Crow South subjected Italian immigrants to some of the same old hat xenophobia that was all too familiar to African Americans. Italian immigrants didn't inherit unabridged whiteness until the turn of the twentieth century. After the 1892 lynching of eleven Italian Americans in New Orleans, Louisiana, and other such atrocities, Italian immigrant organizations appealed for protection against "racial violence."[20] Racial recategorization was a strategic shield. The process was gradual, but today, Italian whiteness is a foregone conclusion. The opportune change— one of many of its sort—discloses the arbitrariness of race.[21] It is an artificial, uncredible means of grouping human beings.

A BEGRUDGING CONCESSION

While writing a book that includes racialized issues, I wrestled with a looming question: What does one do when a biological fiction is almost universally embraced as fact? Racial language is misleading, but it is pervasive. Today, race is like a feral horse that has never known restraint. It is out of the gate and corralling it is a formidable chore. Moreover, rectifying the fallacious connotations of race falls beyond this book's scope. I've concluded, begrudgingly, that the semantics are unavoidable here, so I use common racialized terms like "black" and "white." I'm encouraged by Paul's thoughtful use of pagan poets as he addressed the Areopagus (Acts 17:26–28). I hope to be lucid without giving credence to fraudulent racial notions. It's not ideal, but I pray it is fruitful.

Readers will note, whenever possible, I avoid referring to anyone as "master" or "slave," preferring, instead, "enslaver" and "enslaved." Calling someone a slave recognizes them as such; it almost legitimizes the term. But the word enslaved concedes a crime committed against a human being. I am willing, reluctantly, to use racialized language throughout this work, but never at the expense of human dignity and worth. Referring to real human beings as slaves is, for me, a bridge too far.

THE SCOPE OF THIS BOOK

N. T. Wright observes, "When you're writing theology, you have to say everything all the time, otherwise people think you've deliberately missed something out."[22] My experience sustains Wright's insight. I only add that theology is not the sole casualty of casual reading. *A Burning House* is not a book about "everything," so I did not write everything. If it is beyond this book's scope, I treat it with silence, which I believe is an act of intellectual integrity.

I am writing expressly about American evangelicalism, so I use the term *evangelical* according to the American connotation. This is relevant because various generations, countries, and cultures define the term varyingly. Historically, the word is roughly synonymous with *Protestant* and many global evangelicals still use the term in this manner.[23] But in America, evangelical describes a specific wave within the Protestant stream. It is a sub-movement within the broader, global movement. Depending on whom you ask, American evangelicalism has either evolved or devolved. Regardless of whom you ask, change has occurred. I maintain that much of the morphing was unhealthy; it took us off mission. In many ways, the American evangelical wave now defies the flow of the global evangelical stream. Evaluating the defiance is a sacred responsibility and the agenda of this book.

VIRTUOUS DECONSTRUCTION

Evaluating evangelicalism is an act of virtuous *deconstruction*. I use this language knowing it will provoke ire, but I choose the word unashamedly. Adulterations burden American evangelicalism, so vigilant critique is required. It is an arduous but beneficial task.

As a four-year-old, my brother, Edmond, hated the training wheels on his bicycle. They were needless encumbrances. So he set out to remove them, declaring, "I am too old for these." Our father came home to find, on our back patio, a haphazard collection of bicycle parts and a tearful boy. While capable of bike disassembly, my brother could not reassemble the requisite parts. Our father insisted Edmond restore the bicycle as he offered his unique brand of strident supervision. A half hour later, the bike reappeared—sans training wheels. From that day, my brother rarely consulted our father on bicycle repairs. A week later, he decided the kickstand was "dead weight," and he removed it without aid. He was able because the process of disassembly and supervised reassembly acquainted him with the bicycle's essential mechanics.

Aimless deconstruction can be devastating. It may result in tears shed over a mass of disjointed theological parts. But virtuous deconstruction is a fruit of good theological method and Christian apologetics. It acquaints believers with the mechanics of their faith. Virtuous deconstruction equips us to confront challenging questions about Christianity, even when the questions are our own.

Who supervises virtuous deconstruction? God does! Without blushing, I cite God as the vital actor, and doing so is no cliché. We have access to Scripture which is "God-breathed" and is thus the incomparable source of "teaching, rebuking, correcting and training in righteousness" (2 Tim. 3:16). Moreover, we have the "Spirit of truth" who "guides" us "into all truth" (John 16:13–16). It is from God that we receive our theological guardrails. But we also have human tutors—Christian ancestors who have done the heavy lifting. Generations of godly predecessors have codified our mission and values. We benefit from the catholicity (universality) of the church. It allows for the "longstanding posture of reception and transmission." Our Christian foreparents made a "deposit of faith."[24] If we hope to thrive, we must make withdrawals against their investments. We benefit from the intergenerational dialogue that allows for "theological retrieval."[25] We advance by carefully reclaiming and deploying credible, enduring values.[26] This is a salvage mission, and virtuous deconstruction is a requisite tool. *A Burning House* is a record of my process; it is also my theological deposit for future generations of believers (1 Tim. 6:20).

Part One

EVANGELICALISM AND RACE

DISCUSSIONS REGARDING THE CHRISTIAN IDENTITY CAN BE PLAGUED WITH rhetorical landmines. Ambiguity kills good conversations because we may talk at, instead of to, one another. When such an exchange is over, we've made little headway. To avoid such pitfalls, part I is a primer that, prayerfully, will prepare us before we delve into some contentious points. It summarizes the problem, clarifies key terms, and explains the historical method I use throughout this book. It is my attempt at orientation toward empathetic reading and irenic dialogue.

Chapter One

FRATERNAL TWINS BUT ALOOF STRANGERS

American culture is still reeling from the effects of the
[black] inferiority myth. Although the African-American
Church has its own distinctive and valuable appeal,
Christian whites presume that the brand of Christianity
that comes through the broader evangelical community is
the most significant vehicle of Christianity in America.
—ANTHONY T. EVANS[1]

I AM AN *EVANGELICAL*—AN ASSERTION RIFE WITH COMPLEXITIES. WITH EACH passing day, it grows more taxing, but I am unmoved.[2] In subsequent chapters, I will define and qualify what I mean by "evangelicalism." I am aware of the tarnished public image; in many regards, it is well-earned. Credible evangelicals persist and perhaps always will, but, as a movement, American evangelicalism is on life support. I maintain that the wound is self-inflicted—the product of a truncated gospel message and a self-lauding understanding of history.[3] It is an offense committed by a camp that plausibly professes to be Christian.

They are my eternal siblings, so I seek their repentance instead of my exit.[4]

My assessment is not that of a stranger speaking into this matter from the outside. I ask that you hear my critique with my evangelical pedigree in mind. I graduated from an estimable evangelical seminary where I now serve on the board of trustees. I am an alumnus of a respected church planting residency and I gratefully partner with my mentors to train the next generation of church leaders. I am also the cofounder and preaching pastor of a Bible-believing church; expository preaching is a tenet of our corporate worship gatherings. Doctrinally, I fall squarely within the pale of evangelical Christian orthodoxy, and, due to deliberate theological and apologetics studies, I do so with conviction. I am not immodestly laying out a résumé, but in Pauline fashion (Phil. 3:4–7), I provide this biography to assert that if evangelicalism has poster children, I am among them.

Here's the rub: I am also *unapologetically black*![5] I maintain that my ethnicity and culture, along with the ethnicities and cultures of all my brothers and sisters, are deliberate facets of God's divine plan to gather a mosaic of worshipers.[6] My evangelicalism and my blackness are not at odds. Instead, they move cooperatively toward "a great multitude that no one could number, from every nation, from all tribes and peoples and languages, standing before the throne and before the Lamb" (Rev. 7:9 ESV).[7] God relishes an array of voices that rehearse his glory back to him.[8] Our diverse cultural expressions and theological lenses mingle with our understanding and applications of the gospel; the Bible sustains this mingling. Scot McKnight plays this note well while commenting on Paul's letter to the Romans:

> Ethnicity, then, is at the heart of both the tension in Rome and the gospel message itself. One's theology and one's

ethnicity cannot be segregated, and neither can one's ethnicity and one's identity be separated. There is, then, a
dialectical relationship between ethnicity and theology
throughout the entire letter.[9]

Overlooking ethnicity and culture is exegetically irresponsible
and theologically shortsighted.

A FAMILY DIVIDED

Within American evangelicalism, there are divergent views of
mission, especially regarding the gospel's relevance to systemic
injustice and racism. The divergence prompts a poignant question: Must I choose between evangelicalism and my cultural
identity? Esteemed black leaders have spotlighted this dilemma
by publicly challenging American evangelicalism's inward-
looking take on history, culture, and theology. Many of these
leaders have concluded that dissociation is their healthiest
choice.[10] Despite shared doctrine, white and black evangelicals
generally split regarding social ethics.[11] The rift is so old we
treat it as fated.[12]

Many of my dear friends—all orthodox Christian leaders—
suggest I eschew the evangelical label. They argue that the
movement dishonors my blackness, personal story, and the history of black people in America. Through public tears, I affirm
their concerns. Historically, the black evangelical's perspective
has been relegated to a backseat voice, occasionally recognized
but lowly regarded.[13] American evangelicalism invites black
Christians to come along for the missional ride, but rarely
as the driver. We can now partake in the purported honor
of attending an evangelical seminary where we learn to do
theology through cultural lenses other than, and often at the

expense of, our own. Hard-line evangelical institutions may promote a black leader to the role of ethnic minority spokesperson on the condition that they toe the line.[14] Whispers of observed racism are spurned and written off as ingratitude. For many, including me, it is a paternalistic backhanded slap under the pretense of a father's right hand of fellowship.

In my experience, daring to challenge evangelicalism's cultural myopia is deemed inappropriate. Some have even branded me a "false teacher" despite our near-identical doctrinal stances. This behavior only unveils the role that culture plays in mainstream evangelicalism. Erroneously, we perceive the movement as merely theological, independent of cultural influence. I challenge the belief that our biblical and systematic theologies escape our cultural biases. While I acknowledge that theology is a defining aspect of evangelicalism's identity, I also recognize that everyone does theology through experiential and cultural lenses.[15] Integrity compels us to concede American evangelicalism's preoccupation with the white cultural perspective.[16] The "false teacher" charge is rarely about doctrine. It is typically a reaction to my critiques of the American evangelical penchant for radical culturalism and its blinkered interpretation of the world.

Fixation on one cultural lens results in a poor understanding of history, which has implications for theology and mission. Past atrocities are revised, diminished, justified, or even erased from our historical narrative to maintain the aura of exceptionalism.[17] This trend is scandalous because many of the overlooked offenses of the past shaped America. They are formative, so ignoring them results in a grossly flawed view of the present.[18] It is the reason, on the whole, that black and white evangelicals see the world in such fundamentally different ways. For instance, racial marginalization readied the black church to lead from societal margins with an eye toward justice.[19] Conscious black Christian leaders remember and value this past. They did not fabricate the link between the Bible and justice (Amos 5; Mic. 6:8; Matt. 25:34–40; Luke 4:16–19; cf. Isa. 61:1–2). But centuries of ostracism made the black church sensitive to the gospel's relevance in an unjust, racialized world.[20] Deliberately forgetting the past only obscures present injustices and shrinks the gospel's pertinence.

Despite our seemingly shared message, there is a shocking gulf within evangelicalism. If evangelical representatives of non-white and non-Western peoples were recognized in church history and theology, American evangelicalism may see racial and social brokenness as gospel issues. Instead, the twentieth century saw the rise of calloused arguments to the contrary. So the relationship between black and white evangelicals progressively erodes. We share language regarding the gospel, but we divide on many of its implications. We engage one another from opposite sides of a yawning gulf, so our so-called oneness is, at best, dubious. Many black evangelicals wonder if we have been little more than distant cousins in a dysfunctional family.[21] We are kin, but we are divided.

WHY WRITE A BOOK?

Formative childhood experiences drive me to tackle ethnic discord. As a twelve-year-old, I esteemed the Nation of Islam (NOI), which was not uncommon among black male teens during the late 1980s and early 1990s. Hip-hop messengers— skilled wordsmiths like KRS-One and ably conscious groups like Public Enemy—breathed life into the pseudo-Islamic sects, which, at the time, were more than a decade into their decline.[22] The sects acquired traction amid post-civil rights frustrations. My roused interest led me to read a paltry biography of Malcolm X and, ultimately, his more excellently written autobiography—a collaboration with Alex Haley.[23] His story is compelling. I was captivated by proud, ostensibly well-read black men. They answered questions regarding my history and worth. They were bold, well spoken, and willing to say unpopular things. I was smitten—a moth to a flame.

At the time, I lacked theological insight and oversight. I was unequipped to appraise the NOI's tenuous theology. Still, even as a boy, I was taken aback by odious language like "blonde-haired, blue-eyed devils" and the daft story of Yakub, a renegade scientist who fashioned "the white man" through selective breeding.[24] NOI theology is compellingly absurd; even my untrained adolescent mind noticed. However, in my experience, the NOI pondered critical questions on history, inter-ethnic conflicts, and systemic injustice. Though the NOI's theological propositions were usually a disturbing dance back and forth between doubtful and bizarre, many of their questions were legitimate. They deserved honest pondering. Where the NOI had dismaying answers to valid questions, American evangelicalism, by and large, disregarded the questions altogether or provided equally disconcerting retorts. I was taught, repeatedly, that we need only endure until Jesus returns. I could easily ignore Christianity because it turned a blind eye to my heartache.

I was delivered from the NOI during my senior year of high school and became a Christian during my sophomore year of college. My introduction to Christianity occurred under a pastor-mentor's watchful eye. He possessed a carefully reasoned faith, which allowed him to be calm and unmoved in the face of opposition. It pleased me to meet a regular person who knew what and why he believed. He was, for me, custom made. Because of his guidance, I am among the rare birds who knowingly benefitted from Christian apologetics *before* conversion. I will not go so far as to say that my transformation was solely intellectual; that would be an unbiblical take on salvation (1 Cor. 12:3). However, while the Spirit engaged my hard heart, my Spirit-led mentor engaged my mind with explanations and defenses of the Christian faith. He taught me that biblical faith and sound reasoning are not in conflict; they are cooperative. Accepting Christ as my redeemer was a *rational act of Spirit-led surrender.* The God of creation confronted me in both heart and mind. My route to conversion taught me that submission to Christ does not occur at the expense of thinking. On the contrary, my mind experienced a turn toward God, so I am to "take captive every thought to make it obedient to Christ" (2 Cor. 10:5; cf. Col. 2:8). I still savor the moment when I committed to thinking publicly for my king.[25]

If thinking is an act of worship, then even my faith should be examined (1 John 4:1–6; 2 Cor. 13:5), which created problems. Bear in mind, I spent the entirety of my adolescence as a sympathizer of the NOI, where segregation is a divine value. I was running away from such notions. So I could not overlook the peculiar gap in the church's message and practices. They reminded me of the absurdities I'd hoped to escape. We are one body, under one God, redeemed by one Christ, and empowered by one Spirit (Eph. 4:4–6; 1 Tim. 2:5–6). So I was dizzied by our tendency to, without apparent irony, celebrate our oneness while thoughtlessly modeling apartheid. This behavior prompted me to ask, "Why is the church, the messenger of a unifying gospel, as segregated as the siloed cults that proudly preach antigospels?"

I suspected the church viewed segregation as beneficial—even virtuous. The succeeding decades have substantiated my suspicion. In the first year of planting The Embassy Church, a well-regarded missiologist read our proposal at the behest of a respected pastor in our city. The pastor hosted a meeting between the missiologist and me and suggested bringing a legal pad to note his "expert counsel." The missiologist, a white seminary professor, wasted no time criticizing our church's emphasis on *diversity and integration*. He said, "You are black; if you wish to be successful, you should target only the black people in your neighborhood." His advice showed ignorance or indifference toward the intensifying gentrification occurring in northeast Denver. In his defense (assuming there is such a thing!), he was applying a value. As an "expert," he suggested segregation as a tactic toward numeric success. He sincerely advised leaning into our sinful divisions. That was his strategic plan—our kingdom witness be damned.

Church planting and numeric growth were the missiologist's areas of expertise. Both research and experience taught him that my blackness would effectively draw black people, so I should use it to that end. He believed that if I "attempt to pastor white people, the church will close its doors within five years." "Don't worry about integrating the church," he quipped, "just get people saved. God will make us one when we are all in heaven. Surely you agree with that." It aggrieved me that he was simultaneously smug and enthusiastically wrong. I replied, "Yes, I agree; we will be one when Christ returns. Until then, I feverishly pray '[God's] kingdom come, [God's] will be done, *on earth as it is in heaven*' (Matt. 6:10). Surely *you* can agree with *that*."

The missiologist did not sift his advice through a biblical filter, but that was not his sole blunder. His counsel lacks real-world viability. It values cultural and theological myopia, even when the community is multicultural. His strategy appeals to our consumeristic desire to surround ourselves with people who are like us and avoid those who are "other."[26] The decision to divide into ethnic and cultural silos may result in numeric growth, but it also contributes to needlessly divergent views of the world and theology. Consciously or unconsciously, we bend toward empiricism.[27] Cynicism is automatic when we hear testimony that does not align with our personal experiences. For instance, when a minority group laments injustice, a privileged group may, without genuine inquiry, refute the legitimacy of the lament. The tendency is exaggerated in a deliberately segregated society because alien people are easier to ignore.[28] It plagues even the church—a citadel that should provide sanctuary to the stranger (Lev. 19:34; 27:19; Matt. 25:35).[29] I observed this value within months of my Christian conversion. It is, for American evangelicalism, the status quo.[30] Due to either indefensible blindness or malicious indifference, many of my white eternal siblings neglect the history and ongoing experiences that injure people of color. The movement is willfully surrendering its credibility among minority people groups. I maintain that the mass exodus that plagues American churches is a sure result of the lauded status quo.[31]

For me, the reaction to Trayvon Martin's senseless death was the anvil that broke the camel's back. Trayvon did nothing to invite his demise. He was a beautiful boy walking home from a convenience store armed with nothing but tea and candy. He was deemed a threat by a total stranger who, driven by unwarranted and false assumptions, ignored the directive of a 911 operator and followed him. After an inexplicable confrontation, the stranger killed the boy and suffered no pronounced consequence.[32] I never met Trayvon, but I am a black man and the father of a black boy whom I adore. Trayvon's death provoked deep, almost incapacitating empathy. I mourn him as my own. I awaited evangelical voices that would honor the imperative to "weep with those who weep" (Rom. 12:15 ESV). I was disheartened and further wounded by the indolent response.

To be sure, in the aftermath of Trayvon's death, white

kingdom cohorts stood with me and made public commitments to a full-orbed gospel. It would be unloving and negligent to overlook their boldness and their sacrifice. Still, I lament the realization that they are, by far, the minority. Many are still publicly scorned for their empathy. We preach a message that confronts social ills, and detractors deem it "a different gospel." Friends, mentors, and associates broke my heart with socially illiterate public statements, open letters, and utterly irresponsible social media posts. Regarding the American ethnic rift, they'd been mute their entire lives. But as we mourned the senseless death of a beautiful boy, they became authorities and spoke up from the sidelines, disparaging weary players who'd been on the field for years.

Aloud, I inquired, "What does it look like for the gospel to come to bear on this moment?" Many of the responses only salted my wounds. I was asked, "How do you know Trayvon didn't do something that warranted his death?" Let us pause and consider the implications of that question. Instead of mourning, we defaulted to making sense of the senseless by debating explanations of the moment—willing even to blame the boy. It is a knee-jerk reaction to the world's complexities. If we can contrive a simple explanation, we do not need to enter the fray. Another added, "Trayvon's death is unfortunate, but what does it have to do with the gospel?" These questions were eye-opening. They taught me that I'd falsely assumed I was surrounded by empathetic family members.

I've concluded I am an inconvenient guest in American evangelicalism's idyllic house. I believe the gospel compulsorily confronts our eternal condition *and* the world's palpable brokenness—a message I'd long believed was shared (Eph. 2:1–22). I was wrong. We are woefully askew of one another. Many who sound an alarm are written off as emotional reactors instead of rational believers with legitimate observations and coherent concerns. We are accused of reading "a new canon."[33]

Thankfully, we worship a king who knows and sees the "other" (John 4:4–42).[34] We are blessed with a gospel message that is both heavenly-minded and of earthly good. When we emphasize the gospel's eternal fruits while disregarding its implications on the world's struggles, we are guilty of reducing the message. We have lost our kingdom way. The problem is old and tenacious. I must address it—thus, this book.

A COUNTERINTUITIVE SOLUTION

While adjusting to the realization that I am a guest in the house that I'd previously deemed the family dwelling, I must discover how it occurred. It cannot go unexamined. It is among the reasons I, for this season, defy the appeals of brothers and sisters who insist I leave and join the movement of "exvangelicals." I concede their observations, but my conscience compels me to stay and struggle. What if the movement they are leaving is not evangelicalism at all? What if it has been co-opted by masqueraders cloaked in evangelical garb? Maybe American evangelicalism has abridged the global evangelical message and is, therefore, off mission. I am not saying they are preaching an accursed gospel, but if it has little regard for systemic racism and injustice, the message is truncated and temporally inadequate.[35] If we leave, we may be surrendering our house to interlopers. It is inappropriate for us to relinquish the moniker evangel—"The gospel"—to those who will reduce it. So I submit a question that has long engrossed me: Should we abandon the house or reclaim it?

An examination of American evangelicalism is a historical and theological venture. I suspect the ethnic rift within the movement results from divergent theological and historical methods based on cultural distinctions. I am not contending that cultural identities are innately wrong. On the contrary, culture and experience are unavoidable influencers that, when properly deployed, are advantageous.[36] However, they are catastrophic when someone blindly universalizes their version of Christianity without considering the observations of other Christian forms. This tendency contributed to America's racial rift. In theological terms, black evangelicals and white evangelicals are fraternal twins in *orthodoxy* (beliefs) but aloof strangers in *orthopraxy* (actions). By and large, they espouse the same foundational views, but they apply them in different, often conflicting, ways.

Generally, American evangelicalism espouses a culturally isolated view of the world. For instance, Christianity is commonly parceled as an embodiment of Western values. I've spoken on more than one Christian university campus that lauds Westernization as uniquely indicative of God's character. But the Bible is decidedly non-Western.[37] In an act of fascinating hubris, American evangelicalism attempts to improve upon the original model by roughly forcing Christianity in a Euro-American mold. This is unfortunate because there is much to glean from Christian groups that better embody the Bible's non-Western communal values.[38] When American evangelicalism carefully incorporates the credible perspectives of non-Western evangelicals, it will become a more robust Christian worldview.

By and large, our impaired orthopraxy results from segregation. Siloed Christianity robs its participants by depriving them of fellow believers and their theological perspectives. The upshot is stark: *We do not segregate due to theological conflict; we are in theological conflict due to willful segregation.* If we recognize this, then integration, though counterintuitive, is the obvious solution. We must sacrificially run toward, not away from, one another. Integration confronts corporate ignorance by exposing us to theological ideas and cultural contexts other than our own. In our siloed condition, we have an impaired view of the mission field, so we are falling short of our kingdom potential.

A BURNING HOUSE

I am no fool. I know of the elephant in the room. Evangelicalism is not merely a house divided; it is a house ablaze. Black people are legitimately suspicious of integration.

After civil rights progress in the mid-twentieth century, desegregation was America's professed norm. Still, Martin Luther King Jr., paraphrasing James Baldwin, admitted, "I've come to believe that we are integrating into a burning house."[39] I empathize with King's realization. I've often confessed the same of the evangelical house. King recognized that mere interethnic proximity is inadequate. If the house is divided— plagued by racism—then a seat inside is no better than the torrential storm outside.[40] His 1963 "I Have A Dream" speech is his most cited message. But many who quote it appeal to one or two self-serving lines to the exclusion of the speech's broader, indicting tenor. What's worse is the disregard for King's hindsight critique of those oft-quoted lines. In retrospect, he conceded, "The dream that I had that day has, at many points, turned into a nightmare." He confessed, "Some of the old optimism was a little superficial, and now it must be tempered with a solid realism."[41] While new laws expressed desegregation, integration was still unrealized.[42]

American history is blotted by segregation because the nation prioritized the dignity and worth of one racial group at the expense of the others. The end of slavery was only the

prelude to Jim Crow—an elaborate racial caste system that
openly enforced "separate but equal," an outright lie.[43] Then,
as the civil rights movement agitated the country toward desegregation, Jim Crow laws were less viable, so society fell back
on its organic norms and maintained racial divisions. Dr.
King summed it up when he deemed desegregation "enforce-
able" while conceding that integration is "unenforceable."[44]
Desegregation was a matter of law, but integration fell victim
to national norms and values.

After the Supreme Court's unanimous decision in *Brown
v. Board of Education* (1954), touted as the death knell of Jim
Crow, racial segregation remained a de facto cultural norm.[45]
Even churches willfully resisted the legal imperative to deseg-
regate.[46] The cultural values were so effective that the nation
needed the Civil Rights Act of 1964, the Voting Rights Act
of 1965, and the Fair Housing Act of 1968! Notwithstanding
the nation's professed allegiance to the US Constitution, the
thirteenth, fourteenth, and fifteenth Amendments were pow-
erless against de facto segregation in the post-Reconstruction
era.[47] Even after 1960s civil rights legislation reinforced these
amendments, armed federal officers had to escort black children into disingenuously desegregated schools amid perilous
protests. Actions did not align with words. The "melting pot"
was the declared value, but a racial caste system was the actual
value. So regarding integration, black people can be predict-
ably cynical.

Both history and common sense teach that it is foolish to
integrate into a house that is ablaze. If the structure is burning
to the ground, who cares if we are all together! Self-preservation
is a rational act, so potentially injurious integration is counterintuitive. I understand and even share the concerns of those
who resist integration, especially if many occupants of the
burning house are relational arsonists. However, unlike the

world, we have the gospel—a comprehensive, effectual, and compelling message. Holding American evangelicalism to standards set by a fallen world results in sinfully low expectations. We should strive for the virtues of Christ, our king. The world cannot, and should not, determine our ethical values! We have a message of reconciliation, so deliberately living without one another is "not in step with the truth of the gospel" (Gal. 2:11–14 ESV). Willful segregation is the fruit of an "antigospel."[48] It condones and even adopts the world's sin, which is theologically incoherent. The cross unifies kingdom citizens so they may jointly laud our unifying king (Eph. 2:11–22).[49]

In many respects, I concede that integration has failed. Often, it is a disingenuous façade—an attempt to show health where illness abounds. But some missions are vital; they compel us to persist. Unity around a comprehensive gospel message is such a mission. We cannot cite a history of half-hearted desegregation as justification for disunity. Christ purchased our union at the highest price. Embodying his kingdom, though taxing, is "true and proper worship" (Rom. 12:1–2).[50]

SACRIFICIAL INTEGRATION VERSUS DISHONORING ASSIMILATION

Many of my friends who reject integration cite the poor way we've done it. But I contend they've never experienced a genuine attempt. We've known only disingenuous desegregation. Integration, especially on a global scale, is exponentially more communal. Desegregation means I can no longer legally reject you, but integration prompts me to engage you willingly. The former values legal and ethical loopholes, while the latter values people and community.

Assimilation occurs when a dominant group sits idle as

all other groups huddle around and espouse their take on the world. Integration occurs when all of the groups sacrificially move toward one another. More often than not, a dominant culture reigns over a diverse group. Those who fall outside the dominant culture must assimilate the dominant language and norms to thrive. My education in the evangelical world regularly necessitated "code switching," traversing back and forth between cultures.[51] By and large, my white classmates did not experience this. There was no need because American evangelicalism generally fixates on white cultural norms.

In my first semester of seminary, the cultural rifts were impossible to ignore. I had to discuss it more often than I wanted. One conversation stands out. It was with a classmate who is now my friend. But our relationship had a complicated launch. Within weeks of our meeting, he asked, "Why do I have to see you as a black Christian? Why can't I just see you as a Christian brother? Isn't our faith more important than our race?" His queries were sincere but tremendously naïve. They underscore an often-overlooked state of affairs. My classmates were oblivious to their culture's ubiquity. It is so common that they overlook its influence on their Christian education and values.[52] As a fish in water is inattentive to its wetness, my classmates were so immersed in their culture that they were insensible to it. They believe they espouse a virginal Christianity—uninfluenced by culture. They treated our studies as a collection of universal facts. But, in reality, we were straightforwardly learning Euro-American Christianity, and few seemed to notice. Moreover, they obligated me to uncritically adopt the culturalized theology. More than once, my suspicions were met with, "Isn't our faith more important than race?" It may have been unwitting, but they were subjecting me to dishonoring assimilation.

I will not waste this moment by ignoring the difference between diversity and integration. Ethnically diverse worship gatherings make for first-rate photo ops, but in the absence of genuine integration, some in the photo are not reciprocally valued. They are merely assimilating the dominant culture. If integration will work, the house's occupants must receive mutual honor (Phil. 2:1–11). Cultural integration, especially on a global scale, is foreign to American evangelicalism. It should not be; Christianity is innately global.[53] So we should not merely battle theological error; we should repent of theological isolationism.

Our options are limited. We can divide into separate homes or perish together in a needless housefire of our own making. These decisions dishonor God; we have seen the rotten fruits they bear. A third option, mutually honoring cultural integration, may be counterintuitive, but the alternatives are sinful. American evangelicalism is a burning house. Do we find an exit or honor Dr. King's proposal to "become firemen"?[54]

MY PLEA AND MY PRAYER

Confronting sin is an evangelical imperative. So, ironically, where American evangelicalism has sinned, I am compelled to speak and act. But *redemption* is also an evangelical value. I desire to honor God by upholding these complementary duties without compromise. Assuming I have the means to douse the flames, I am derelict, or worse yet, disobedient, if I abandon the burning house. I plead with you: read the following work while mindful of the balance between confronting sin and desiring redemption. I pray that God's sovereign plan will be honored and that our corporate contrition will contribute to Christ's fame.

Chapter Two

THE EVANGELICAL MARKERS

*When I refer to evangelicalism, I am referring to a
historic and global phenomenon that seeks to achieve
renewal in Christian churches by bringing the church
into conformity to the gospel and by making the
promotion of the gospel the chief mission of the church.*
—MICHAEL F. BIRD[1]

SINCE HER INFANCY, MY DAUGHTER HAS BATTLED AN ENIGMATIC CHRONIC illness that we now know as "Cyclic Vomiting Syndrome" (CVS). The ailment's tag is hardly imaginative, but it is apropos—indicative of its symptoms. On a predictable cycle, she endures dizziness and a migraine that nauseates her. Food consumption is impossible for days; even water will not stay down. My wife and I took her to specialists in two different states, each of whom ran a battery of tests. I assumed discovering my daughter's ailment was the aim. I was wrong.

A father can endure only so many blood tests, ultrasounds, and CAT scans on his ailing child before emotions boil to near eruption. I would not be handled by muddled medical jargon. I insisted they explain procedures in fine detail. We sat in the office of a "board certified" physician as she explained that the tests will not discover the problem, "they will only omit suspects." The strategy is called "diagnosis by exclusion." She said, "We will not be absolutely certain of the diagnosis; but, once we know *what it is not*, we can cautiously speculate regarding *what it is*." My daughter's treatment hinged on an admittedly educated guess. In contrast, toward the end of a routine annual check-up, my wife described the symptoms to our family pediatrician, who, with hardly a moment's pause and almost disturbing confidence, declared, "Reese has CVS."

What was the difference between the specialists and our family pediatrician? First, our pediatrician has treated our daughter since birth and is acquainted with her medical *history*. Her use of my daughter's name during the diagnosis was deliberate. She has known the child from birth. Second, our pediatrician is familiar with CVS. She knows its *markers*. Whereas the specialists hoped to discover a list of candidates to perhaps explain the symptoms, our pediatrician recognized the ailment *by* its symptoms. She diagnosed the illness by confidently fixing her conversant mind on *what it is* instead of unsurely sifting through *what it is not*.

A FIXATION ON WHAT WE ARE NOT

I may have furrowed some brows with my evangelical avowal in chapter 1. Consider that my confession may not mean what you suppose. Unfortunately, both advocates and detractors casually characterize evangelicalism according to *what it is not*.[2] Disregarding the movement's critical markers results in educated guesses and gaffes—errors (sometimes well-intended) that take the movement off course. The gaffes are mingled with

Christian values. They appear authentic, but they are unduly culturalized and partisan.[3] When evaluating evangelicalism, we cannot focus on *what we are not*. In this chapter, I will offer a list of evangelical markers and a working definition. A finespun list of characteristics is essential to diagnosing our enigmatic condition.

When a familiar word is unclear, we will, for good or ill, invent a definition. Even when it is wrong, a term's popular use becomes its favored connotation.[4] This was American evangelicalism's plight. It occurred in plain sight. Evangelicalism is a centuries-old movement, but its current iteration is relatively new. After a gestation period, it came to fruition in the 1970s.[5] Mission drift plagues this new form, and the movement is ironically out of step with some historical evangelical markers.

THE CATCH-ALL GAFFE

In America, the term *evangelical* is nearly unserviceable. In the Global South, *evangelicalism* usually refers to some Protestant Christians. But in America, because of culturalization and partisanship, the term is little more than a catch-all category. In its popular use, it almost evades a clear and defensible definition.

When some political surveys provide the opportunity to identify as "evangelical," they are merely asking if the survey-taker subscribes to loosely defined, Christianized theism. The catch-all gaffe scarcely delineates what evangelicalism is, but it emphasizes the few things it is not. It's an error that opens American evangelicalism up to non-evangelicals. Casual survey-takers assume the label applies to them because they *are not* atheistic, Roman Catholic, Jewish, or Muslim.[6] If an American falls outside these limited categories, they can freely identify as evangelical. Genuine markers, like a sincere confession of faith and embodied sanctification, are scarcely considered in such a survey. According to this gaffe, we are evangelical based on *what we are not*. There is little consideration of *what we genuinely are*.

The unserviceable definition should prompt wariness when a poll reports an inordinately high evangelical population. Regarding the consequences of laxly defining "evangelicalism," John Dickerson observes,

> Chances are, you've heard the claim that 40 percent of Americans are born again. Many evangelicals assume we are a supermajority in the United States because we've heard the figures recycled and recited by leaders we trust. . . . At best, according to the most optimistic reports, we are two in every ten Americans. And now, a consensus of the most dedicated researchers pins the number at *less than* one in ten.[7]

An over-inclusive definition is among the causes of misleading polls. In America, "evangelical" is a bastardized theistic classification. It is a theological catch-all resulting from a tragic oversimplification of monotheistic religions. Many Americans choose "evangelical" only because it is the most applicable option. Inevitably, this gaffe misrepresents both evangelical numbers and values.[8]

THE "CHRISTIAN NATION" GAFFE

The Christian nation gaffe exacerbates the catch-all gaffe. We tend to conflate faith and patriotism—often to the detriment of both.[9] This springs from the tenuous assertion that we are, and have always been, a "Christian nation." We treat faith and citizenship as a package deal, which lulls us toward nationalistic pseudo-Christianity and allows those with no credible Christian devotion to self-identify as evangelical.[10] Partisan values now define American evangelicalism. Votes in a national election can weigh as heavily as a genuine confession of faith.[11] Because the bar is so low, masqueraders are polled and licensed to speak representatively—marring the evangelical image.[12]

In the eighteenth century, William Wilberforce confronted this drift among his compatriots. As Christianity was a cultural norm, many assumed they were Christians *because* they were British. But Wilberforce countered that such a person might be only a "cultural Christian," which may not be Christianity at all.[13] Generally, when national identity and religious values are at odds, religion loses.[14] We force our faith to conform to patriotic values like a square peg into an unremitting round hole. We've reinvented evangelicalism according to personal preferences, cultural biases, and political partisanship with little regard for credible history, sound theology, or biblical insights. Because of this gaffe, evangelicalism is now misrepresented by Americanized knockoffs.[15]

THE REACTIONARY GAFFE

The eighteenth-century Enlightenment, an era that prioritized "reason and science as the criteria for truth," gained prominence in the Global West.[16] Theology and the supernatural were spurned in favor of human reason. American evangelicalism is, in part, a reaction to the Enlightenment and its effects. This is not necessarily a bad thing. Christian apologetics, a deliberate defense of the faith, is an onus of the church. We should graciously but boldly engage theological and philosophical trends (2 Cor. 10:3–5; Col. 2:8; 1 Pet. 3:15).[17] But, as with all things, we must be careful in how we do apologetics. Retorts to errors must be measured if we will avoid new errors. The Enlightenment prompted a fit response as it birthed modernity—a worldview that centralizes humanity and decentralizes God. Such a worldview merits a response and respond the church did! In fact, conservative Christians became obsessed. Modernity became the benchmark of unbelief and American evangelicalism retooled and reoriented itself to respond to modernist thinkers (see chapter 7).[18]

When driving a narrow path, fixation with the cliff on the left may lead to an unconscious drop into the ditch on the right. When a measured response reduces to an ill-advised reaction, it replaces the first set of problems with a new set, resulting in well-meaning, though dangerous, ideas and practices. Such carelessness made modernity our ideological reference point. In many respects, American evangelicalism became the *anti-modernity movement.* (This is a bit ironic because, as we will see, Christianity is in a long, complicated romance with the Enlightenment. We reject it while honoring many of its terms.) When faced with modernity, the American church panicked and gradually morphed into today's post-Enlightenment fundamentalism.[19] Our mission devolved into a spooked reaction and contributed to our present dysfunction.

THE MARKERS

There is a well-worn sermon illustration about the Secret Service Agency and counterfeit currency.[20] The Secret Service protects key officers of America's executive branch—most notably, the president of the United States. They are known for their trademark security measures, but they have a lesser-known responsibility that predates their bodyguarding duties. The United States Treasury Department founded the Secret Service Agency in 1865 because, in the aftermath of the Civil War, an estimated third of circulated US currency was bogus.[21] Agents took on the responsibility of tamping out counterfeiting. If they are incapable of recognizing a forgery, they are unequipped for their mission. At their Washington, DC, headquarters, in a "specimen vault," the Secret Service has a sample of every effective forgery dating back to the late nineteenth century.[22] But they are not charged with mastering fakes; that would result in investigative rabbit trails as novel forgeries are ever-coming. They fixate on the real thing. They are skilled at recognizing imitations *because* they are experts on authentic bills.

Defining evangelicalism according to what it is not has led only to theological and missional rabbit trails—aimless debates regarding the movement's identity. Studying the genuine article is vastly more productive. Like an authentic bill, evangelicalism has markers that make it recognizable, so we must orient our eyes toward them. Our missional identity cannot be an educated guess.

Much of the disdain for evangelicalism results from repeatedly shifting the movement's values. We have so corrupted the term that non-evangelicals now sincerely claim it.[23] In America, "evangelical" is in a prison of ambiguity. We use it often, but its meaning and values are furtive. The term now provokes a bitter taste in the mouths of disillusioned Christians. Noting this, Carl F. H. Henry writes,

> Several opposing schools of thought vie for the use of the term *evangelical*. Appropriation of the word by those who do not hold to its biblical and historical content has caused some hesitancy on the part of those who hold to the doctrines of revealed Christianity as to its proper use. They fear misunderstanding of their theological position.[24]

Henry observed that many evangelicals steer clear of the term because it is blemished by impostors who use it as a cloak. He penned these words in 1957, but he may as well have published them this morning. We are not noticing an abrupt missional shift that lay dormant for decades only to rouse in our lifetime. Instead, it is a generations-long debate over who we are and what we value.

Instead of sifting aimlessly through a mass of potential definitions, we should heed the testimonies of credible historians and theologians. This method provides insight into the movement's history, mission, and message; it underlines evangelicalism's distinctiveness. For me, knowing the markers before delving into the history proved vital; it assisted in appreciating the story of the mission drift. While several historians and theologians played a role in this process of definition, David Bebbington, Timothy Larson, and Alistair McGrath took the lead.

BEBBINGTON'S QUADRILATERAL

David Bebbington offered four markers that have long served as a trustworthy checklist.[25] According to Bebbington, an evangelical is someone who prioritizes:

1. CONVERSIONISM—the belief that lives need to be changed;
2. ACTIVISM—the expression of the gospel in effort;
3. BIBLICISM—a particular regard for the Bible;
4. CRUCICENTRISM—a stress on the sacrifice of Christ on the cross.[26]

Conscious evangelicals laud these priorities, dubbed "Bebbington's Quadrilateral," as foundational. Mark Noll, an evangelical historian, called it "the most serviceable general definition . . . for the purposes of the history of Christianity."[27] I am inclined to use the word *description* over *definition*, but Dr. Noll's appraisal is nonetheless valid. Bebbington did not create the quadrilateral; he codified it. He is a historian observing evangelical markers revealed by history. He did not *prescribe* evangelical values; he *described* the movement's historical values.

In my estimation, Bebbington's Quadrilateral is exceptional and worthy of respect. In four brief points, Bebbington paints a picture of evangelicalism's basal essence. It is so good that it summarily indicts our apathy. I am inclined to believe we know this because we've circumvented the markers by redefining the terms. Furthermore, we treat them as irrelevant to our context—discounting their implications on the American ethnic rift. I have two suspicions as to why.

First, Bebbington's Quadrilateral may be too concise—probably because he makes assumptions about his original audience. Perhaps he anticipates they would infer broader theological points from his summary.[28] This assumption is no longer feasible. We are only one generation removed from Bebbington's work, and in that brief span, we've managed to subject his terms to unwarranted revisions. For example, we've relegated *activism* to little more than "getting people saved," but, historically, it means more than that: the activist seeks worldly wholeness![29] This would explain why Bebbington lists "conversionism" and "activism" as distinct markers; the former regards gospel conversions, the latter regards gospel actions. Bebbington recognizes the gospel as eternally *and* temporally relevant. They are both evangelical values upheld by history. Activism is "an energetic, individualistic approach to religious duties *and social involvement*."[30] Bebbington avoids confusion by including examples. He writes,

> But activism often spilled over from beyond simple gospel work. . . . Shaftesbury's efforts in such causes as public health provided a further outlet of evangelical energy. Wilberforce's campaign against the slave trade and Nonconformist political crusades around 1900 are but the

most famous instances of attempts to enforce the ethics of the gospel. A host of voluntary societies embodied the philanthropic urge. Hannah More, the evangelical authoress of the turn of the nineteenth century, summed up succinctly the prevailing evangelical attitude. 'Action is the life of virtue,' she wrote, 'and the world is the theater of action.'[31]

When noting historical examples of activism, Bebbington cites leaders who fought for "public health," opposed the "slave trade," and were philanthropic toward the communal good. Evangelical activism sustains the discipleship mandate of Matthew 28:16–20 *and* the social directive of Matthew 25:31–46. The movement seeks to add to the fold of disciples, and it upholds the present-day, sacrificial "ethics of the gospel."[32]

We preach a message of heavenly reconciliation *and* earthly conciliation (Eph. 2:1–22); choosing either at the expense of the other truncates our message. The evangelical identity carries ethical imperatives. The activistic marker has worldly implications. The church is the kingdom's embassy on earth, so "the world is the theater of action."[33] Fixation on our eternal destiny with no regard for temporal brokenness is an abdication of a vital evangelical marker.

Second, in the Global West, evangelicalism filters through individualism at the expense of the collective.[34] While we can infer certain assumptions from "conversionism" and "crucicentrism," Bebbington's Quadrilateral is silent regarding the church.[35] I maintain that excluding it was an act of intellectual integrity. Bebbington's historical evaluation of evangelicalism is limited to the era that began in the eighteenth century and culminated in the twentieth century. During that period, evangelicalism emphasized conversions, not the church. It was a revivalist movement embodied by itinerate preachers like George Whitefield, D. L. Moody, and Billy

Graham.[36] During this era, by and large, the church was not a central marker of the evangelical movement. Decentralizing the church only contributed to the movement's mission drift. Without the accountability of a global community of kingdom citizens, voices that traverse regions and history, individuals and local churches isolated themselves and incorporated their region's cultural norms—even when the norms were sinful.[37] Contextualizing the gospel is biblical, but willfully ignoring the voice of the universal church is shortsighted. Evangelical mission drift was all but inevitable.

THE LARSON PENTAGON

Timothy Larson deferentially builds upon David Bebbington's work by drafting language cleverly tagged "The Larson Pentagon," which pays clear homage to Bebbington's Quadrilateral.[38] Larson avows that an evangelical is:

1. an orthodox Protestant
2. who stands in the tradition of the global Christian networks arising from the eighteenth-century revival movements associated with John Wesley and George Whitefield;
3. who has a preeminent place for the Bible in her or his Christian life as the divinely inspired, final authority in matters of faith and practice;
4. who stresses reconciliation with God through the atoning work of Jesus on the cross;
5. and who stresses the work of the Holy Spirit in the life of an individual to bring about conversion and an ongoing life of fellowship with God and service to God and others, including the duty of all believers to participate in the task of proclaiming the gospel to all people.[39]

As with Bebbington's Quadrilateral, conscientious evangelical peers affirm the Larson Pentagon. Larsen has not supplanted Bebbington; his work is a helpful amendment. In my estimation, Larson fills in language that Bebbington could omit a generation ago.

Supplementing Bebbington's work with Larson's results in a near-unassailable characterization of historical evangelicalism. Their summaries can stand alone, but together, they are a *tour de force*! In his first two points, Larsen specifies a lineage of Protestant Christianity, which mitigates the catch-all gaffe mentioned above. From there, the overlap between Bebbington and Larsen is palpable. Larson's third point affirms *biblicism*; his fourth point sustains both *conversionism* and *crucicentrism*; while carefully identifying the Holy Spirit as the star actor, the fifth point supports *conversionism* and *activism*. According to Larsen, evangelicals are Spirit-led, Bible-believing Protestant Christians who serve God and humanity, armed with Christ's comprehensive gospel message.

Like Bebbington, Larsen recognizes activism as a key marker. Expounding on this point, he writes,

> Evangelicalism is a tradition marked by a mobilized laity as well as a highly energized clergy. This activism has produced a rich tradition of social action, including, for example, the movement in Britain guided by the evangelical William Wilberforce to abolish the slave trade and the work among the poor of the evangelical organization, the Salvation Army.[40]

I wish to be clear: Bebbington and Larsen are not being accusatory. They are simply identifying evangelical markers as revealed by history. Conversely, based on their work, and my observations of American evangelicalism, I am making unambiguous accusations. I maintain that, among American evangelicals, social activism stands out as a selectively orphaned marker. To be sure, we are activistic and vocal regarding issues that align with conservative values (e.g., abortion, traditional marriage). However, by and large, the ongoing racial rift receives a fraction of our activistic fervor. Later, when we consider the evangelical narrative, we will examine why this could occur, but, for now, suffice it to say that social activism is a marker that carries less weight than the others.

On the whole, evangelical churches, with variations, affirm the Bible (*biblicism*), the significance of the cross (*crucicentrism*), and the need for human conversion (*conversionism*). American evangelicals or, more accurately, "fundamentalists" narrowly define these markers, and violators can be stamped with a scarlet letter—dubbed heretics or, at least, "false teachers."[41] In contrast, the American ethnic rift, which is among America's longest running social afflictions, carries less weight.[42]

EVANGELICAL AS A WORD AND A KINGDOM PEOPLE

Bebbington's Quadrilateral and Larsen's Pentagon are overlapping lists of values, but there is no universal confession of faith. We need an overarching characteristic, a theological north star shared by all evangelicals to keep us on a common course. Blessedly, there is no need to invent one; the theological plumb line already exists.

The word *evangelical* derives from the Greek term *euangelion*, which means "good news."[43] First-semester Greek students know that appealing to a term's etymology has potential failings. The passage of time nuances—or outright changes—a word's meaning. However, I maintain that *euangelion* experienced no significant change; it is often tethered to the biblical concept of "good news" or "gospel."[44] So, etymologically, *evangelical* still refers to a person, institution, or movement *of the gospel.*[45]

Later, I will have to clarify what the "gospel" is, but, for now, suffice it to say that the gospel is the fruit of Christ's incarnation, extraordinary life, death, resurrection, and *ascension.* He is not merely alive; he is presently seated at the Father's right hand (Eph. 1:20)! We woefully overlook his reign, but it is essential to the gospel. His present-tense reign as king is our theological north star, our defining marker. *Christ's kingdom is the overarching characteristic through which we must filter evangelicalism.*

When I use the word *evangelical,* I refer to an orthodox Christian worldview—a framework of theological ideas with corresponding affections and practices, and they are all subject to Christ! Evangelicals are citizens of an eternal monarchy with no geographical borders. We are diverse and united in our eternal residency. Christ's dominion frames our theology and practices. His reign is the nitty-gritty of the *euangelion.* If the gospel is central to the movement, then the kingdom, the culmination of the gospel, is paramount. The kingdom of God overrules sinful partiality, oppression, or indifference to human suffering (Luke 4:16–21). A movement that is not Christocentric is decidedly *not* evangelical (Rev. 2:4; 19:11–12, 16)!

We overlook Christ's current reign as an essential aspect of the good news (*evangel*).[46] While conceding that his enthronement is inevitable, we behave as though he has not yet been crowned. I am not inclined to find theological controversies under every rock. Still, I must avoid ambiguity here: acting as though Christ is not presently king is an abject error, a debasement of the gospel (Col. 1:15–20).[47] Presently, we are the king's ambassadors (2 Cor. 5:16–21).[48] Hence, activism, the embodiment of his kingdom's values, is an evangelical imperative. Because he reigns, we are *activists* commissioned to engage the world and proliferate the kingdom's holy culture (Matt. 28:16–20). We will not accomplish this before he returns, so we preach a message of eternal hope. But in the meantime, we persist in bringing the kingdom agenda to earth. As evangelicals, our mission includes conversionism *and* activism.

SO WHAT IS AN EVANGELICAL?

When I identify as evangelical, I am not championing the popular brand. On the contrary, I contend that the present form of American evangelicalism is an unsafe, reactionary caricature of the real thing. We've shaped the movement in a cultural image rather than aligning ourselves biblically and surrendering to the kingdom (Mark 1:15). Our infraction can be overturned through theological retrieval—revisiting our core values. I cannot improve upon Gavin Ortlund's take:

> Sometimes the best way to go forward is, paradoxically, to go backward. This is true in solving math problems, executing military operations, navigating relational conflict, and (here I suggest) doing theology. Contemporary evangelical theology can be enriched and strengthened in her current task by going back to retrieve classic theological resources.[49]

A theological reset is difficult. It is an act of repentance that calls us back to long-abandoned seasons of the church. But the heavy lifting is done. The ideas are drafted. We need only reembrace and contextualize deserted values.

In search of solid language, I found solace in Alistair

McGrath's definition of *evangelicalism* as "the term chosen by evangelicals to refer to themselves, as representing most adequately the central concern of the movement for the safeguarding and articulation of the *evangel*—the good news of God which has been made known and made possible in Jesus Christ."[50] McGrath's definition is admirable; he spotlights "the *evangel*—the good news." It is authentically evangelical. Still, it needs real-world characteristics—markers that concretize his language. My take on these markers is not novel because of the careful work of scholars like Bebbington and Larsen.[51] I amend their lists only to spotlight a long, diverse lineage of evangelical stalwarts—a family tree that predates the 1970s by centuries. We should recognize our ethnically and culturally diverse theological foreparents and their holy contributions to the movement. Also, our present dysfunction obliges the recognition of a Christocentric, overarching marker that underscores the kingdom. The amendments in the list below are not mine; they are longstanding descriptions of evangelicalism, retrieved and highlighted out of necessity.

While previous generations could treat these markers as foregone conclusions, it is now necessary to explicitly mention them to combat our mission drift. I avow that an evangelical is:

1. A genuinely confessing Christian
2. who is in the spiritual lineage of figures like John Wesley, Richard Allen, Jarena Lee, Charles Spurgeon, Harriet Beecher Stowe, Francis J. Grimké, and Carl F. H. Henry;
3. who prioritizes the Bible as inspired and authoritative revelation—divine insight regarding God, humanity, the universe, faith, and kingdom practices (*biblicism*);
4. who stresses the effectual incarnation, life, death, resurrection, and ascension of Christ (*crucicentrism*);

5. who recognizes the intervening Holy Spirit as the Lord over Christian conversion, sanctification, and progressive transformation, enthusing sacrificial living for God and fellow human beings, which includes proclaiming the gospel toward eternal salvation *and* temporal wholeness (*conversionism* and *activism*);

6. and who identifies with the global church, the gathering of the summoned (*ecclesia*)—communal citizens and stewards in the eternal, boundaryless kingdom where we joyfully serve under Christ's reign (*Christocentric ecclesiology* and *kingdom ethics*).

I long for an evangelicalism instantiated by these six markers. Dare I say it, they are my beloved theological hexagon.

Without the kingdom, we reduce evangelicalism to a bauble of our own making. But under Christ's reign, these markers serve as our blessed contribution to the *missio dei*—God's undefeatable mission to publish his dominion. It fixates on a full-orbed message that orients us toward *who we are* instead of *who we are not*. I desire to embody the *euangelion*, to be a man of the gospel. When I identify as evangelical, this is what I mean. I willfully reject the *modern-day* caricature, so it is essential at this point for us to look to history. Knowing where we went astray might contribute to a missional course correction.

Chapter Three

HISTORY HAUNTS THE PRESENT

*History, as nearly no one seems to know, is not merely
something to be read. And it does not refer merely, or even
principally, to the past. On the contrary, the great force of
history comes from the fact that we carry it within us, are
unconsciously controlled by it in many ways, and history
is literally present in all that we do. It could scarcely be
otherwise, since it is to history that we owe our frames
of reference, our identities, and our aspirations.*
—JAMES BALDWIN[1]

IN AUGUST 2019, THE *NEW YORK TIMES MAGAZINE* PUBLISHED *THE 1619
Project*, a long-form journalistic endeavor and brainchild of
journalist Nikole Hannah-Jones. It sought to "reframe the
country's history by placing the consequences of slavery and
the contributions of Black Americans at the very center of the
United States national narrative."[2] August 2019 marked the
four hundredth anniversary of enslaved Africans arriving at
Virginia. *The 1619 Project* treats August 1619 as a flashpoint,
maintaining that it triggered a shockwave of racial marginalization in American history.[3] According to Jake Silverstein,

editor-in-chief of the *New York Times Magazine*, the arrival of enslaved Africans in 1619 launched "a barbaric system of chattel slavery that would last for the next 250 years." "This is sometimes referred to as the country's original sin," he writes, "but it is more than that: It is the country's very origin."[4]

The 1619 Project triggered a foreseeable backlash. Treating slavery as essential to the nation's formation runs afoul of a prized narrative that stresses American exceptionalism. By executive order, the 1776 Commission convened in September 2020, chaired by Larry P. Arnn. President Donald Trump deputed the commission to produce a curriculum that promotes "patriotic education."[5] In January 2021, they published *The 1776 Report*, candidly intended to counter *The 1619 Project*.[6] They maintain that the Declaration of Independence articulates national values, so those who seek to typify the nation should look not to seventeenth-century slavery but to July 4, 1776. The national identity is revealed in the creed that "all men are created equal."[7]

If truth be told, these two works of popular-level history align on many details. The *New York Times Magazine* recognizes the assertion of "unalienable rights," and the 1776 Commission concedes the enslavement of Africans. But while these projects are exposed to the same data, they came to strikingly different conclusions regarding the cultural imprint of these events. They concur on many aspects of the past but irreconcilably split on the national story.

A PRIMER ON HISTORICAL NARRATIVES

The study of the past is so common that students can take it for granted. Our glibness is worsened by how history is generally taught, fixating on temporary, rote memorization of names, places, and dates. Instead of esteeming history as a formative story that shapes our present, it is a collection of isolated factoids used to afflict students via exams. Upon receiving an acceptable grade, pupils deem the information useless, and, to avoid mental clutter, they vacate the space it occupied in their minds. We discount the benefits of reading history as a true chronicle scripted in "artistic" prose.[8] Fixating only on dates relegates the past to episodic snapshots, but a historical narrative is an insightful high-def motion picture.

The past is most useful when framed as the engaging story of the real world.[9] Flouting it amounts to starting a book at the midpoint and, upon completion, deeming oneself an expert. In like manner, knowing only a fraction of a historical narrative ends in a patchy view of the world. History is more than something we possess—it is also something we must do. Unfortunately, we do it haphazardly. Good narratives are innately complex.[10] Complicated narratives are off-putting. They nuance conclusions and force us to honor the perspectives of others. In America, we have chosen and, for the most part, universalized a national story. But what if such an approach to history is unduly simple and revisionist? Journalist Amanda Ripley confronts this tendency head-on, saying:

> The lesson for journalists (or anyone) working amidst intractable conflict: *complicate the narrative.* First, complexity leads to a fuller, more accurate story. Secondly, it boosts the odds that your work will matter—particularly if it is about a polarizing issue. When people encounter complexity, they become more curious and less closed off to new information. They listen, in other words.[11]

Before reading the historical narratives in the ensuing chapters, we must consider what we mean by "history." This chapter is not an exhaustive essay on historiography; that would go beyond this book's scope. Instead, it is a layman's introduction to historical narratives that underlines four points:

1. History is a coherent, nonfiction narrative—a truthful story that gives context and meaning to the present.
2. Experiences influence our hermeneutics, forming our interpretations of the past.
3. Memories—both personal and communal—preserve our experiences and our hermeneutics.
4. A plurality of credible, complementary narratives offers a more thorough understanding of history and honors historical characters.

SEQUENTIAL TIMELINE VERSUS TRUTHFUL NARRATIVE

Generally, we treat the terms "past" and "history" as synonymous, but using them interchangeably can be misleading.[12] The *past* is a sequential collection of moments we can mark as dots on a timeline; it places events in chronological order. But it does not necessarily underline *why* the moments occurred or their connections to one another.[13] The past provides reliable data, but if we do not arrange it as a coherent, elucidating plot, we may have only disjointed facts.

HISTORY MAKES THE PAST PORTABLE, RELEVANT, AND APPLICABLE

Historians exhume facts from the past and shape them into a nonfiction narrative—a credible story.[14] Whereas the past can provide the sequence of events, a historical narrative underlines the unobserved consequences buried within the sequence. For instance, the American Revolution predates the French Revolution. That is the order of events, but what of the story?[15] France treated the American Revolution as proof of concept. American liberation made independence viable for many French patriots. Ultimately, America's Declaration of Independence was a loose template for France's Declaration of the Rights of Man and Citizen; Thomas Jefferson consulted.[16] The result was a French republic of citizens instead of a monarch reigning over subjects.[17] The American Revolution was an influential forerunner of the French Revolution.[18] A timeline honors the sequence, but the story discloses an unforced correlation between the two events.

HISTORY IS TRANSFERABLE

Historians are storytellers.[19] They write a memo that makes history transferable across generations.[20] A historical narrative allows the past to be resident in our present, where it shapes our ideas, values, and conduct. Conversely, a flawed view of the past generates a reciprocally poor interpretation of the present.

I recently read an essay that hinged on a timeline. The author treated the end of the Civil War as the launch of an inexorable trek toward ethnic equity. He argues we achieved parity over a century ago. The essay unduly simplified the narrative. America was dragged—often kicking and screaming—to the civil rights decisions of the 1960s. His timeline dishonors the complexities. The author ignored the hard-fought progress of the civil rights era, which trudged onward despite policies aimed at rewinding society to the pre-Reconstruction era.[21] Treating the Civil War as a direct cause of civil rights is a historical blunder—*post hoc ergo propter hoc* (Latin: after this, therefore because of this).[22] This blunder is a common shortcoming of a sequential timeline.

HISTORY IS FACT BASED

In 1943, Mortimer J. Adler, a philosopher and bibliophile, cocreated the Great Books Foundation.[23] He hoped to enlighten readers by exposing them to the classics. He was aware of the need to tutor through the process, so he proactively published *How to Read a Book*, an introduction to literary genres. The book is a jewel in my library. However, the 1972 edition of *How to Read a Book*, written in collaboration with Charles Van Doren, maintains that history is closer to "fiction" than "science." They believed historical facts could be "elusive" and skewed by a historian's bias, so they treated history as near-fiction.[24] I believe Adler and Van Doren overstated their case.

While fiction can warn of what may be, history recalls what was. Fiction can caution against bad ideas and laud good ideas, but history reminds us of what occurred when good and bad ideas came to fruition. Good fiction artistically echoes the real world. But for the historian, the past does not merely inspire a story; it *is* a story.[25] The historian sketches a literary image that captures critical and relevant moments from former times; those who read it are peering into the real world. The past is the skeletal frame of history, but the historian goes a step further, providing the flesh, muscle, and ligaments of a narrative. Because past facts are the historian's framework, good history is always factually based.[26] Respectable historical narratives are deeply rooted in reality, so they must emit the unmistakable aroma of truth. Adler and Van Doren underestimated the extent to which biased historians can be impartial.

Biases do not automatically disqualify a historian. The dance between objectivity and subjectivity, though intricate, is achievable. Historians have long recognized that it is possible to be partial and yet write history with a requisite measure of impartiality. To this point, Carl Trueman writes, "Most historians would, I believe, both acknowledge the biased nature of the history they write and also maintain that they aspire to be objective in what they do."[27] Patent facts are a dispassionate harness on the historian's passions; even those with predispositions can provide an honest narrative.

The Gospels are ideal examples of subjectivity and objectivity coexisting. Luke, for instance, was commissioned by a patron named Theophilus to write Luke-Acts, a two-volume historical work that chronicles the ministry life of Christ and the rise of the church (Luke 1:1–4; Acts 1:1).[28] As a Christian, Luke was perhaps inclined toward a story that shines a favorable light on Christ and the church, but he honored the norms and standards of ancient historiography.[29] He interviewed witnesses to sustain the story, incorporating content from trustworthy sources.[30] He did the work of a historian (Luke 1:1). He did not contrive a story; he disclosed one and scripted it as a truthful, compelling saga that allowed Theophilus to "know the certainty of the things [he'd] been taught" (Luke 1:4). Luke-Acts is not a fabricated tale but an authentic and formative narrative relevant across generations.[31]

HERMENEUTICS, EXPERIENCE, AND MEMORY

Hermeneutics is our means of comprehension—the lenses we use to interpret information.[32] Among Christians, the term is typically associated with the interpretation of texts, principally Scripture, but it goes beyond the written word and applies to all "concepts."[33] Hermeneutics is how we select relevant facts and determine their meaning.[34] Jens Zimmerman writes, "One is engaged in hermeneutics whenever one tries to grasp the meaning of something—be it conversation, a newspaper article, a Shakespeare play, or *an account of past events.*"[35] Historians, like all interpreters, read the past through their hermeneutical lenses. Divergent hermeneutics would partially explain how two people groups can assess the same past and sincerely script diverging histories. Historical truths are *not* relative; all truths are absolute! However, our hermeneutics determines which facts we readily see and how we weigh them. If we overlook or downplay pertinent information, our interpretation is adversely affected.[36]

EXPERIENCE AND HERMENEUTICS

Hermeneutics can vary from person to person and group to group because our interpretive lenses are shaped, in part, by our diverse experiences. So any discussion regarding interpretation must honor the fact that we evaluate history through an array of experientially formed perspectives. Just as glasses improve eyesight and allow us to see previously unseen objects, experiences shape our hermeneutics and open our eyes to facts that, though always present, were previously obscured.

In 2004, when Cheri and I married, I promised her I'd never buy a minivan. Then we had children, and our midsized sedan was inadequate. We needed to do something. Coincidentally, I rented a Chrysler Town & Country for our annual Christmas trip from Denver to Dallas. While en route, my wife became a convert. We purchased a Town & Country soon after returning to Denver. As we pulled out of the dealership, a twin van drove by, and we saw four more on our short drive home. We could not help but see them! Before, they'd gone unnoticed, but we had new lenses. Our purchase did not create reality; the minivans had always been there. But the experience amended our hermeneutics, allowing us to notice the previously unobserved vehicles.

Hermeneutical amending is not limited to minivans; we

apply it daily. While watching *Peanuts* cartoons, we are bewildered when Lucy repeatedly challenges Charlie Brown to kick a field goal, only to snatch the football away at the last moment. As Charlie Brown flies through the air, we share a thought: How does he fall for it repeatedly? It is funny to us because it is inconceivable. We are rapt because his interpretation of her invitation is unchanged. He does not allow prior experiences with Lucy to amend his hermeneutics.

Experiences have, to some degree, epistemic authority. In other words, they can influence what we know. They have a legitimate and authoritative effect on our perceptions of objective reality. *The 1619 Project* and *The 1776 Report* are diverging perceptions of the same past; the former stresses the implications of slavery while the latter lauds the nation's language regarding human rights. I maintain that divergent hermeneutics are among the causes of their disagreements. They read the past—and the present—through different, experientially formed lenses. The two camps are the products of the same moments experienced in divergent ways.

For instance, on July 4, 1776, America declared independence from Great Britain. However, during their merriment, America legally upheld racialized slavery. It was a day of declared freedom for some and, for others, just another day of bondage.[37] It stands to reason that the two groups will have divergent interpretations of the moment.

Cognizant of the brazen hypocrisy, many black people gingerly protested Independence Day.[38] Frederick Douglass, a renowned abolitionist, deftly underlined the holiday's pretentiousness. In 1852, he received an invitation from the Rochester Ladies Anti-Slavery Society to speak at the Corinthian Hall. They requested a speech commemorating seventy-six years of American independence. He used the opportunity to illuminate the disparate ways black and white people experienced

July 4, 1776. His message is aptly called, "What to the Slave is the Fourth of July?" He stood before an audience of nearly six hundred and, true to form, he was unsubtle:

> I am not included within the pale of this glorious anniversary! Your high independence only reveals the immeasurable distance between us. The blessings in which you, this day, rejoice, are not enjoyed in common. The rich inheritance of justice, liberty, prosperity and independence, bequeathed by your fathers, is shared by you, not by me. The sunlight that brought life and healing to you, has brought stripes and death to me. This Fourth July is *yours*, not *mine. You* may rejoice, I must mourn. To drag a man in fetters into the grand illuminated temple of liberty, and call upon him to join you in joyous anthems, were inhuman mockery and sacrilegious irony. Do you mean, citizens, to mock me, by asking me to speak today?[39]

Douglass was an "outlaw," a repeat violator of America's Fugitive Slave Act![40] He rarely lost the opportunity to remind, "I appear before you . . . a thief and a robber. I stole this head, these limbs, this body from my master and ran off with them."[41] On the day of the 1852 speech, he was wanted for stealing himself from a Maryland enslaver.[42] He observed Independence Day by stressing its acute irony![43]

American independence was a singular event experienced by a plurality of groups in fundamentally different ways, which resulted in correspondingly disparate interpretations of the moment. The conclusions of the 1776 Commission reflect the experiences of the eighteenth-century aristocracy— namely, white male property owners. For them, July 4, 1776, is a day pivotal to freedom. But what of those for whom the Declaration of Independence was an ironic blade that inflicted an unremitting wound? For enslaved black people, it was only a reminder of their real-world dystopia. Imagine the assault of watching your enslavers celebrate *their* freedom! The phrase "all men are created equal," which was avowed by flagrant enslavers, only reiterated for the enslaved that they were not honored as "men." The two groups experienced one event in two poignantly disparate ways. Reducing history to only one of their experiences is "inhuman mockery and sacrilegious irony."[44]

EXPERIENCE AND MEMORY

I anticipate some readers will protest my emphasis on experience, specifically its influence on *The 1619 Project* and *The 1776 Report*. Objectors will observe that none of the authors participated in the histories they wrote, so experience could not influence their historical narratives. But such a critique overlooks inherited memory.[45] Experiences can be communal and, in conjunction with corporate memory, have ongoing implications that affect a group's interpretation of the past.[46] When a person or group experiences a historical moment, their descendants and empathizers inherit their interpretation of the moment. Hermeneutics follow in the wake of inherited memory.

Our inherited hermeneutics influence how we interpret the world and the historical characters with whom we identify. *The 1619 Project* memorializes the authentic and formative experiences of the enslaved, underlining slavery's objectively seminal role in nascent America. *The 1776 Report*, advocating for the accomplishments of the founding fathers, deems slavery an incidental, ethical blip committed by noble men. This is the mainstream narrative taught to children in elementary schools. Here's the problem: even if the mainstream narrative is sincere, it is intolerably incomplete. A historical narrative that highlights relevant heroism and downplays relevant oppression is unethical. Integrity compels us to honor the whole story and include all relevant details in our corporate memory—even when those details are inconvenient. Otherwise, the historical narrative is mythical nostalgia and is not factually based.[47]

HERMENEUTICS AND "THE OTHER"

Not all experiences are firsthand. Some occur indirectly through candid dialogues with those who are "other." Even indirect experiences can amend your hermeneutic. We know this intuitively, which is why we associate wisdom with experience and treat understanding as "transferable."[48] Again, the agenda is not to create truths, but empathizing with the experiences of others can allow us to see previously unseen realities. Hans-Georg Gadamer, one of the twentieth century's foremost experts on hermeneutics, calls it "keeping oneself open to what is the other."[49] Availing ourselves of "the other" and their experiences broadens our perspective and enhances our perception of reality.[50] Surrounding ourselves with like-minded thinkers is comfortable, but it does not hone our ideas. Exposure to "the other" allows for a transference of experiences and, thus, an amended perspective on the world.[51] Amended perspective explains how a person can genuinely change their perception despite unchanged facts. Truths are static, but, ideally, interpreters are not. When our hermeneutics are amended credibly, we may see the facts more clearly, and unseen realities come into focus. When this occurs, integrity requires a corresponding change in our opinions and perceptions of the world.

In 2011, I planted a church in collaboration with Derrick Kelsey, one of my dearest friends. I've revered his mother, Janice Kelsey, since I met her. Her stories of the Birmingham campaign of 1963 have left an indelible mark on me. She shared a photo of herself as a sixteen-year-old in a make-shift jail with "fellow marchers." A desire for "a level playing field" was their crime.[52] I once inquired, "Considering the potential consequences, what drove you to participate in the campaign?" She was brief and poignant, "I had no children yet," she said, "but I wanted better for the children I'd have." Segregated Alabama was so crippling that a young girl took a sacrificial stand for children she'd yet to bear. I do not have firsthand experience of the event, but I have Mother Kelsey. Before our conversation, I was aware of details, but now, my understanding is patinaed by her experience, which I've inherited as transferred memory.[53] During the civil rights era, James Baldwin famously observed, "White people are end-lessly demanding to be assured that Birmingham is really on Mars."[54] He averred that the white populace wanted racialized segregation to be a distant evil committed by extraterrestrials. But Janice Kelsey's experiences make Birmingham proximate, destroying the Martian delusion. Her perspective is essential to the American narrative.

Intuitively, we know the need to memorialize moments for the betterment of future generations. It is, after all, why history courses, biographies, and documentaries are worth-while. We've sated our country's landscape with monuments that commemorate former days. Erroneously, we assume they merely preserve information, but they do more than that.[55] Transferred memories influence our interpretation of the world. In the Bible, memorials are means to hermeneuti-cal ends (Gen. 35:14; Isa. 19:19; 55:13). The psalmist directs us to "remember the deeds of the LORD" (Ps. 77:11). Why? Because recalling God's *past* faithfulness informs our interpre-tation of the *present*. Even generations that did not experience God's deliverance firsthand have indirect experience through memory transferal. When they encounter trials, they can cite the testimonies—nonfiction stories—of their predecessors as evidence of God's faithfulness, which informs their assessment of life's trials. Memory transference tacitly shapes the hermeneutics of descendants.[56] When done well, this is a virtuous thing.

MEMORY AND WILLFUL AMNESIA

After my first encounter with Janice Kelsey, I posted photos of the Birmingham campaign on social media. It was a gallery of appalling images—German shepherds and firehoses depravedly repurposed to assault human flesh. I submitted them without comment, hoping others would inherit the memory. The backlash was disheartening: "Brandon, you insist on creating division by digging up long-forgotten days." The person who wrote this did not deny the events, but they insisted we forget them. It is willful amnesia, a desire to "disremember" the past.[57] The timing of this response is noteworthy. I'd posted the photo montage within days of September 11. That same week, many of my deriders posted montages of their own, memorializing 9/11. They conveyed one message: "Never forget!" Remembering honors the victims and their foreverchanged families. Moreover, it shapes how future generations will understand September 11, 2001. Since remembering is a virtue, the backlash to my social media post prompts a pressing question: If 9/11 is worthy of memorialization (and it is), then why is memorializing the Birmingham campaign considered an act of "division"?

This incongruity brings two points to light. First, victims and victimizers weigh memory differently. A victimizer wishes to forget an experience that a victim cannot.[58] We memorialize 9/11 because we identify with the victims. The sins of 9/11 are memorable and significant. In contrast, because we identify with the founding fathers, we treat their racialized sins as incidental. It preserves their heroic reputations but does so at their victims' expense. Willful amnesia dishonors real human beings.[59] As mentioned above, memorialized experiences amend our hermeneutics. We write history and interpret the present based on our recollections of the past. Consciously forgetting or downplaying slavery, Black Codes, and Jim Crow only revises history, which blurs our view of the present. We mitigate this error only by carefully remembering.

Second, we seek oneness by improperly simplifying our story.[60] We are wooed by stories of heroism. The narrative of America's brave founding fathers, who launched a new kind of nation, is romantic and mesmerizing. Alternative views that may nuance the story can be disorienting. So we choose self-serving simplicity—cleanly dividing historical figures into groups of villains and heroes. We fear that conceding their demonstrable sins will put us on shaky ground. But real-world characters are complex. They may not neatly fall into our naïve categories.[61] A hero to some can genuinely be a terrorist to others. Our historical narrative should reflect this complexity.[62] Otherwise, we lose credibility. Selective storytelling spreads a tale and rewrites history.

In his book *History in Three Keys*, historian Paul Cohen adeptly explains three ways we evoke the past, "*event, experience*, and *myth*." "Event" is the objective history—the story drafted by credible historians with the benefit of hindsight. "Experience" is how the array of participants endured the moment. Not all groups experience a moment the same way, so they have varied observations and emphases.[63] "Myth" is a strategic story written by those who hope to justify a cause. Mythologizers reduce the historical narrative to strategically selected highlights. They may be sincere, but they cherry-pick the facts—selectively choosing details that affirm the calculated story they wish to tell. Cohen writes:

The past treated as myth is fundamentally different from the past treated as history. When good historians write history, their primary objective is to construct, on the basis of the evidence available, as accurate and truthful an understanding of the past as possible. Mythologizers, in a sense, do the reverse. Certainly, mythologizers start out with an understanding of the past, which in many (though not all) cases they may sincerely believe to be 'correct.' Their purpose, however, is not to enlarge upon or deepen this understanding. Rather, it is to draw on it to serve the political, ideological, rhetorical, and/or emotional needs of the present.[64]

"Myth," as Cohen uses the term, is not necessarily a lie, but it is often the product of selective memory or disremembering. It is unabashed confirmation bias. While good historians look for the story, a "mythologizer" looks to confirm a predetermined message by ignoring or diminishing history's inconvenient episodes.

THE BENEFITS OF A PLURALITY OF TESTIMONIES

In 2003, I was one of six witnesses to a hit-and-run car collision; police officers secluded us and asked what happened. After giving my report, the officer believed he had a "good understanding," but the accident scene was chaotic, so I was sure I'd missed vital details. He settled my concerns by assuring me that the "cumulative accounts" of the event tell the story. "The witnesses are not contradicting one another," he said, "they just have different points of emphasis. You gave us the make and model of the car and a description of the driver.

Others provided details that you omitted, like a partial license plate number. When we combine the testimonies of all credible witnesses, we can confidently identify the car and, eventually, the driver."

The existence of alternative testimonies can be troubling for some. We treat history as a brute fact immune to interpretation. So we find diverse testimonies disturbing. But the police officer summarized an important lesson. Choosing only one report can lead to an incomplete story. To avoid this, we garner reports from an array of trustworthy witnesses. *When we combine the credible testimonies, we have a more thorough account.* No person or group can interpret a moment from every perspective; their hermeneutical lenses will pick the relevant facts and determine their significance to the story. I fixated on the car and its driver; others ignored the car and attended to the license plate. Each of us gave partial reports that, when combined, provided a "good understanding." We have different hermeneutics, but our testimonies complemented one another. We should not assume that two different reports are contradictory; they may merely see one event from various angles and with unique emphases.

For instance, the Bible includes four Gospel narratives, biographies of Christ. But they have different emphases. They tell the same story from four harmonious angles.[65] None is superfluous; they are mutually beneficial, inspired, and "useful" (2 Tim. 3:16). Matthew and his audience were Jewish, which explains his approach to Jesus's genealogy (Matt. 1:1–16). He tracked the lineage from Abraham (v. 1), through King David (v. 6), to Joseph (v. 16). The genealogy qualifies Jesus as an heir to David's throne. He is the Messiah the Jews were anticipating. Luke, a gentile writing predominantly to gentiles, approached the genealogy differently (Luke 3:21–38).[66] He traces the lineage from Joseph (v. 23), through King David

(v. 31), then Abraham (v. 34), and he culminates with Adam, the "son of God" (v. 38). Luke traces the genealogy to Adam because Christ is the second Adam, the new "federal head" of all humanity—including gentiles (Rom. 5:12–17; 1 Cor. 15:45). The two biographies are contextualized according to their distinct original audiences—one Jewish, the other gentile. But they are complementary. Together, they provide the fuller story; Jesus is the anointed king of both Jews *and* gentiles. Choosing only one perspective of the past tells a partial tale.

RECAPITULATION

A historical narrative is the cumulative story of real people, so we must make their formative experiences known. We are charged with valuing the communal memoirs of image bearers. We are ethically compelled to respect their implications on history and the present; ignoring them falsifies a nonfiction story and dishonors historical figures. Theologian Miroslav Volf calls it "remembering rightly," and historian Beth Barton Schweiger counts it a loving "relationship with the dead." They both base this value on the biblical imperative to "love your neighbor as yourself" (Mark 12:31).[67]

Retaining the stories of previous generations is a loving act. When applying this idea to our depraved historical episodes, Dr. Volf follows it to its noble conclusion. "Many writers, artists, and thinkers," he writes, "are soldiers of memory."[68] To tell a story that willfully forgets the inconvenient and formative hardships of real human beings is, at best, mythologizing. At worst, it is thinly veiled, self-serving deceit. Either way, it is an unjust act. A historical narrative that does not vigilantly reflect the relevant details results in a skewed take on the present. It may fulfill an agenda, but it does not do the work of a historian. "Remembering rightly" enables us to see history more thoroughly, which frees us to correct exaggerations and purge myths. As we proceed, we must retain and honor this pivotal lesson while considering the historical and cultural context of American evangelicalism.

Part Two

HISTORY AND CULTURE

AMERICAN EVANGELICALISM HAS A DETERMINATIVE STORY. BEFORE EFFEC-
tively evaluating our condition, we must appreciate the
historical events that gave rise to our present. To that end, part
II is a survey of American evangelicalism's origins and consequent values. I begin the historical narrative *before* the era of
evangelicalism's emergence. We must start earlier because evangelicalism's birth had a formative gestation period—a *prequel*.
It is a historical runway that reveals a tendency to spotlight
Euro-centric culture to the exclusion of others. Though this
tendency predates evangelicalism, we willingly inherited it as
foundational. Also, I consider world and American history
while pondering American evangelical history. I maintain that
such an approach is right and even necessary because of the
inevitable mingling of Christian and non-Christian narratives;
the latter contextualizes the former.

Chapter Four

THE GESTATION PERIOD AND A SEMINAL IDEOLOGY

History, despite its wrenching pain, cannot be unlived,
but if faced with courage, need not be lived again.
—MAYA ANGELOU[1]

I HAVE A LONGSTANDING LITERARY AFFECTION FOR THE LATE TONI MORRISON. It started as an academic fascination, but it became more. If you're familiar with Morrison's work, you know words were, for her, instruments akin to Picasso's brushes. She wrote in high-def, using vivid, sometimes ominous imagery. She took precious time introducing her characters. Morrison *walked* her readers to pivotal moments; she avoided hasty *jumps*. While writing a novel, Morrison attends to what I call the "gestation period"—the series of events and ideas that culminate in a pivotal moment.

Memorable events are like childbirth. They result from conception and a somewhat obscure gestation period. (Genesis 1 is an exception that proves the rule.) The past is a series of seemingly peripheral, interwoven, unobserved occurrences culminating in episodes that garner our attention. Morrison's care for gestation is not—or shall I say, should not be—unique to fiction. It is an essential quality of good stories, including historical narratives. Rushing to a moment without considering its causal runway gives only the illusion of understanding. While a timeline *jumps* from one moment to the next, a historical narrative *walks*. If the past is a foreign land, we are oblivious tourists. To benefit from a trip across time, we must know the relevant languages, customs, worldviews, and ideologies. Otherwise, we have only what W. E. B. Du Bois dubbed the "propaganda of history."[2]

WHERE TO START

When writing an American evangelical history, we must consider relevant world and national history. Faith and context are symbiotic; for good or ill, the two sway one another. But where do we start? It is impossible to write everything. With that in mind, recall that I am addressing the ethnic rift that plagues American evangelicalism. This rift—the product of a seminal ideology that predates America—sets my starting point and establishes which details are pertinent to *this* book. We must start at its conception and subsequent gestation.

THE SACROSANCT STORY

I don't know when I first heard the popular account of America's discovery. Teachers told us the critical points with no context, so I was intuitively suspicious. The story was like an invalid answer to a math problem; at a glance, you may not know why it's wrong, but you know enough to ask questions.

The American "discovery" story was sacrosanct, so my inquiries were judged disrespectful. Even now, when I hear the word *exasperated*, the face of a specific teacher comes to mind. She was at least a decade younger than any teacher I'd ever had and little more than a decade older than her students. I recall her as kind, patient, and attractive, an example of subtle Southern charm—accent and all. She was doubtless the first crush of many preteen boys. Her appeal did not provoke mannish feelings. Instead, it nurtured trust, which, for me, was often marred by her absurd accounts of American history. I barraged her with questions, the only device available to a puzzled student. My raised hand provoked poorly veiled sighs. Whenever we broached the subject of American discovery, I queried: "If people were already on the land, how could Columbus 'discover' it?"[3] To my young mind, the "discovery" story glorifies a robber, and everyone seemed okay with it. Sometimes it takes a child to admit that "the emperor has no clothes."

THE "DISCOVERY" MYTH

For generations, the American story began with the whimsical tale of Christopher Columbus, an Italian explorer speciously credited with "discovering" the Americas in 1492 while on a crusade to prove Earth's "roundness." The tale is a nineteenth-century story composed primarily by novelist Washington Irving.[4] Irving's account is better classified as *historical fiction* because it is loosely (very loosely!) based on actual events and characters. If readers keep this in mind, it has potential as an escapist story, but when read as tried history, it is dangerous.

Credible historians have debunked much of the Columbus myth, but some of its aspects have staying power. The space that Columbus occupies in our minds is best exhibited by the cities, provinces, and countries that pay him homage: America's District of Columbia (Washington, DC), Canada's British Columbia, and South America's Colombia are among the examples.[5] Historians are amending the fib, so Columbus's luster is diminishing.[6] But he espoused an ideology that still plagues us and needs confrontation.

WHAT IS IDEOLOGY?

Broadly speaking, an ideology is a value or set of values held by an individual or group. I am using *ideology* in a pejorative sense—untested presuppositions based on egocentric ideals, utopian superstitions, or "myths."[7] Such ideology is not merely a belief; it is a dubious conviction treated as fact. Ultimately, it serves as the framework for desired social norms.[8] That is to say, a person or group wishes the world were a certain way, so they adopt or devise foundational values that corroborate their desired world. They then stand firm on the values, even if they misrepresent or oversimplify reality.[9] Such ideologies are dangerous because, though they are not always entirely wrong, they are always incomplete and reductionistic. Because it oversimplifies society and values, it can reduce godly virtues to a vice by turning them into idols.[10]

I maintain that *the assumption of European Christian superiority was the seminal ideology behind the aggressive expansion of Eurocentric Christian culture.*[11] European culture is not necessarily bad, but turning it into an idol is dangerous. To be clear, I am *not* critical of the missional spread of the gospel. The Great Commission is both a joy and an imperative (Matt. 28:18–20; 2 Cor. 5:16–21). However, the assumption of European culture as the premier vessel of Christianity is the result of a virtue descended to a vice. Self-worth has merit, but in isolation it descends to sin—domineering supremacy.

THE AGE OF DISCOVERY

Upon acquiring the technology for long-distance seafaring trips, Europe commenced the "age of discovery" or the "age of European expansion."[12] Portugal and Spain were among the exploratory front-runners, and the supremacy ideology received a boost from distinguished Christian authorities—Catholic popes and European monarchs. Historian Justo González partially associates the Roman Church's steep moral decline with the Great Schism of 1054—a split within the church that had *theological, political,* and *organizational* instigators.[13] It resulted in a plurality of authorities and, thus, confusion. There were occasions when two—and even three—claimants declared themselves head of the church. The chaos exposed the Catholic Church to discord and ensuing corruption. To this point, González writes:

> Almost as soon as the schism was healed, the papacy fell into the hands of men who were more moved by the glories of the Renaissance than by the message of the cross. Through war, intrigue, bribery, and licentiousness, these popes sought to restore and to outdo the glories of ancient Rome. As a result, while most people still believed in the supreme authority of the Roman see, many found it difficult to reconcile their faith in the papacy with their distrust for its actual occupants.[14]

The disunity amounted to a leadership vacuum as unscrupulous men took advantage.[15]

Some popes fell to the lure of power grabs and conquests. They sought new lands to garner resources, discover trade routes, expand national boundaries, and spread "the Christian Empire." As they encountered new peoples, they evaluated them, and the assessments were hardly favorable. Throughout colonialism, there was the austere need to defend indigenous peoples against assumptions that they were naturally "slaves," "barbarians," and "animals."[16]

PORTUGAL

King Alfonso V of Portugal, a poor European nation, sought to procure African territory. The land was inhabited, so Alfonso V, who was Catholic, appealed to Pope Nicholas V for authority to occupy the land, harvest its resources, and expand trade opportunities.[17] Portugal's Prince Henry the Navigator branded the conquest of the indigenous peoples as charitable, an opportunity to Christianize and, therefore, civilize them.[18] The Christianization included European culturalization.

Nicholas V honored Alfonso V's request in 1452 by issuing a papal bull, *Dum Diversas*, granting Portugal sovereignty over the "discovered" African lands. A papal bull is an authoritative decree from the pope. According to Roman Catholic theology, the pope is in the apostolic line of succession that began with the apostle Peter.[19] As the "vicar of Christ," he wields the keys of the heavenly kingdom. A papal bull is, thus, received as a divine decree through God's representative.[20] With this assumed authority, Nicholas V gave Portugal sovereignty over the African land *and* its inhabitants.[21] In 1455 he supplemented his first bull with a second, *Romanis Pontifex*, which authorized Portugal

To invade, search out, capture, vanquish, and subdue all Saracens [Muslims] and pagans whatsoever, and other enemies of Christ wherever placed, and the kingdoms, dukedoms, principalities, dominions, possessions, and all movable and immovable goods whatsoever held and possessed by them *and to reduce their persons to perpetual slavery*, and to apply and appropriate to himself and his successors the kingdoms, dukedoms, counties, principalities, dominions, possessions, and goods, and to convert them to his and their use and profit. . . . The said King Alfonso . . . *justly and lawfully* has acquired and obsessed, and doth possess, these islands, lands, harbors, seas, and they do of right belong and pertain to said King Alfonso and his successors.[22]

Pope Nicholas V's bull hearkened back to the Crusades—aggressive campaigns sanctioned by Pope Urban II. The "First Crusade" was a response to Islam. In the name of "holy war," Muslim armies laid siege to Christian holy lands. In 1095, Urban II commissioned Christian pilgrims to take up arms and reclaim sacred soil. For the Crusaders, the aggressions were a substitute for penance. Historian John Dickson writes that Crusaders "willing to . . . fight the Muslims, and reclaim Jerusalem for the Lord would receive full pardon for sins and the promise of salvation."[23] Nicholas V cited the Crusades as license to take militaristic action against a land's inhabitants. But his papal bulls sanctioned unprovoked aggression against noncombatants. Under the banner of Christ, he authorized Portugal to confiscate land and enslave indigenous African peoples.

PORTUGAL AND THE SLAVE TRADE

Even if spreading the Christian faith was a sincere goal, it quickly succumbed to another mission. Because the papal bulls condoned "perpetual servitude," financially strapped Portugal parlayed slavery into an economic boon. According to historian Martin Meredith,

> The trade in slaves soon turned out to be the most profitable part of their business . . . To finance their purchase of gold, the Portuguese began to participate in the domestic slave trade off west Africa. Their usual trade goods such as cloth had limited value in an equatorial climate; horses could not survive the trypanosomiasis virus carried by the tsetse fly in the rainforest belt. Firearms were in good demand but selling them was banned by the Papal bulls to prevent them from reaching Muslim adversaries. *The Portuguese solution was to act as middlemen in the slave trade.*[24]

The church prohibited trading firearms but had no restriction on trading human beings. So the indigenous inhabitants became a profitable resource of the newly "discovered" land.

Slave traders, both African and European, obtained humans who were either kidnapped or prisoners of intertribal African conflicts. Europeans purchased them and set them to perpetual servitude throughout Northern Africa, the Middle East, and Europe.[25] It was a lucrative business for Portugal and the inception of the large-scale intercontinental slave trade. The freedom to "justly and lawfully" treat human beings as commodities results from the supremacy ideology, and Portugal recognized the Roman Church as the authority behind their ventures with offerings from the land's proceeds. Theologian Willie Jennings notes, "Prince Henry, following his deepest Christian instincts, ordered a tithe be given to God through the Church. Two black boys were given, one to the principal Church in Lagos and another to the Franciscan convent on Cape Saint Vincent."[26] The boys were treated as property, a sampling of the commodities harvested from the land.

SPAIN

King Ferdinand and Queen Isabella of Spain observed Portugal's ventures and desired similar expansion.[27] But if Spain openly attempted to harvest African territory, they would violate the papal bulls that granted African land exclusively to Portugal. They were Catholic, and violating the bulls could be penalized with excommunication from the church.[28] So after years of reluctance, the Spanish monarchs were open to Columbus's petitions for patronage.[29] They granted Columbus the title "High Admiral of the Ocean Sea" and assured him he would be "viceroy and perpetual governor" of any "discovered" lands. But, leery of Columbus's potential for "discovery," Spain's investment was nominal. They provided only three ships, and Columbus set sail with approximately eighty-six men.

Columbus purportedly set out to find a westbound route to Asia for easier trade with Japan, China, and India.[30] Doing so would avoid the lands already "discovered" by Portugal. He did not find the route, and he never set foot on the land now known as the United States. In 1492, he came upon the Caribbean Islands. Columbus erroneously believed he'd sailed west from Europe, circumnavigated the planet, and arrived on the eastern shores of South Asia. Because of his false belief, the indigenous peoples of the Americas were wrongly tagged "Indians," and the islands located at the convergence of the Atlantic Ocean and the Caribbean Sea are still known as "the West Indies."[31]

Columbus spent months mapping the islands and searching for precious resources. They named one of the islands Hispaniola (modern-day Haiti and the Dominican Republic), where they encountered indigenous peoples. Columbus garnered their trust by trading trinkets like copper bells and colored glass.[32] The indigenous peoples accommodated the Europeans and came to their aid, providing food and serving as tour guides.

Initially, the proceeds of the land were sparser than

Columbus had hoped. The indigenous peoples wore gold as jewelry, but Columbus could not find it in abundance. The expedition experienced a setback when the *Santa Maria*, Columbus's flagship, ran aground and was beyond recovery.[33] The two remaining vessels were too small to accommodate the men, so they built a makeshift fort on the eastern shores of Hispaniola. Thirty-nine men remained on the island while Columbus surveyed the other islands and returned to Spain to report his "discovery." On his return, Columbus brought "samples" of New World commodities. The cargo included gold, exotic birds, plants, and kidnapped human beings—many of whom died during the trip. The samples were promising enough for Spain to sponsor a second voyage. They provided seventeen ships, and Columbus returned to the Caribbean with approximately twelve-hundred "conquistadors," which means "conquerors."[34] Historian Thomas Kidd calls them "soldiers of fortune, looking for the treasures hidden in the New World."[35]

SPAIN AND THE "NEW WORLD"

Like Portugal before them, Spain petitioned the church for rights to the "discovered" land, and Pope Alexander VI accommodated them in 1493, issuing a papal bull, *Inter Caetera*.[36] Spain was concerned about conflicting interpretations of the various papal bulls, so ultimately, Alexander divided the non-European world between Spain and Portugal. He marked a location approximately three hundred miles west of the Azorean islands, off the western coast of Europe, and drew a vertical line through that mark from the north pole to the south pole. "Discoveries" east of the line were Portugal's, and "discoveries" west of the line were Spain's. Portugal observed that the division favored Spain (Alexander VI was a Spaniard). Portugal took offense, so the pope resolved the matter by moving the line westward. The new line granted the easternmost part of South America (modern-day Brazil) to Portugal. Spain and Portugal recognized the revised boundary via the Treaty of Tordesillas (1494).[37]

SLAVERY IN THE "NEW WORLD"

Upon returning to Hispaniola, Columbus discovered the makeshift fort burned and the thirty-nine conquistadors killed. Bartolomé de Las Casas, a sixteenth-century Spanish priest and historian, argued the conquistadors were abusive while Columbus was away. They enslaved the natives and sexually assaulted the tribal women.[38] Moreover, they ate excessively. The natives resorted to hiding food, and, according to Las Casas, the conquistadors tortured and even killed natives until they disclosed the reserves. The natives eventually responded to the abuse by killing the men.[39] Columbus and cohorts took vengeance by enslaving the natives—setting them to servitude in gold and silver mines and on sugar plantations.

Though the deaths of the conquistadors was an instigator, slavery was always the plan. In 1482, a decade before "discovering" the "New World," Columbus observed Portugal's lucrative business on Africa's Gold Coast (modern-day Ghana). They'd built the port of Elmina, an active trade post for precious metals, ivory, and enslaved humans.[40] While Columbus is known for exploration, financial gain was his priority. According to historian Andrés Reséndez, Columbus, noticing Portugal's economic gains, "could observe how a European stronghold on another continent could thrive by trading various products, including humans."[41] Hispaniola was a candidate for such a stronghold. Colonial presence in the "New World" would make slave labor a precious commodity, an observation that was not lost on Columbus.

THE HOLLOW JUSTIFICATION FOR SLAVERY IN THE "NEW WORLD"

Savagery, specifically cannibalism, was cited as validation for conquering and enslaving tribes of the "New World." Columbus and his men may have encountered at least one tribe, the Caribs, that allegedly practiced cannibalism, and enslavement was the purported means of civilizing them. Science journalist Jake Page argued there is no evidence of cannibalism, which is noteworthy.[42] However, even if the dubious allegations of Carib cannibalism were true, it does not explain the sweeping enslavement of overtly peaceful tribes. For instance, after the loss of the *Santa Maria*, the Taino tribal chief offered assistance to recover the ship. He tearfully mourned its loss and provided gifts to boost Columbus's morale. Hernando Colón, Columbus's son, described the tribe's response as "great kindness." They even offered their homes to store the sunken ship's contents.[43]

The Arawak and Taino were, by all accounts, initially timid, then accommodating and sacrificially hospitable. Despite this, they were among the first enslaved.[44] The enslavement of the natives was hardly a police action; it was the realization of a decade-old plan. Columbus was moving toward a slave trade stronghold on the eastern coast of Hispaniola, a replica of the Portuguese port Elmina.

THE TRANSATLANTIC SLAVE TRADE

Queen Isabella advocated for the humane treatment of indigenous peoples, but while Spain hotly debated the specifics, Columbus dispatched cargo vessels to Spain. In 1495, he sent three ships with five hundred fifty humans stored in their cargo holds—"The best men and women" chosen from a lot of sixteen hundred kidnapped natives. The rest were released or offered to conquistadors who would remain in the "New World." On the trip to Spain, many of the five hundred fifty succumbed to disease or extreme cold, and the sailors tossed their bodies overboard. Columbus also gave indigenous women as gifts. His childhood friend Michele da Cuneo tells of receiving "a beautiful Carib girl [*bellisima Camballa*] who was brought to [his] cabin . . . and seeing her completely naked as is their custom, the desire to have her came over [him]."[45]

Reminiscent of Portugal in Africa, Spain identified the "New World's" indigenous peoples as commodities. The Spanish presence in the "New World" took a toll. Historian David Abulafia notes that few descendants of the indigenous peoples remain today. The population was devastated by harsh labor, malnutrition, and, worst of all, European illnesses to which the natives had no immunity.[46] Spain needed enslaved people to harvest resources from the land, so the steep death rate was problematic. Initially, they supplemented the depleted numbers by shipping enslaved people from Spain, which inaugurated the large-scale transatlantic slave trade. Then, in 1580, Spain and Portugal formed the Iberian Union, which granted Portugal a monopoly on the slave trade to the "New World."[47] The transatlantic slave trade became a lucrative business in itself.

ROMAN CATHOLICISM IN CHURCH HISTORY

I anticipate American evangelicals will review the content of this chapter and observe that Roman Catholic popes authorized the iniquitous behavior. That observation is sensible. However, while the boundary between Catholicism and Protestantism exists, it is a dotted line. Whether or not we wish it true, the Roman Catholic Church is American evangelicalism's foreparent. It is, therefore, inappropriate to study church history by jumping from the third century to the sixteenth, writing off all that occurred in the intervening centuries. Evangelicals almost universally recognize and value the investments of Catholic theologians like Augustine and Aquinas, and they are right to do so. But Augustine and Aquinas are not the only Catholics from whom we inherit our identity. Whole cloth disassociation from the Roman Catholic Church is impossible because history, theology, and ideology tether us.[48]

Portugal and Spain acted with the consent of, and even at the behest of, the Roman Church. There are bold procedural similarities between the Roman Empire and the Roman Catholic Church; among them is *imperialism*, the expansion of a nation through diplomacy or military force. While it is not unique to Rome, imperialism is associated most with the Roman Empire, and Rome influenced the church. Justo L. González observes, "The Church imitated the uses of the [Roman] empire, not only in its liturgy, but also in its social structure." The Roman Catholic Church was a Christian facsimile of the Roman Empire. Popes were to the church what emperors were to Rome. The overlap between them dates back to Emperor Constantine, who confessed Christianity. Because of this affiliation, Christians went from enduring extreme persecution to enjoying influence in the Roman Empire. Many, like the historian Eusebius, interpreted this as evidence of God's favor and an affirmation of the Roman Empire.[49] But Christian values were compromised by the union. Yes, Rome was Christianized, but the church, in many regards, was unsuitably Romanized. History is a blaring alarm confronting unexamined Christian nationalism; this will prove relevant later.

Historian Will Durant's summary of the symbiotic relationship between the church and the empire is estimable; it justifies a lengthy quote. He writes,

By the middle of the third century, the position and resources of the papacy were so strong that Decius vowed he would rather have a rival emperor at Rome than a pope. *The capital of the empire naturally became the capital of the Church.*

As Judea had given Christianity ethics, and Greece had given it theology, so now *Rome gave it organization*; all these, with a dozen absorbed and rival faiths, entered into the Christian synthesis. . . . *The Roman gift was above all a vast framework of government, which, as secular authority failed, became the structure of ecclesiastical rule. Soon the bishops, rather than the Roman prefects, would be the source of order and the seat of power in the cities*; the metropolitans, or archbishops, would support, if not supplant, the provincial governors; and the synod of bishops would succeed the provincial assembly. *The Roman Church followed in the footsteps of the Roman state; it conquered the provinces, beautified the capital, and established discipline and unity from frontier to frontier. Rome died in giving birth to the Church; the Church matured by inheriting and accepting the responsibilities of Rome.*[50]

The intermingling of the Roman Empire and the Roman Church survived Rome's descent. Roman Catholicism preserved many Roman norms. European empires, led by Catholic monarchs, had the church as a relic of Roman imperialism. Keeping this in mind may elucidate the pronouncements of popes like Urban II, Nicholas V, Innocent IV, and, expressly, Alexander VI.[51] These men were not, by any means, representative of all popes. Still, they were legitimate ambassadors of Roman Catholicism, and they embodied imperial values that the church co-opted from the empire. Just as Rome militarily expanded its borders, the Roman Catholic Church condoned militarily expanding European Christianity and felt justified as they enslaved indigenous peoples in the process. In the next chapter, we will note that the Roman Church policies of colonialism and conquests were inherited by her Protestant progenies. And even now, we are reaping the consequences.

Chapter Five

COLONIALISM AND SLAVERY

My part has been to tell the story of the slave. The
story of the master never wanted for narrators.
—FREDERICK DOUGLASS[1]

IN 1963, MARTIN LUTHER KING JR. WROTE *LETTER FROM BIRMINGHAM JAIL,*
a response to clergymen who published a critique of civil rights
demonstrations in Birmingham, Alabama. They believed the
protests were "unwise and untimely."[2] Patiently waiting,
they maintained, would bring justice. King, incarcerated for
his role in the campaign, read the statement while in a jail
cell, where he promptly drafted a reply. He wrote of children
expected to "wait" patiently while bigoted adults unhurriedly
embraced universal human dignity. He mentioned a parent
watching their child's self-worth receding as "ominous clouds
of inferiority . . . form in [their] little mental sky."[3] I was the
child of whom he wrote—a boy battling the notion that he is
peripheral.

Only months before I read *Letter from Birmingham Jail,*
a teacher told me that "black people have American names
because they forgot their African names." She claimed that

enslavers kindly provided identities for the pitifully anonymous. With no apparent malice, she avowed that Africans
"couldn't take care of themselves, so someone more capable
did." She said it matter-of-factly. But who forgets their name?
Her words were seeds of inferiority planted in the heart of a
boy who adored her. My "little mental sky" was overcast.

That same year, I watched *Roots*, a miniseries based on
Alex Haley's novel *Roots: The Saga of an American Family*.
The story is historical fiction inspired by Haley's African foreparents, chiefly Kunta Kinte, who was kidnapped and enslaved
as a teenager, then shipped to America. Those familiar with the
saga will recall the moment Kunta had his name involuntar-
ily changed to "Toby."[4] Kunta scoffed at the reidentification,
so the overseer had him flogged until he yielded under the
whip. Haley's novel truthfully echoes the historical practice of
stripping newly enslaved humans of their names. Sociologist
Orlando Peterson observes,

> [A] major feature of the ritual of enslavement involved the
> changing of the slave's name. A man's name is, of course,
> more than simply a way of calling him. It is the verbal signal
> of his whole identity, his being-in-the-world as a distinct
> person. It also establishes his relation with kinsmen. . . . In
> every slave society one of the first acts of the master has
> been to change the name of the new slave. . . . The changing
> of a name is almost universally a symbolic act of stripping
> a person of his former identity. . . . The slave's former name
> died with his former self.[5]

Enslaved Africans were not victims of bizarre amnesia!
Their names—their former selves—were pilfered and cast off.
Whips, shackles, iron collars—all manner of inhumanity—were

tools of plunder. Society empowered enslavers to declare a person's indigenous identity void. A comprehensive history would stray from this book's scope. However, ignoring formative parts of American colonialism and slavery only allows the supremacy ideology to thrive. This chapter spotlights *some* aspects of the story to set up the theological evaluation that follows.

THE DOCTRINE OF DISCOVERY

In the previous chapter we discussed fifteenth-century papal bulls that set precedents for international law. A principle now known as the "doctrine of discovery" classified any territory, even inhabited land, as undiscovered until a European Christian nation "discovered" it.[6] It was the legal basis for European colonialism—consent to discard non-European cultures and languages and take their "geophysical bounty."[7] The doctrine of discovery answers the question I'd posed as a child. Columbus could "discover" occupied land because he represented Catholic European monarchs who were sanctioned by Roman Catholic popes; it gave him the ostensible prerogative to conquer in Christ's name.

The doctrine of discovery mitigated conflicts among monarchies by delineating territorial lines between Europe's expanding empires. As new land was "discovered," popes determined whose it was. Steven Newcomb, the cofounder of the Indigenous Law Institute, asserts that "what is generally referred to as the doctrine of discovery might be more accurately called the doctrine of Christian European arrival, or, better still, the doctrine of Christian European invasion."[8]

Conscious Christian voices contemporaneously opposed

European "discovery" practices. Bartolomé de Las Casas, a sixteenth-century Spanish Roman Catholic priest, witnessed cruelty toward indigenous peoples. In response, he dedicated most of his life to opposing enslavement and abuse. "To subject them first by warlike means," he maintained, "is a form and procedure contrary to the law, gentle yoke, easy burden and gentleness of Jesus Christ." Las Casas compared Spain's policies to the conquests and imperialism common to Islam and European empires, noting:

> It was the same method used by Mahomet and the Romans to upset and despoil the world. . . . Therefore it is most evil, tyrannical, libelous of the sweet name of Christ, and the cause of infinite new blasphemies against the true God and the Christian religion . . . because of it, the Indians consider God to be the most cruel, unjust and pitiless of gods, and consequently it impedes the conversion of many unfaithful, giving rise to the impossibility of infinite people in the new world ever to become Christians.[9]

Las Casas argued that Spain's pope-sanctioned conquests were an embarrassment to Christ's name, undermining the Christian witness to indigenous peoples of the "New World." The professed mission of Christianizing the Americas was subsumed by imperialism, making Christian conversions increasingly improbable.

The United States' founding fathers affirmed the doctrine of discovery and recognized it as the divine basis for "American exceptionalism" and "Manifest Destiny."[10] German philosopher Immanuel Kant retrospectively criticized colonizing and conquest practices. He challenges his readers to consider:

The inhospitable actions of the civilized and especially of the commercial states of our part of the world. The injustice which they show to lands and peoples they visit (which is equivalent to conquering them) is carried by them to terrifying lengths. *America, the lands inhabited by the Negro, the Spice Islands, the Cape, etc., were at the time of their discovery considered by these civilized intruders as lands without owners, for they counted the inhabitants as nothing.*[11]

The objections of ethicists notwithstanding, "discovery" became European policy. From the fifteenth century, it was established international law, and many of the details were set by the Roman Church, sanctioned by unscrupulous popes. The church was in need of reform.

ENTER MARTIN LUTHER

Reformation does not occur in a moment. Before Martin Luther, vocal dissidents addressed the theological and ethical descent of the Roman Church. But the sixteenth-century Protestant Reformation bore extraordinary fruit. Luther, a Catholic monk, rejected many of the church's teachings and openly criticized papal corruption. On October 31, 1517, he published his critiques, tacking his "Ninety-Five Theses" to the door of the Castle Church in Wittenberg, Germany.[12]

Among Luther's concerns was the church's practice of selling indulgences, but he also questioned the scope of papal authority. A series of popes believed they'd inherited authority first consigned to the apostle Peter. According to historian Eamon Duffy, popes assumed "both spiritual and temporal power, *exercising spiritual power directly, and temporal power indirectly through obedient Christian rulers.* The Pope, like Christ, is supreme in both spheres."[13] The popes' presumptuous authority explains why Catholic European monarchs appealed to them before conquering new lands.[14] The popes and the monarchs had a symbiotic relationship. The monarchs were the popes' means of "temporal power," and the popes provided a divine co-sign for the monarch's conquests. Luther's critique of papal authority could potentially upend a longstanding and lucrative arrangement.

It takes little imagination to anticipate how the pope would respond to Luther's public appraisal. Pope Leo X appealed for an order that Luther rescind his critiques of the papal office. Luther refused, so Leo issued a papal bull (*Decet Romanum Pontificem*) excommunicating him. Luther maintained his criticisms at an imperial trial (The Diet of Worms), so Emperor Charles V, who was catholic, declared him an "outlaw." Ostracism led to no substantive change in Luther's resolve. He spent much of his life inventively insulting the pope and challenging the scope of papal authority.[15]

THE ENGLISH STREAM OF THE REFORMATION

The Reformation was not a monolith; it contextually splintered into at least four streams: the Lutheran, the Swiss or Reformed, the Anabaptist, and the English or Anglican.[16] The English Reformation is relevant here because it set the stage for North American colonialism. When popes defined "discovery" practices in the fifteenth century, England was a Catholic nation bound by papal bulls and the Treaty of Tordesillas.[17] But Henry the VIII, the petulant King of England, quarreled with a pope and their tiff led to a split between England and the Roman Catholic Church. Henry responded by starting the Church of England, and English Parliament appointed him head of the church. England had the occasional Catholic sympathizer on the throne, but the kingdom was decidedly *not* Catholic.[18]

ENGLAND'S NORTH AMERICAN COLONIALISM

Because of England's disassociation with Catholicism, English monarchs had no compulsion to submit their North American colonial plans to the pope.[19] Still, they conveniently applied international "discovery" policies. Robert J. Miller, a doctrine of discovery specialist, notes that England carefully interpreted "discovery" to justify their right to North American land.[20] English lawyers argued that "discovery" requires occupancy. It would not be enough for Spain merely to know North America existed; they had to stake a claim and take up residence to uphold the claim. In direct violation of papal bulls, which they no longer recognized as authoritative, England started establishing colonies on the eastern shores of North America.

JAMESTOWN AND THE OTHER ENGLISH COLONIES

England founded Jamestown, Virginia, in 1607, sustaining their discovery rights; Virginia was the first of thirteen successful colonies. Settlers received free land in return for seven years of labor. The circumstances were grueling. After the winter of 1609–10, most English settlers were dead. Conflicts with Native American tribes were devastating, and food was in low supply. Whispers of cannibalism among the English settlers abounded.[21] The survivors planned to abandon the colony, but reinforcements arrived. They brought an infusion of labor, leadership in the form of a provisional government, and a legal code to establish order among the settlers. The code reflected Protestant Christian values; historian Paul Johnson dubbed it "distinctly puritan," noting that "Sabbath observance was strictly enforced, immodest dress was forbidden and idleness punished severely." Johnson also notes the product that provoked the rise of North American slavery:

The colony was not yet self-supporting even in food, however, and had nothing to export to England. But, the year after the code was promulgated, a settler named John Rolfe, fearing prosecution for idleness, began experiments with tobacco. After trying various seeds, he produced a satisfactory crop, the first sweet tasting Virginian tobacco, and by 1616 it was already exportable.[22]

Rolfe discovered the cardinal crop that would be central to the nascent Virginian economy.

NATIVE AMERICAN SLAVERY AND INDENTURED SERVITUDE

Plantation owners grew wealthy by shipping their tobacco harvests across the Atlantic.[23] Virginia was prospering in less than a decade, competing with Portuguese and Spanish colonies established in the "New World" a century earlier.[24] While tobacco harvesting was lucrative, it was also laborious. The English settlers sought to conscript slave labor among the Native Americans, but the indigenous tribes resisted bondage. English settlers labeled them lazy. They assumed slavery was the natural order, so Native Americans were considered "haughty" because they did not comply.[25]

Capturing and keeping Native Americans proved difficult. They were familiar with the lay of the land, so they could escape and disappear into the countryside. The settlers concluded that capturing and selling them to plantations in unfamiliar regions allowed for easier enslavement. But Native Americans were willing to fight. The tribes were members of a confederacy called the Powhatans, making them formidable. Historian Thomas Kidd notes that the Powhatans "demonstrated repeatedly that they were capable of countering and even defeating English power in Virginia."[26] While the settlers were able to subjugate some Native Americans, the enslaved numbers could not meet the demand of the bountiful tobacco harvests.

Plantation owners supplemented slave labor with "indentured servitude." An *indenture* is a contractual agreement between a servant and a patron. Poor Europeans served for an agreed-upon time, usually four to seven years, in return for the cost of travel from Europe to North America. Their labor went toward paying their debt. The work was arduous, and deadly diseases like malaria were rampant. Many indentured servants did not survive the duration of the contract. Upon fulfilling the agreement, indentured servants were released and, ideally, were free to pursue the "New World's" opportunities. Unlike African and Native American enslaved people, European indentured servants had rights. Though they were often mistreated, they were *not* property. They had recourse in courts of law.[27]

THE ARRIVAL OF AFRICANS

On August 20, 1619, John Rolfe recorded the arrival of a ship, the *White Lion*, that had "20 and odd negars" available for sale or trade.[28] According to historian Lerone Bennett Jr., the ship was "manned by pirates and thieves" who had hijacked the vessel while it was en route to the Caribbean.[29] The "20 and odd" human beings were the first recorded Africans in North America. Sir George Yeardley, provisional governor of Virginia, traded "victuals" (food and provisions) for at least fifteen of the Africans and set them to work on a one-thousand-acre tobacco plantation.[30] Whether the Africans were enslaved or indentured is unclear.[31] They were in debt to no one, were in Jamestown under duress, and probably did not live long. Owning them was no violation of the "distinctly Puritan" moral code upheld by the colony. The English settler's understanding of Protestant Christianity did not preclude human bondage.

In the first generation of the colony, some African indentured servants gained freedom. Still, they were second-class
members of the colony. They were lower in the human hierarchy, with landowners at the top and indentured servants
and slaves at the bottom. "'Gentlemen' not only expected to
receive the deference of their social inferiors but were willing
to expend considerable force to ensure it."[32]

The colonies honored a de facto social caste system that was
not initially confined to "race." Native Americans, Africans, and
the Irish were all, to varying degrees, considered subordinate.
Inferiority was *not* determined by *what one was*; it was decided
by *what one was not*. For instance, the English deemed Africans
"savage or uncivilized" because African "culture was very different from that of Europeans and appeared to the English to
be manifestly outlandish and inferior."[33] In other words, they
were *lesser* because they were *other*. The supremacy ideology
traveled from Europe to North America. More to the point, it
was no longer limited to the Roman Church, it was now the policy of many Protestant English settlers. The caste system was a
social presupposition during the brief window between colonial
founding and institutionalized slavery in North America.

AFRICANS AND THE "RIGHTS OF ENGLISHMEN"

1619 also marks the year that the settlers received the
"rights of Englishmen." With Sir George Yeardley serving as
governor, Virginia organized a legislative machine that was
a "miniature parliament." But the settlers denied citizenship
to Africans who were in Virginia. This is an unambiguous
embodiment of the caste system. Paul Johnson writes:

Thus in 1619 the first English colony in America embarked
on two roads which bifurcated and led in two totally different directions: representative institutions, leading to

democratic freedoms, and the use of slave-labor, the 'peculiar institution' of the South. . . . The bifurcation was real, and it eventually produced a society divided into two castes of human beings, the free and the unfree. These two roads were to be relentlessly and incongruously pursued, for a quarter of a millennium, until their foundational incompatibility was resolved in a gigantic civil war.[34]

Even before slave-sustaining laws, the colonies established castes for humans, an instantiation of the supremacy ideology. Because they were *other*, African indentured servants who, despite the odds, survived the duration of their contract would earn no rights of citizenship or equal protection under the law.

THE CORRELATION BETWEEN SLAVERY AND RACE

The correlation between slavery and race can be nuanced, but it is real. Historian Peter Kolchin writes:

Indeed, what we now know suggests that the most appropriate question is not whether slavery caused prejudice or prejudice caused slavery (a false choice, since the evidence sustains neither of these two conjectures) but rather how slavery and prejudice interacted to create the particular set of social relationships that existed in the English mainland colonies.[35]

The English were atop the colony's social hierarchy; they placed themselves there. They needed a workforce to uphold their agriculturally based economy. Slavery was the chosen means of low-cost labor because *perpetual* bondage is cost-efficient. Enslaving a European for life was not an option because they ranked too high on the artificial hierarchy and had the protection of European nations. So the English settlers self-interestedly branded Africans and Native Americans worthy of bondage. Historian Joseph Harris writes, "It was *a combination of European attitudes about blacks and the demand for cheap labor* that sired the Atlantic slave trade and New World black slavery."[36]

SLAVERY CODIFIED

In 1667, only forty-eight years of the *White Lion*'s arrival, Virginia drafted laws relegating Africans to a condition of perpetual bondage. Blackness and whiteness took on meaning, and racial distinctions became policy. The racist social structure was in place *before* the invention of racial distinctions, but the codification of slavery relegated black people to taxable property.[37] Moreover, a black child inherited the mother's status, so, for enslaved Africans, *slavery was both lifelong and generational*. The law also determined that conversion to Christianity did not rescind perpetual slavery, which is noteworthy because the papal bulls limited slavery to non-Christians, and European legal precedents "suggested that only 'heathens' could be enslaved." English colonial law made Africans an exception to the bulls and European jurisprudence.[38]

English settlers mingled Christianization and imperialist conquest; imperialism often dominated the blend. A zeal for colonial expansion determined the policies of the colonists. Kolchin sheds light on the settlers' mindset: "In many ways, the world from which early colonists came was a world of pre-modern values, one that lacked the concepts of 'cruel and unusual,' equal rights, and exploitation; it was a world that instead took for granted natural human *in*equality."[39] The English brought the supremacy ideology with them to North America. *Race*, as we now use it, was invented to emphasize

the artificial human hierarchy, and racialized slavery was codified within one generation of colonial founding.

THE TRIANGULAR TRADE AND CHATTEL SLAVERY

Before 1700, a supply of enslaved Africans was readily
available. Spain and Portugal had refined the "transatlantic
slave trade" in the previous century. The English colonies
only accelerated the rate at which ships traversed the Atlantic.
Vessels traveled intercontinentally according to trade routes
determined by their cargo. The three-legged exchange was
known as "the triangular trade":

1. Settlers in North America garnered their profits by
   shipping raw goods like tobacco, sugar, and cotton to
   Europe;
2. African colonies received shipments of Europe's
   manufactured goods like fabrics, guns, and rum; and
3. ships traveled from Africa to the Americas carrying
   enslaved black humans.

The route that carried enslaved Africans to the Americas was
called the "middle passage," the most profitable of the three
legs. It was such a lucrative trip that many slave traders became
specialists, acquiring larger ships and customizing their holds
to accommodate tightly packed human cargo.[40] Slavery was
fundamental to colonial finances. Thomas Kidd observes,
"Although the Middle Colonies and New England were less
suited to plantation agriculture, *all of the English colonies had
connections to the slavery economy.*"[41]

In August 1619, there were "twenty and odd" enslaved
Africans in North America; in 1700, there were 27,817; in
1740, there were 150,024. By 1770, the enslaved African population grew to more than 462,000, about one-fifth of the

populace.[42] The remarkable boom in the enslaved population is indicative of slavery's essential role in the development of the English colonies. Slavery was an institution. Much commerce among the colonies and nations on four continents, occupying both sides of the Atlantic ocean, was built on trade driven by conscripted slave labor.[43] Africans were a means to an end, victims of what the Bible calls "man-stealing" (Gr. *andrapodistēs*; 1 Tim. 1:10; cf. Ex. 21:16; Deut. 24:7). They were taken under duress while theologians, Catholic and Protestant, cited God as the authority.

"NITPICKY" CAN BE A VIRTUE

In North America, Africans were initially enslaved because *they were not European*, but soon after, they were enslaved because *they were African*. The difference is subtle, and the outcome is essentially the same. But there is a need to highlight the nuance. I am picking at nits, but in history and theology, being *nitpicky* is a virtue. Initially, African slavery did not result from fixating on the assumption of African inferiority but from believing in the ideology of European supremacy. Gradually, but relatively quickly, these errors became two sides of one coin; while discussing one, the other was an assumption. Nuancing the two errors is necessary because, as we will see, even after slavery's abolition, the supremacy ideology remained a societal value. The supremacy ideology was deeply entrenched; it existed prior to, and independent of, chattel slavery. So it is a gross miscalculation to treat slavery's abolition as the death knell of systemic racism. The supremacy ideology remained a societal value, and prominent advocates of the racial caste system cited Protestant Christian theology as justification for their racialized notions.

Chapter Six

REASON OVER THEOLOGY

*Racial ideologies are insidious. They instruct
in intricate ambient teaching systems. The
country is their classroom and everyone is in
school, whether they choose to be or not.*
—ELIZABETH ALEXANDER[1]

ON APRIL 3, 1905, W. E. B. DU BOIS RECEIVED A LETTER FROM ALVIN
Borgquist, a graduate student at Clark University in Worcester,
Massachusetts. Borgquist researched crying, specifically its
correlation to emotions. He inquired of Du Bois, then teaching
at Atlanta University in Atlanta, Georgia, regarding weeping
among "colored people." In Du Bois, Borgquist accessed a
scholar par excellence, the first African American to receive a
Ph.D. from Harvard University. Even apart from such a feat,
he ranks among America's premier intellectuals. Du Bois was
chiefly adept regarding the black American experience. It is,
to me, peculiar that Borgquist consulted a thinker of such heft
with a question so inane as, "Does the Negro shed tears?"[2]

Du Bois conducted no research to answer Borgquist's
question; he was privy to black heartache, and it served as

anecdotal yet iron-clad evidence of black weeping. He replied, in part, "The negro sheds tears. . . . Our waters contain our sorrows."[3] Borgquist's letter was par for the course in the early twentieth century. The ethnic gulf kept understanding at bay, so he was reprehensibly unaware.

TWO PITFALLS OF IDEOLOGY

Reading Borgquist's inquiry in its context may allow for a brief moment's grace. In the aftermath of the Civil War and Reconstruction, the supremacy ideology manifested as sweeping segregation. Two pitfalls ensued: *obliviousness* and *reverse-engineered self-fulfilled notions*.

To be oblivious is to be ignorant of the world around you. Segregation created a chasm that allowed Borgquist to be ostensibly unaware of black tears. To be unconscious of the world around you is bad enough, but to be irrationally ignorant of mournful weeping—a common human experience—is worse still. Black people were *other*, observed with unseeing eyes. Borgquist asked a long-ignored question. Most were content not knowing the answer, deeming inquiries about the *other* absurd wastes of time. When people consciously segregate, brazen ignorance thrives and is perhaps even valued.

Witlessness and bad ideas are proximate—even chummy; where there is one, the other is usually nearby. In addition to starving people of mutual understanding, supremacy-fueled segregation feeds egregious ideas about the *other*. Baseless opinions cause immeasurably more damage than hushed ignorance. When the rubber meets the road, reality asks questions that should make us suspicious of the supremacy ideology: Why is racialized slavery acceptable? Who said segregation is the natural order? How do we reconcile our racist behavior with universal human dignity? "Does the Negro shed tears?" Alas, instead of allowing these questions to refine or purge our bad ideas, we invent justifications for the ideas. Instead of scrutinizing our bigotry, we hold fast to false notions of the *other*, then we *reverse-engineer baseless defenses of our assumptions*. The defenses are usually *self-fulfilled*, and manufactured out of whole cloth to prove supremacy. If we are not careful, even our Christian theology will be reshaped to justify our racialized ideologies. I maintain that has already occurred.

THE ENLIGHTENMENT

As we've seen, the Age of Discovery marked the era of European expansion, and the Protestant Reformation set the stage for Europe's presence in the Americas (see chaps. 4 and 5).[4] Also key to our discussion is the Age of *Enlightenment*, which molded Western intellectual method.

The Enlightenment was a movement that began in Europe during the seventeenth century; it prioritized human reason as the *chief* means to knowledge. Formerly, Europe recognized religion *and* reason as the one-two punch that shaped culture.[5] But the Enlightenment promoted reason. Religion became either irrelevant or supplemental to philosophy and science. Describing the Enlightenment, Philosopher Michael Inwood writes, "Beliefs [were] to be accepted *only on the basis of reason, not on the authority of priests, sacred texts, or tradition*."[6] According to historian Edmund S. Morgan, "The element of divinity had not entirely departed, but it was a good deal diluted."[7]

The Enlightenment contributed to the intellectual method known as *modernity*, a framework characterized by "secularization" and "naturalistic reason" that rejects or diminishes the supernatural.[8] Since God is, by definition, *supernatural*, modernity assesses the world through a lens that either denies God's existence (atheism) or downplays God's temporal relevance (deism).[9]

CHRISTIAN MODERNITY

Some Protestant thinkers responded to modernity by embracing it.[10] Such a strategy is not necessarily unsound, but it can limit Christianity to the boundaries of human reason, which may occur at the expense of good theology and ethics.[11] Theologian Michael Bird describes this tendency as "a *reaction* to Modernity *and* an *appropriation* of it."[12] He is rather critical of the strategy, writing:

> It might seem clever to try and outplay modernity at its own game. It is perhaps a necessity to take captive the usable elements of modernist philosophy and to press them into the service of Christian theology. . . . [Charles Hodge] and others *tried to walk the line between being in modernity but not of modernity*. The problem is that *they allowed modernity to define the rules of the game. They enabled modernity to set the agenda for theology, including the beginnings, task, and method. They also ran the risk that the failings of modernity, with its claim to unbridled access to absolute truth, could also become the failings of Christian theology*. By showing that the Word of God aligned with "reason," *they were in the end subjecting the Word of God beneath reason*.[13]

THEOLOGY AND PHILOSOPHY

Theology does not abhor philosophy; they can and, I maintain, should coexist. But "*theology is the queen . . . and philosophy is her handmaid*." Good theology is the logical starting point because insights hinge on credible revelation.[14] Philosophers will come to lousy conclusions if deprived of a good theological starting point. Theology is principal, and philosophy, though vital, is supplemental. Otherwise, we may reason our way toward bad ideas. Our disregard for this order had consequences. Modernity skulked into the church, disguised as Christian theology, and it brought its social failings.

REASONING *FROM* IDEOLOGY

The church's appropriation of modernity normalized Europe's intellectual method and egregious cultural values. Inevitably, subordinating theology to reason led to reasoning *from* ideology; it treated unexamined notions as foregone conclusions, then retroactively justified (Christianized) them.

Aristotle predates the Enlightenment by two millennia. But the Enlightenment breathed life into the intellectual *ethos* of Greco-Roman philosophy. In many regards, modernity, a product of the Renaissance, is a rebirth of old ideas, and Aristotle was among the consulted ancients.[15] His influence is such that some historical Christian thinkers reverentially crowned him "*the* Philosopher."[16] His ideas, despite his brilliance, were not always good, but they bear on the Western church. For instance, Aristotle believed a human hierarchy was essential to a healthy society, arguing that some humans are "natural slaves."[17] He did not devise this idea but stamped it with an intellectual's endorsement. Aristotle's notions were later packaged in Christian terms by acolytes. Saint Thomas Aquinas, one of the church's greatest minds, writes, "And so it is clear from the foregoing that it is advantages for slaves and masters, *fit to be such by nature*, that one be the master and the other the slave."[18]

Centuries later, the European Enlightenment contextualized the idea of natural slavery. Christian leaders followed the idea to a self-serving conclusion, arguing that enslaving Africans was essential to European expansion and civilization. Reasoning *from* unexamined ideology, the church sloppily adopted and affirmed depraved ideals of non-Christian intellectual champions.

AMERICAN REPRESENTATIVES OF THE SUPREMACY IDEOLOGY

The Enlightenment was not all bad; it was a basis for evaluating monarchies, natural law, and human rights.[19] In no small part, America is a government "of the people, by the people, and for the people" because representatives of the Enlightenment carefully pondered these matters. But there was a shadow side: the Enlightenment espoused a human caste system.[20] While pondering human rights, they gazed into a cultural mirror to define "human." Anyone unseen in the mirror (e.g., black Africans) was *other*—not necessarily subhuman, but a lesser human. Despite gallons of ink expended waxing eloquent on human rights and natural law, many Enlightenment thinkers, including Christians, *conveniently* rationalized the inferiority of non-Europeans.

THOMAS JEFFERSON

Thomas Jefferson was the chief drafter of the Declaration of Independence, an adamantly egalitarian document that maintains that "all men are created equal . . . endowed by their Creator with certain unalienable Rights." It stands defiantly against accusations of the supremacy ideology.[21] So why is it problematic?

Jefferson was a product of the Enlightenment who prided

himself on his capacity to reason. While he saw slavery as an abomination, he rationalized it as a *necessary evil*. The incongruity between his words and deeds provoked historian Edmund S. Morgan to quip, "[Jefferson's] attitude toward black slavery verged on *hypocrisy*. . . . If his actions are any evidence, he placed a higher value on collecting books and drinking good wine than he did on freeing his slaves."[22] Jefferson's antislavery rhetoric was duplicitous; he spoke against slavery *while* living luxuriously on the stolen toil of enslaved black people.

Reasoning *from* his low view of black people, Jefferson believed freeing the hundreds enslaved at Monticello, his five-thousand-acre Virginian plantation, amounted to "abandoning children."[23] He argued they were incapable of caring for themselves, a fascinating assertion considering black people facilitated Monticello's day-to-day operations. As gourmet chefs, stonemasons, carpenters, livestock wranglers, etc., they fulfilled tasks beyond Jefferson's own competence.

Jefferson drafted the Declaration of Independence as a prototypical revolutionary document to proclaim *his* human rights *while* consciously depriving black people of theirs. To his mind, this was no conflict. It was rational because he sat atop the human caste system. His ethics stemmed from his lifelong adoption of the supremacy ideology and subsequent notions of black inferiority.[24] By conjoining his low view of black people with his high self-view, he convinced himself of slavery's reasonableness. In *Notes on the State of Virginia*, he writes:

> Love seems with them [black people] to be more an eager desire, than a tender delicate mixture of sentiment and sensation. *Their griefs are transient.* Those numberless afflictions . . . *are less felt, and sooner forgotten with them.* In general, their existence appears to participate more of sensation than reflection."[25]

Jefferson's critique is a pristine example of *reverse-engineered notions*. Setting aside the demonstrable falsehood of his ideas, he provides a convenient pass for his inhumanity. Destroying an enslaved family by selling loved ones is palatable when their emotions are "transient," "less felt," and "sooner forgotten."

Jefferson maintained that black people are "much inferior" thinkers. He describes black people as "dull, tasteless, and anomalous." He asserted:

> Never could I find that a black had uttered a thought above the level of plain narration; never see even an elementary trait of painting or sculpture. . . . Religion indeed has produced a Phyllis [Wheatley]; but it could not produce a poet. The compositions published under her name are below the dignity of criticism.[26]

Jefferson deprived black people of education and artistic outlets beyond what benefited him, and with no apparent appreciation for the irony, he derided them for their illiteracy and lack of creativity! His notions were *self-fulfilled*; he created oppressive circumstances, then cited them as grounds for oppression. While he conceded the accomplishments of Phillis Wheatley, he promptly dismissed her as an outlying product of religion. And even then, her work was beneath consideration. He started with the assumption of his supremacy, which fostered the byproduct of black inferiority. He then created circumstances that, to his mind, corroborated his baseless beliefs.[27]

Jefferson recognized black people as human and acknowledged slavery as an atrocity. However, using reason, not theology, as his intellectual starting point, he was able to rationalize slavery and contrived ideas of black inferiority. He was not alone. Nearly 75 percent of the Declaration signers (forty-one of fifty-six) and almost 50 percent of the delegates to the Constitutional Convention (about twenty-five of fifty-five) were enslavers. Eighteen of the first thirty-one United States Supreme Court justices were enslavers. Twelve of the first eighteen presidents enslaved human beings during their lifetimes; eight of the twelve did so while in office.[28] The prevalence of slavery among national leaders is telling. It is imprudent to assume these men made, interpreted, and enforced laws independent of their values and life choices. The supremacy ideology made the human hierarchy normative, and national leaders cited their Enlightenment shaped Christian theology as the foundation. Prominent Christian theologians walked in lockstep.

JONATHAN EDWARDS

While in seminary, I took an interest in biographies; a theologian's backstory contextualizes their theology. Jonathan Edwards's story divulged a pertinent point; he, like Jefferson, was an incongruous enslaver! He could reconcile it because, despite his intellect, sinful reason supplanted good theology and determined his anthropology, specifically his doctrine of race. Observant of the biblical prohibition against "man-stealing," he would not purchase a kidnapped African. However, with no qualms, he purchased American-born African descendants.[29] Historian Kenneth Minkema writes, "Whatever questions Edwards had about the institution of slavery, he accepted it. In fact, he owned several slaves."[30] He is suspected of stripping them of their names. For instance, he procured a fourteen-year-old girl called Venus, and it seems he recast her "Leah," a biblical name better suited to a minister's home.[31]

He enslaved black humans to fulfill household and field duties, their stolen toil affording him unencumbered time for Christian missions, pastoring, and theological work. The irony of his choices hardly hampered him. Instead, he excused himself with an ethical loophole—chattel slavery vs. transatlantic slavery—and a paternalistic view of black people. He believed he was doing what was best for those he'd enslaved; if nothing else, their bondage provided an opportunity to hear the gospel.[32]

Edwards recorded his views in a letter written in defense of a proslavery pastor who was under the scrutiny of antislavery congregants. He conceded slavery's inequality but believed it was innate to the social order. Minkema observes, "Though he himself owned slaves, he did not wholeheartedly defend slavery; rather, his letter acknowledged its inequities and disturbing implications. At the same time, however, Edwards felt that slavery was a necessary evil that served some positive good in the natural order that God had decreed."[33]

Edwards argued that criticism of the enslaving pastor was *an injustice committed against the pastor*! He made this assertion based on a human hierarchy. As a pastor, he had high social ranking. Minkema notes, "As a clergyman and a member of the social elite, Edwards was representative of the slave owning class in New England. . . . A significant number of ministers owned slaves as a symbol of social status."[34] Edwards, a premier evangelical theologian, sustained the supremacy ideology and unashamedly Christianized it. While his *theology* allowed him to recognize the evils of bondage, he *reasoned* that bondage was essential to the divine plan and the common good.

For Edwards, slavery was not ideal, but it was not innately sinful. A benevolent enslaver could implement the institution well. By way of illustration, he argued that excessive "eating and drinking" can be sinful, but abstaining from food and drink is absurd because eating and drinking honorably is possible. Similarly, it is possible to own a person either sinfully or humanely. According to Edwards, enslavers should do the latter. His perspective overlooks the implications of the *imago dei*; human beings are God's image bearers. Treating them as property demotes them beneath their station as divine vice-regents. It is sweepingly unethical and innately inhumane to own a human. American chattel slavery was lawful. If an enslaved person escaped, they were a fugitive from the law. Such injustice should shock the conscience. An institution that lawfully upholds bondage is an abject violator of human dignity and worth (Ex. 21:16).

We cannot overlook the remarkable similarities between Jefferson's ideas and Edwards's. Often, national values shaped evangelical theology and ethics. Edwards attempted to Christianize the supremacy ideology and practice a brand of slavery that he believed was God-honoring. However, his take on his own supremacy did not allow him to honor the enslaved. He justified his actions by assuming and asserting the inferiority of black people, arguing that they would benefit from being enslaved. The behavior of Jefferson and Edwards differed in degree but not in essence. Slavery is an example of Edwards, a Christian stalwart, embracing an unsifted worldly ideology and stamping it with Christ's name.

GEORGE WHITEFIELD

Many of Edward's colleagues, most notably George Whitefield, shamelessly benefited from black slavery. During the height of his ministry, Whitefield was among the most famous men in the world, lauded in Europe and North America.[35] He was once an abolitionist, but the pragmatic desire for inexpensive labor changed his message. He argued that slavery's benefit to white people, specifically the children of his orphanage, is adequate justification for black bondage. His view was the societal norm.[36]

One can only imagine how the voice of the world's most recognized preacher could have stemmed the tide of racialized slavery. We will have to imagine because Whitefield used his platform to promote imperialist colonialism in the state of Georgia. As slavery would contribute to Georgia's thriving, he rejoiced to see it legalized. Historian Peter Choi notes:

> The long and winding path Whitefield traversed in search of a viable strategy in Georgia helps us understand his response to the legalization of slavery in 1751. Upon hearing the news, he burst into doxology. "Thanks be to God, that the time for favoring that Colony seems to be come," he wrote to a colleague in ministry. In addition to praise of his almighty, his letter mingled relief with regret as it revealed the extent of his involvement in Georgia affairs. Relief because slave labor would provide a much-needed boost to Georgia's ailing economy. Regret because the decision had come after long and costly delay. He could not help looking back and lamenting the many lost opportunities: "What a flourishing country might Georgia have been, had the use of [slaves] been permitted years ago?"[37]

Whitefield, an esteemed preacher of "the gospel," and celebrated evangelical, weaponized his voice to prolong human bondage. He did not do so out of rejection of black humanity. He believed black people had access to Christ and suggested a "school for the negro."[38] But after years of opposing slavery, Whitefield adapted the supremacy ideology as a pragmatic means of staffing his school and orphanage for white children. He willfully benefitted from black bondage and justified it as the African's lot. He compelled black people to dutifully endure slavery until Christ's return.

ROBERT L. DABNEY

Robert Lewis Dabney, a Southern Presbyterian theologian, maintained that black people were "of an alien race and lower culture" and were plagued by "ignorance, indolence, and thriftlessness."[39] He believed slavery was an act of Christian graciousness, writing, "For the African race, such as Providence has made it, and where he has placed it in America, slavery was the righteous, the best, yea, the only tolerable relation. . . . Domestic slavery here has conferred on the unfortunate black race more true well-being than any form society has ever given them."[40]

Dabney's ideas were formative. Biographer Sean Michael Lucas observes that his teaching "turned the tide against racial equality in the Southern Presbyterian church . . . and set the 'racial orthodoxy' of the Southern Presbyterian church for the next hundred years."[41] Dabney has contemporary endorsements from men like John MacArthur and Douglas Wilson, who have influential platforms in fundamentalist/evangelical circles.[42]

Assuming the best of his endorsers, which I choose to do, they would perhaps reject Dabney's views on race. But systematic theology is a framework that interconnects doctrines. Theological notions bear on one another, so omitting one of them may not be so simple. For instance, Dabney's low view of black people expresses his anthropology (doctrine of humanity). Good social ethics always hinge on a good view of humanity. Unsound ideas inevitably lead to objectionable behavior.

Dabney's disturbing anthropology allowed for and even applauded slavery and segregation. For Dabney, "An organic society that was just and equitable would preserve moral equality but also *insist on civil inequality*."[43] According to Lucas, Dabney averred that in "every society there had to be a laboring class, 'a social sub-soil to the top soil,' that would work and not read."[44] His understanding of humanity and society hinged on the supremacy ideology. For Dabney, human beings may be equal in essence but not in rank. Social standing was determined, at least partially, by race. Accordingly, Dabney advocated for a God-sanctioned racialized caste system that required segregation. He deemed anything else an "anti-biblical [theory] of rights."[45] To his credit, Dabney was honest. He recognized the far-reaching inferences of his anthropology. His endorsers would do well to do the same.

THE SUPREMACY IDEOLOGY AND PROTESTANT DENOMINATIONS

The Southern Baptist Convention (SBC) was founded to mollify Southern enslavers who desired a Christian sect that endorsed the supremacy ideology and its implications, specifically slavery. Using remarkably unambiguous terms, theologian Albert Mohler writes, "the SBC was not only founded by slaveholders; it was founded by men who held to an *ideology of racial superiority and who bathed that ideology in scandalous theological argument*."[46] In 2018, the Southern Baptist Theological Seminary issued a seventy-one-page report that acknowledged slavery's relevance to the school's history. It concluded:

> The founding faculty of this school—all four of them—were complicit in slavery and segregation. Many of their successors on this faculty, *throughout the period of Reconstruction and well into the twentieth century, advocated segregation, and the inferiority of African-Americans*, and openly embraced the ideology of the Lost Cause of southern slavery.[47]

Regarding the long-ignored implications of their history, Mohler, president of the seminary since 1993, conceded:

> We have been guilty of *a sinful absence of historical curiosity.* We knew, and we could not fail to know, that *slavery and deep racism were in the story.* We comforted ourselves that we could know this, but since these events were so far behind us, we could move on without awkward and embarrassing investigations and conversations.[48]

The report concedes that the Southern Baptist Convention, the largest evangelical network of churches globally, was complicit in systemic racism and oppression from the day of its founding and for over a century. The SBC is only one of the malefactors. The Presbyterian Church in America (PCA), which is among the largest Presbyterian Christian sects in America, valued segregation and white supremacy. They resisted ethnic wholeness during the civil rights era. The PCA was founded nine years *after* the Civil Rights Act of 1964, but admit their founders spent the preceding decades opposing "racial reconciliation," "actively" working "against it."[49]

The African Methodist Episcopal Church (AME) exists, in grand part, *because* of segregation. It is peculiar, to say the least, that evangelical rites and ordinances of worship were subjected to society's apartheid norms. The prayer altar, baptism, and even worship gatherings were segregated in both Northern and Southern states. These conditions gave rise to the AME Church (see chapter 11). The National Baptist Convention (NBC), the Progressive National Baptist Convention (PNBC), and a distressing share of black American churches and denominations have similar origin stories. They exist in response to the normalization of a racial caste system.

Even after the abolition of slavery, the supremacy ideology was common to national and evangelical orthodoxy. Segregation was an inevitable fruit of longstanding racial values. To borrow poignant language from Eric Mason, "the black church exists, not as an entity that was born out of a willing missiological effort, but out of heretical theology and practice."[50] On the whole, the black church was necessary because, as a movement, American evangelicalism took a hard stand against the comprehensive unifying gospel. By and large, segregation was valued *because* Eurocentric culture was beloved. Mingling with the culturally *other* was ideologically and, therefore, theologically, unacceptable. Treating the supremacy ideology as historically incidental is willful self-delusion. A meaningful measure of Christians and sizable denominations systemically deployed Enlightenment Europe's racialized segregationist values. The values were not occasional; they were normative and pervasive.

EVANGELICALISM, FRIEND AND FOE

To be sure, American and European Christians played a significant role in the abolition of slavery and the civil rights movement. I would be remiss if I implied otherwise, and I will address it later. But it is reckless to ignore that the abolitionists' efforts met resistance from lauded evangelical personalities and the nation's most prominent Christian denominations. Eurocentrism led to the descent of social ethics and a yawning racial chasm, and the church was not immune. We presently reap the consequences of this history.

Part Three

DIAGNOSIS AND RECOVERY

EVANGELICALISM HAS UNDENIABLE PROBLEMS, LEADING MANY TO ESCHEW the movement. But a good physician seeks a diagnosis before treatment. Likewise, we must diagnose evangelicalism's condition to determine a prognosis, avoiding reactionary decisions. If the bad actors are interlopers who misrepresent evangelical values, then scrapping the movement is tantamount to euthanizing a patient when effective treatment is available. Maybe the movement shouldn't be discarded but reoriented toward the longstanding kingdom values it once claimed. Turning away from fallen strategies and reincorporating the comprehensive gospel can be our saving grace.

Chapter Seven

CHAMPIONS, MONSTERS, OR BOTH?

*In the world today we have a confronting picture of the
two faces, the Jekyll and Hyde, of church history. There
is the humble servant cheerfully bearing pain rather than
inflicting it, and there is the morality policeman eager
to bully the culture for the cause of 'righteousness.'*
—JOHN DICKSON[1]

A FEW YEARS AGO, A BELOVED FRIEND INVITED ME TO LUNCH TO GIVE ME
notice of a forthcoming announcement. He was resigning from
his pastoral post, but he assured me that he'd *yet* to decide if
his resignation was the first phase of a categorical repudiation
of evangelicalism. His sharp use of the word *yet* was conspicuous; it forced the rest of his remarks to the background and
made his resignation almost trivial. My first question was *not*
sophisticated: "Yet?" He replied, "I need to reevaluate my alle-
giances. I suspect we are complicit in a manipulative lie. At
some point, 'evangelicalism' became something else. I need to
know when and why that happened."

My friend's announcement was old hat; he was not the first to initiate such a conversation. He was, however, the most shocking. He is a theologian, a good one. Theology is his predisposition and the culmination of years in school. He is among the most theologically astute people I've ever met, and here he was questioning it all. I affirmed his decision to reevaluate, but I asked what he hoped would come of it. He said, "I have to consider how much of our faith is crippled by undue tribalism. How much comes from the Bible, and how much do we impose on the Bible. We may now be more political than Christian. Our camp is a culturally tribalized movement; we must consider how that happened and its implications."

I had no rebuttal to my friend's apprehensions. Frankly, I was coming to grips with similar concerns. Then in a conversation that already qualified as serious, he somehow achieved a sterner tone. "*Brandon*," he whispered, "we spend our lives standing firm against black conscious cults who accuse us of representing a 'white man's religion.' Our evangelical colleagues are behind us—albeit disgracefully distant—cheering us on. Meanwhile, many of *them* teach Christianity as a *white man's religion*! At what point do we turn and stand firm before them? Our silence is a tacit co-sign of corporate sin."

To underline his point, he produced five social media posts—oblivious statements on the American ethnic rift. They were the public opinions of an individual I know personally. His posts grossly oversimplified critical points of American history and, therefore, downplayed the formative experiences of black people. While I attribute the content to his obliviousness, which allowed for some clemency, his historical revisions were too extreme to overlook. Needless ignorance is negligence. None of his content was novel, I was aware of his views, but over the years, he'd escalated his rhetoric. A realization came over me like a flood. I wrestle, even now, with the near certainty that our relationship provided moral license for his obtuse social media posts. With my silence, I'd freed him to speak and write irresponsibly. That realization changed my course.

THE ADULTERATED DEFINITION

I pastor in northeast Denver, Colorado, a community known for its acute gentrification. We chose the neighborhood because its diversity, new as it was, aligned with our church's vision. In retrospect, I cannot overstate our naïveté. Gentrification is usually little more than *resegregation*. A community that was, for decades, predominantly African American, historically dubbed "the Harlem of the West," is now a bastion of socioeconomic retrofitting.[2] The transition provoked a *cold war*—hardly hidden animus between the exiting black community and the incoming socially climbing gentry.

As a church, our gospel mission is to bring an array of disparate people together under a kingdom umbrella, empowered by the comprehensive gospel. Such a gathering need not occur at the expense of our ethnic, cultural, and socioeconomic distinctions. On the contrary, God has commissioned us to commune under his reign and put our blessed peculiarities on display. The directive to "praise the Lord" is to "all you nations" and "all you peoples" (Ps. 117). A cosmopolitan neighborhood is an excellent opportunity to join together and embody the psalmist's imperative, but it proved more taxing than we'd anticipated. Never have I met opposition while preaching a message of ethnic conciliation. Ephesians 2 provokes an affirming commotion from a room of Bible believers. However, when confronting the history and hurdles of racism, the affirming commotion morphs into a bullish rebuke of the preacher. Untested biblical theories feed applause, but real-world applications of the Bible can provoke moans because there are idols to which we hold tightly—even at the expense of our kingdom values.

In the early days of the Embassy Church (2012–13), I met with people in the community who were considering us a potential church home. Such meetings are par for the course when planting a church, but I was not merely answering questions; I was receiving an education. Several white parishioners asked, "Who did you vote for in the last election?" The question came up so often I suspected they'd collaborated. I'm still suspicious. Deliberately, I never answered, and nearly everyone took offense to my unabashed dismissal of the question. In other meetings, sometimes on the same day, I was asked by black parishioners if the church was evangelical. I always answered, "Yes." *Evangelical* is a theological identity, so it did not appear to be an inappropriate question. However, after a few months, I realized that the two groups were making the same inquiry! *Evangelicalism* is now a co-opted word that needs qualifiers to avoid confusion. Otherwise, it indicates a political tribe and corresponding social ethics. Redemption requires pondering how this occurred. This chapter considers how "evangelicalism" received its adulterated definition.

THE SETTING

Amid the Revolutionary War, the United States' founders had to wrestle with North American slavery. It was, at that point, over a century old and deeply entrenched in the economy. As mentioned earlier, tobacco played a vital role in the thriving of English colonies. After recognizing the benefits of an agricultural economy, plantation owners expanded to other crops, notably sugar and cotton. All of the harvestings were markedly profitable due, in no small part, to unpaid low-overhead labor—primarily chattel slavery.

While the founders carefully avoided slave language in the United States Constitution, there are two unambiguous references to slavery. The language reveals compromises that allowed the South to maintain a "slavocracy," have a voice in the national culture, and obligated non-slave states to participate in Southern slavery. Such compromises seem indicative of the role that slavery played in the nation at the time of its founding.

THE THREE-FIFTHS COMPROMISE

The first constitutional reference was the "Three-Fifths Compromise." A state's population determines its representation in Congress and the Electoral College. Pro-slavery delegates argued that enslaved people should count toward representation despite their lack of citizenship. Northern delegates rejected this suggestion on the basis that enslaved people were "property with no political rights." The United States Constitution afforded black people no citizenship and, consequently, no representation. In the South, the black population was immense. Because of slavery, many states were at least 50 percent black. Counting the enslaved would give the South disproportionate representation in Congress and the Electoral College. The delegates resolved this issue by agreeing to count three-fifths (60%) of the black population toward the total population of each Southern state.[3]

The Three-Fifths Compromise is noteworthy for at least two reasons. First, it is the delegate's inadvertent recognition of slavery's relevance. Slavery had implications on the Southern states' economy and political standing. In 1808, the transatlantic slave trade was formally outlawed, but chattel slavery was not. Illegally smuggling Africans into the country was a bustling business, and selectively breeding enslaved people, treating them as livestock, was legal and lucrative.[4] The Three-Fifths Compromise collaterally stimulated smuggling and breeding because a large and growing slave population emboldened the agrarian culture and added to population-fueled political power.

It is also noteworthy that Southern delegates displayed a self-serving perception of black people. When convenient, the enslaved were property, a commodity that contributed to an enslaver's net worth. They were assets unworthy of rights and privileges. However, when it came to the South's political representation, the enslaved were opportunely human and worthy of counting toward the state's population. This is an example of Southern delegates strolling both sides of an ethical street. They chose which side based on self-serving convenience.

FUGITIVE SLAVE ACTS OF 1793 AND 1850

In addition to the Three-Fifths Compromise, Southern states insisted on Northern participation in their slavery practices. It was another act of peculiar behavior and double-dealing. The South insisted on a state's right to legalize bondage; they abhorred interference from the federal government on the issue of slavery. But they insisted on a federal law that "provided for the seizure and return of runaway slaves who escaped from one state into another or into a federal territory." The Fugitive Slave Act of 1793 allowed Southern enslavers to pursue and recover enslaved persons who'd escaped to a non-slave state. The law was later expanded by the Fugitive Slave Act of 1850, which obligated Northern law enforcement to capture and return escapees. It was a federal crime to steal oneself from bondage. It was considered an offense against an enslaver that deprived him of property.

A SLAVE SOCIETY

Historian David Blight identifies America, particularly the South, as one of history's five "true slave societies." He defines "slave society" as

> any society where slave labor . . . the relationship between ownership and labor—is defined by slavery. By a cradle to grave...human bondage. Where slavery affected everything about society. Where whites and blacks, in this case—in America in a racialized slavery system—grew up, were socialized by, married, reared children, worked, invested in, and conceived of the idea of property, and honed their most basic habits and values under the influence of a system that said it was just to own people as property.[5]

Blight's view forestalls and undermines the assertion that slavery was incidental. In actuality, slavery was innate and, therefore, culturally formative.

A slave society will neither quickly nor voluntarily abolish bondage. It is too essential to the society's economic wellbeing. According to Blight, "Slaves were the single largest, by far, financial asset of the American economy."[6] Blight was *not* speaking of the raw goods harvested by the enslaved. He was referring to the financial worth of the enslaved people. As commodities, they were appraised and, in many cases, insured by their enslavers. Blight notes that in 1860, "the nearly 4 million American slaves were worth some *$3.5 billion, making them the largest single financial asset in the entire U.S. economy*, worth more than all manufacturing and railroads combined."[7]

Because of the appraised value of the enslaved and the proceeds from slave labor, "there were more millionaires (slaveholders all) living in the lower Mississippi Valley than

anywhere else in the United States."[8] According to historian
Thomas Kidd, "The expansion of the cotton economy built
thriving business for slave traders and markets in the major
southern cities."[9] Cotton production nearly doubled in each of
the four decades preceding the Civil War, and in 1860 cotton
reached a historically high price. Cotton was the economic
"king."[10] If the financial wealth of the Southern United States
was evaluated as an independent country, the South would
have been the fourth wealthiest nation in the world! The
assessment of economists Fred Bateman and Thomas Weiss is
somewhat telling:

> Despite its presumed similarity to underdeveloped or
> backward economies, the antebellum South fared better
> economically than traditionally believed. The growth of per
> capita income between 1840 and 1860 approximated that
> of other regions in the United States. The level of per capita
> income, while below the national average when slaves are
> included in the population, approximated the average and
> even exceeded that of the North-Central region when only
> the free population is considered. Southern backwardness
> has been defined largely by comparison with the prosperous
> Northeast. But when viewed in a broader context, the South
> appears materially successful, exhibiting the world's fourth-
> highest per capita income in 1860.[11]

The marriage between cotton and human bondage was not
incidental or supplemental to the economy; it was fundamental.

There are often-overlooked implications of this history.
The supremacy ideology mingled with national values, institutions, structures, and even economic systems. Because of the
mingling, the ethnic rift became requisite. It is quite telling that
America fought a Civil War in which more than three-quarters

of a million people died over a state's right to sanction slavery. The racial hierarchy was systemic—maintained by federal and local policies that were codified and normalized well into the twentieth century. Even after emancipation, the racialized supremacy ideology did not fade. Post-Reconstruction efforts to return to an earlier time were more than mere longings for wholesome days of old. For many, the efforts were also a callback to a racial hierarchy, which was a fundamental value. It was one of the causes of ideological, social, and political splits during the twentieth century. The church participated in these rifts, which partially contributed to the movement that we know as American evangelicalism.

THE EMERGENCE OF AMERICAN EVANGELICALISM

While America was in the midst of the Civil War, an unrelated but pertinent phenomenon was smoldering in Europe. Modernity, which emerged from the Enlightenment, had taken hold. Evangelicalism's assumptions and theological method were under scrutiny. Modernity, driven primarily by the Tubingen School in Germany, was functionally atheistic. It called the Bible's veracity into question and considered the notion of miracles dubious. For staunch modernists, the virgin birth and the resurrection, among other biblical concepts, were absurd. Doctrines that were fundamental to Christian theology were challenged. Modernists went about proselytizing in Europe, where modernity had a foothold. It finally arrived in America at the turn of the twentieth century.

In response, staunch American Christians published a series of essays known as *The Fundamentals*, which outlined essential Christian doctrines and served as a direct response to modernists' criticisms of the Christian faith. The split resulted in what is known as "The modernist-fundamentalist controversy."[12]

American Christians and denominations divided over these issues, taking sides in the debates. Some maintained the Christian label while adapting aspects of modernist philosophy. Christians sympathetic to modernism were labeled "mainline" to distinguish them from the fundamentalists.[13] The rift between the two camps lasted decades and persists to this day as "liberal" versus "conservative" Christianity.

THE SCOPES MONKEY TRIAL

As with most controversies, a moment defined the battle's trajectory. Most church historians cite the Scopes Monkey Trial (1925) as pivotal.[14] Across Southern states, it was illegal to teach Darwinian evolution. Darwinism is not modernity, but the two are complementary in that they lend themselves to an atheistic view of the world. In the early to mid-twentieth century, they shared the ire of the Christian fundamentalists. John Scopes, a Tennessee science teacher, was arrested for teaching evolution. The trial was the event of the decade, covered in its entirety by international news outlets and prominent American newspapers. William Jennings Bryan served as the prosecutor, and Clarence Darrow was the defense attorney. Bryan was a staunch fundamentalist and saw the trial as an opportunity to affirm conservative Christian values. Darrow, an agnostic, was a modernist sympathizer. He used the opportunity to publicly undermine fundamentalist Christian doctrines and values.

The trial was real, but it was arranged. Scopes volunteered for the arrest. His trial provided the occasion for an open challenge to the anti-Darwinian laws, and it set the stage for a fundamentalist-modernist showdown.[15] Bryan and Darrow were the stars, which was revealed by their peculiar trial strategies. For instance, Darrow, the defense attorney, called Bryan, the prosecutor, to the witness stand as an expert witness. Armed with modernist arguments against the Bible, Darrow asked questions that caused Bryan, who was not a biblical scholar, to flounder. Despite these oddities, Bryan ultimately won the trial, proving that Scopes violated the anti-evolution law. But the national and international audiences walked away with a lower view of American fundamentalist Christianity, some relegating it to superstition and myth. In response to their diminished reputation, fundamentalists adopted a separation strategy, isolating themselves from the world.[16] To avoid culture's descent and protect future generations from the nation's rampant immorality, fundamentalists erected a cultural bubble around themselves.

FUNDAMENTALIST SCHOOLS

The establishment of fundamentalist schools was one facet of the isolation strategy, and Bob Jones College—later Bob Jones University—was a quintessential example. The school built its curriculum and values on aggressive opposition to modernism, Darwinism, and ethnic integration. These three issues were somewhat interlinked. For the leaders of Bob Jones College, modernity and Darwinism allowed for a context that overlooked the God-ordained separation of the races. Accordingly, the school held fast to segregation. Bob Jones College and schools of its sort were deliberately countercultural, and they could do so because of their willful commitment to isolation. As a result, they disassociated from politics and other platforms dedicated to cultural and social development.

NEO-EVANGELICALISM

The binary divide between fundamentalist and mainline Christianity did not fully represent the Christian population of the United States. There was a notable third camp that split the gap between the two extremes. Theologians like Harold Ockenga, Carl F. H. Henry, and Vernon Grounds recognized that a Christian could be devout without ignoring the observations of science and philosophy. They could affirm fundamentalist doctrines while judiciously conceding any legitimate discoveries of modernity. They called themselves "neo-evangelicals." They had a highly regarded spokesperson in Billy Graham and launched schools and periodicals—notably, Fuller Seminary and *Christianity Today*.[17] They promoted historical Christian values.

It bears mentioning that the neo-evangelicals, a name eventually abbreviated to "evangelicals," were attentive to activism as an essential characteristic of the gospel. Their efforts to retrieve the true sense of evangelical theology shed light on the need for social engagement and the pursuit of justice. They deliberately distinguished themselves from fundamentalism, which valued isolationism and overlooked the imperative to engage the world to seek justice and wholeness. Where fundamentalism embodied the racist policies that were rampant during slavery and post-Reconstruction, neo-evangelicals preached a unifying message and contextually applied it to complexities common to America.

Ockenga actively addressed the conditions caused by the World Wars, launching a mission that aided European war victims. He recognized this as an imperative of his evangelical faith. Vernon Grounds published "Is Love in the Fundamentalist Creed?" which was an outright criticism of fundamentalism's disregard for activism and gospel wholeness. Carl F. H. Henry adroitly observed that "social justice is not . . . simply an appendage to the evangelical message; it is an intrinsic part of the whole, without which the preaching of the gospel itself is truncated." Neo-evangelicalism took a bold stand treating activism as essential to the evangelical identity.

LIBERALS AND CONSERVATIVES

It bears mentioning that a similar rift was occurring in the non-Christian world. Political tribalism gained a foothold, and the nation divided along liberal (read: progressive) and conservative lines. The terms did not have precisely the same meaning they have now; our present understanding of them is the gradual fallout of societal rifts. In the late nineteenth and early twentieth century, *liberal* and *conservative* referred to divergent ideologies regarding societal values. Liberals recognized progress as a value, while conservatives argued that progress was often detrimental, so the social values of the past should be conserved. The two tribes were not yet partisan. Political parties had representatives from both tribes.

Conservativism is relevant to this discussion because it espoused values that aligned with those of Christian fundamentalism. For instance, both value the sanctity of marriage, the nuclear family, and "traditional" gender roles. Conservatism is not necessarily fundamentalism. However, the two groups have overlapping values, so they were allied in a pursuit to redeem American culture.

JERRY FALWELL SR.

Amid the civil rights movement, many fundamentalist values would come under scrutiny, and the camp's leaders sought strategies that resisted the nation's moral descent. Jerry Falwell Sr. was a fundamentalist who avowed opposition to Modernism, Darwinian evolution, and racial integration. Initially, he affirmed the fundamentalist strategy of isolation and eschewed political engagement, but it lost its luster in the 1970s when the Internal Revenue Service (IRS) scrutinized segregated schools. Despite the 1954 *Brown v. Board* decision, which ostensibly outlawed segregation, and the 1964 Civil Rights Act, several southeastern schools were openly segregated well into the 1970s and enjoyed tax-exempt status. After the IRS revoked Bob Jones University's exemption and threatened to do the same to other schools in the southeast, Jerry Falwell Sr. observed the need for fundamentalists to make a national impact through political engagement.

In the 1970s, the term *evangelical* was commonly associated with Americans who identified as "born again." Generally, the term applied to Christians who abided in the healthy balance between fundamentalist and mainline Christianity. The word lost clarity when Falwell and his cohorts brought fundamentalism into the political domain. Aware of the commonality of the term *evangelical*, the fundamentalist camp strategically co-opted it, allowing them to identify with as many American Christians as possible. The strategy afforded the group significant numbers and, therefore, a measured impact on the political sphere. By the early 1980s, "evangelicalism" was associated with conservativism—an ideological tribe. They sought their ethical values using an allied political party as a vehicle, and evangelicalism became a political force that could not be ignored. Falwell's strategy proved effective.

But under Falwell's leadership, the evangelical movement wasn't evangelicalism at all; it was fundamentalism cloaked behind the term *evangelical*. So many of the evangelical values that Ockenga, Henry, and Grounds reinvigorated were overlooked or outright rejected. For instance, social justice as an expression of activism went by the wayside. Applying the gospel to the ethnic rift was even deemed antithetical to fundamentalist Christian values. Schools like Bob Jones University maintained segregationist policies long after they were deemed unconstitutional. For instance, the school took a theological stand against interethnic relationships and banned interracial marriage among students until the year 2000.[18]

EVANGELICALISM AND FUNDAMENTALISM: DISTINCT, BUT OFTEN CONFLATED

Fundamentalism and evangelicalism have overlapping doctrinal views; that should never be downplayed. By and large, they share orthodoxy. However, they embody the orthodoxy in respectably different ways. As defined by Ockenga, Henry, and Grounds, evangelicalism recognized activism as innate to kingdom values. Seeking wholeness in a fallen world is innate to the gospel. Such a view of the message motivated them to toward social justice. In contrast, fundamentalism, as Jones and Falwell defined it, upheld segregation under the peculiar belief that it was a Christian value.

Today, the subtle though salient distinctions between "evangelical" and "fundamentalist" remain buried under mounds of political oratory. Our responsibility is to sift through the rhetoric and identify the unadulterated evangelical message. Abdicating this responsibility has only marred our witness as we are now associated (rightly or wrongly) with the segregationist values of mid-twentieth-century fundamentalists. We chose our current strategy because it seemed to provide power and influence. That was a shortsighted, wrong decision that has come home to roost. Choosing an oversimplified set of notions and aligning ourselves with a political tribe based on a few overlapping values has sullied the evangelical identity; it has taken us off mission and diluted our message. Consider this: The political decision was to maintain temporal influence and power, but it occurred at the expense of the power Christ underlined in the Great Commission. He assured us that all authority—power, influence—on heaven and earth is his. He availed us of himself and his authority. In turn, we gravitated toward political tribalism's shortsighted and shiny power. Too often, the politicized tribe—not Christ, our king—sets our ethical course. Our orthodoxy may be intact, but our ortho-praxy is incoherent because our chosen strategy deviates from the Great Commission. We boast of our theological under-standing while ignoring the compulsion to claim the world with an incomparable, comprehensive gospel message. We chose the wrong strategy and must now repent.

Chapter Eight

ARE WE HITCHED TO A SICK HORSE?

The problem we have in the church today is that people inadequately define God's kingdom. Some people secularize and politicize the kingdom, which means they think the solutions to our problems are going to fly into town on Air Force One.

These individuals believe that political involvement or social action will by itself usher in the kingdom. While there is nothing wrong with entering the political arena as an evangelical—it ought to be encouraged—we need to bear in mind that God's kingdom is not comprised of, or limited to, a political institution of mankind. God is neither Democrat nor Republican. He does not ride the backs of donkeys or elephants.

—ANTHONY T. EVANS[1]

ONE DOES NOT NEED TO BE AN AMERICAN EVANGELICAL LONG BEFORE learning they may have inherited a political legacy. More than one person has informed me that my kingdom identity came with compulsory loyalty to one political camp or another. Early on, I gave this little thought, but I did know enough to ponder how one can choose a party without struggle. For me, the choice is not so simple. It was paralyzing because neither of them adequately overlaps with the kingdom's agenda.

Moreover, I observed that black evangelicals and white evangelicals did not evaluate the decision in the same way. A straw poll of my associates has black and white evangelicals gravitating in two directions, and both cite their evangelical Christian values as justification for their choice. How did that happen, and what does it say about their respective doctrinal views? Do they disagree because they have notably divergent theology? Experience has taught me that they agree more often than not, and their occasional disagreements would not explain the reckonable split in their political choices. So how did we arrive at the present partisan gulf?

POLITICAL TRIBALISM

Before considering the divide, I should clarify some word usage. I am not treating political tribes and political parties as synonymous. Many of the political differences are divergences in historical perspective that are best labeled conservative and progressive (read: liberal). Unfortunately, most who use these terms associate them with today's prominent political parties and give hardly any attention to their origin or higher meanings. Conservative and progressive are notions that once existed independent of political parties. As we will see, there were conservatives and progressives in both parties. "Conservatism" refers to the desire to maintain the social status quo or return to a social norm from a previous generation. Progressivism is the assumption that society should be in a constant state of social evolution, arguing that societal change is evidence of a healthy community.

Both conservatism and progressivism can be guilty of "chronological snobbery," which is particularly true once their historical perception becomes ideology. Once it achieves that extreme, progressives wish to replace the past based solely on the fact that it is the past; conservatives wish to maintain old ways based solely on the assumption that older is better. Both extremes choose a political path that hinges on their perception of former times.

I call these extremes political tribes for two reasons. First, I believe it is necessary to distinguish these groups from political parties. The outright conflation between tribes and parties is relatively new, approximately fifty years, and it only clouds productive discussions. Second, political tribes indicate historical method more clearly than political parties. This is relevant because, while American evangelicalism is presently associated with a party, it chose a tribe before it aligned with a party. The sequence of events will prove relevant.

The chronological snobbery of both groups merits rigid criticism. To simplify our interpretation of society and ethics, we can overstate or understate past values. In actuality, some things need to change, while others need to remain the same. For instance, nineteenth-century racism and women's rights desperately needed progression, while many of the same era's family values should be judiciously conserved. Oversimplifying how one interprets previous generations is a disservice to history and ethics.

Moreover, evaluating previous generations through only one hermeneutical lens is intellectually irresponsible (see chapter 3). These issues are nuanced and should be treated accordingly. For example, a sweeping callback to an earlier time may benefit privileged groups while remarginalizing oppressed groups. Lax historical method can have dire consequences.

DIFFERENT POLITICAL AFFILIATIONS

Abraham Lincoln was America's first Republican president. He presided over the Civil War, which was fought to preempt a permanent split between the Northern and Southern states. Initially, the North did not wage war over the freedom of enslaved people. But the 1863 Emancipation Proclamation did liberate *some* of the enslaved, "those residing in jurisdictions in rebellion against the federal government of the United States." According to Lincoln, the Proclamation was issued "upon military necessity."[2] It was a strategic plan to end the war by weakening the Confederate states.[3] Still, perhaps because of the Emancipation Proclamation, Lincoln was branded the "Great Emancipator." After the war, the nation ratified the so-called "Reconstruction Amendments," one of which—the fifteenth— afforded black men the right to vote. The black voting base in the South recognized the Republican party's role in the emancipation of black people and the partial provision of voting rights. So it is no surprise that the first black politicians elected to office aligned with the party of Lincoln, the touted "Great Emancipator." They voted and ran for office as Republicans.

During the late-nineteenth century, most Southern Democrats were social conservatives. Recall that conservatism was not a political identity but an ideology of conservation, a desire to maintain old norms. Specifically, it was the belief that the culture as it was in former times was ethically and socially superior. So, conservatives called society back to the values and practices of the previous generations. That is noteworthy because, in the 1860s and 1870s, such an ideology meant the reinstitution of bondage, at worst, or, at best, formal recognition of the racial hierarchy. A societal rewind would erase the egalitarian society afforded black people by the Reconstruction era. So black politicians and voters were not merely running toward the Republican party; they deliberately avoided the conservatism of the Democratic party.[4]

RECONSTRUCTION UNDERMINED

Reconstruction was short-lived. Black politicians attained hundreds of local, state, and federal offices, including U.S. Congress. But these advancements were first undermined by Andrew Johnson who became President upon Abraham Lincoln's assassination. He sympathized with the Confederate cause and expedited a reunion between Northern and Southern states. His urgency occurred at the expense of the Reconstruction amendments. He approved clemency for many Confederate politicians and paved the way for their return to office. Upon retaking seats of political power, Confederates strove for a societal rewind.[5] They accused black people of being incapable of adequately managing their new freedom, much less civic duties, and they vied for a return to the racial caste system, which they accomplished by reestablishing post-Civil War policies called the Black Codes.[6] It was an unmitigated move toward rescinding racial advancements. Historian Allen Geulzo maintains that Reconstruction never failed; instead, it was successfully "overthrown."[7] It started under Johnson but came to fruition in a subsequent presidential election.

The outcome of the 1876 presidential election between Republican Rutherford B. Hayes and Democrat Samuel J. Tilden was in dispute; both parties claimed victory. The disputation was so contentious that Congress feared the potential for another nationwide conflict, something to be dreaded so soon after the Civil War. Northern Republican members of Congress had a clandestine meeting with Hayes and assured him they would decide the election in his favor. In return, Hayes promised that, upon becoming President, he'd remove federal troops from Southern states. Most historians call it the "Compromise of 1877." Historian Paul Johnson dubbed it "legalized fraud."[8]

Removing the federal troops had far-reaching implications. The soldiers were more than a military reminder of the North's Civil War victory. They policed the South against de facto oppression and marginalization. Troops stemmed the tide of subversive practices intended to disenfranchise black voters. Their absence coincided with the relaunch of the remodeled Ku Klux Klan, which utilized terroristic and homicidal tactics to suppress black voting in the South.[9]

Hayes wittingly surrendered the region to former Confederates who, only fifteen years earlier, waged war against the Union over the asserted right to enslave black people.[10] Without a Northern presence, the South experienced their sought-after societal rewind. Southern policies dragged the country back to prior racial norms. Essentially, Hayes and Northern Republican members of Congress appeased conservative Southerners at the expense of black citizenship and suffrage. Rayford W. Logan, a black activist intellectual, later dubbed this era "the nadir of the Negro's status in American society."[11]

The rewind foreshadowed the next ninety years; societal bungees perpetually hampered racial advancement. Unashamedly, the South disenfranchised black people using disingenuous and unhidden policies.[12] Black Codes, property requirements, the grandfather clause, literacy tests, poll taxes, Jim Crow, judicial and extrajudicial lynching, abusive sharecropping practices, and vagrancy laws in conjunction with convict leasing are a mere sampling of the strategies deployed to circumvent the thirteenth, fourteenth, and fifteenth amendments. W. E. B. Du Bois adroitly summed up the story: "The slave went free; stood a brief moment in the sun; then moved back toward slavery."[13]

THE GREAT MIGRATION

Fleeing the reinstituted marginalization and persecution in the South, Southern blacks moved northward and westward to metropolitan cities like Chicago, Cleveland, New York, and Los Angeles.[14] Upon reaching the North, they had voting opportunities. Two notable experiences influenced their party of choice. First, they did not forget the betrayal that came with the Compromise of 1877. It left a bitter taste in their mouths as they considered the Republican party.

Second, the Great Depression devastated America, and the unemployment rate among black people was approximately double that of white workers. Franklin D. Roosevelt, a Democrat, addressed the circumstances by introducing the New Deal, which promised employment opportunities. Roosevelt anticipated a swift drop in unemployment rates and a healthier economy that would avoid depression conditions in the future. The New Deal, often touted as a colorblind strategy, was nonetheless shaped by the racialized discrimination of its day. Roosevelt had to compromise with Southern conservative Democrats. Otherwise, the New Deal would never achieve approval. The Social Security Act and the National Labor Relations Act were not applied to agricultural and domestic workers—jobs heavily occupied by African American and Mexican American citizens. Despite this shortcoming, black people had high hopes for Roosevelt's plan.

Just as emancipated black citizens gravitated to Lincoln's Republican Party, black refugees of the Great Migration slowly moved toward Roosevelt's Democratic Party in search of relief from the Great Depression. Civil rights organizations advised black people not to be loyal to either party. Both parties had conservative voices that called for regression to a previous and less egalitarian era, so absolute allegiance to either party was considered unwise. While many black people still voted Republican, they were open to other political camps.

STROM THURMOND

Strom Thurmond was a Southern conservative Democrat who vehemently opposed integration. His commitment to the Democratic Party stood firm until Democrat presidents, starting with Harry S. Truman, proposed civil rights legislation. Thurmond considered such practices a violation of conservative values. He left the Democratic Party and attempted to launch a new conservative movement that would be home to Southern segregationist democrats; he called it "The States' Rights Democratic Party"—nicknamed "the Dixiecrats." His upstart party was short-lived, and he returned to the Democratic Party, where he attempted to make a conservative stand. Ethnic segregation was a standard component of his political platform.

In 1960, John F. Kennedy, a Democrat, was elected president. His win was no small feat considering he was from Massachusetts and may have been judged critically by Southerners. Shrewdly, he chose Lyndon B. Johnson, a Democrat from Texas, as his running mate. Despite initial trepidation, Kennedy made civil rights an aspect of his presidential platform, but he was assassinated only three years into his first term. Johnson inherited the presidency and cooperated with civil rights leaders like Martin Luther King Jr. to establish civil rights progress. President Lyndon Johnson signed the Civil Rights Act of 1964 into law.

Johnson's civil rights legislation throughout the 1960s was the final straw for Thurmond. Seeing a Southern Democrat take action against segregation prompted Thurmond to leave the Democratic Party and join the Republican party. Throughout the decade, many conservative Democrats followed suit. Thurmond's party shift is an often downplayed moment in the trajectory of American political parties. It is misleading to treat Democrat and Republican distinctives as unchanged since 1865. It is here where political tribes are a much more accurate read of political history. Thurmond changed parties but maintained the conservative ideology typical of Southern political leaders. His conservatism motivated his party shift. Many of his peers did the same, which would change the ideological makeup of both parties. Discussing the supremacy ideology in the context of "conservative" and "progressive" is a much more accurate take on America's national values.

WILLIAM F. BUCKLEY JR. AND CONSERVATISM

The debate over desegregation was usually couched as a disagreement over states' rights. Public intellectuals like William F. Buckley Jr. argued that federal laws obliging integration violated Southern rights, values, and sensibilities. Buckley believed the South should be free to gradually move toward civil rights on their terms and in their own time. He argued for this on the assumption that black voters were not yet equipped to fulfill the tasks of citizenship. Buckley suggested the South develop structures that would help black citizens grow toward competency as voters. He insisted the federal government not intervene in the process chosen by the South. In an article entitled *Why the South Must Prevail*, Buckley concludes,

> The South confronts one grave moral challenge. It must not exploit the fact of Negro backwardness to preserve the Negro as a servile class. It is tempting and convenient to block the progress of a minority whose services, as menials, are economically useful. Let the South never permit itself to do this. So long as it is merely asserting the right to impose superior mores for whatever period it takes to effect a genuine cultural equality between the races, and so long as it does so by humane and charitable means, the South is in step with civilization, as is the Congress that permits it to function.[15]

For Buckley, who was Roman Catholic, segregation was not inhumane or immoral. He confessed to learning of benevolent segregation from his mother, who referred to black people as "dear, kind, simple people."[16] Following her lead, he argued that black voters lacked the proper "mores"—customs or values—to be qualified voters. Buckley believed his assertion was not racist; it was obvious. Biographer Nicholas Buccola said of Buckley:

> Few things rankled Buckley more than the conflation of racial attitudes like those of his mother with those of racists motivated by hatred. It was possible, he would insist, to reject racial egalitarianism while at the same time treating those of other races humanely.[17]

Buckley argued that segregation is a defensible product of objective black inferiority. Never one to be unclear, Buckley clarified his opinion of black voters straightforwardly, writing:

The central question that emerges...is whether the White community in the South is entitled to take such measures as are necessary to prevail, politically and culturally, in areas in which it does not predominate numerically? The sobering answer is *Yes—the White community is so entitled because, for the time being, it is the advanced race.*[18]

Buckley suggested the South establish policies to move black people toward a more civilized outlook before giving them the right to vote.[19] And the federal government should not interfere with a state's right to handle such racial progress as they see fit.

THE SOUTHERN STRATEGY

Racial supremacy cloaked in states' rights led Buckley to endorse Barry Goldwater as the Republican presidential candidate in 1964. It is noteworthy that Buckley and his cohorts began using the language of conservativism and republicanism interchangeably. As conservative Southern Democrats moved toward the Republican Party, following in Thurmond's wake, the interchanging of these terms became gradually more standard. Goldwater lost the election, but in 1968, Republican Richard Nixon applied a more effective version of Goldwater's election strategy.

Nixon appealed to Southern states and promised to establish "law and order." He was not necessarily appealing to Republican voters. Instead, he catered to Southern, conservative, white voters without emphasizing a political party. His tactic is nicknamed "The Southern Strategy." With conservativism, he spoke the language of a more extensive voter base that transcended the two major parties. This is another example of conservative and progressive ideologies better reflecting national values. Like Buckley, Nixon characterized the Republican Party as *the* conservative party, which attracted conservative Southerners, despite party allegiance. Social ideology, not partisanship, determined their course.

Nixon's message of "law and order" hit home in the 1960s as civil rights uprisings, even licit protests, were considered violations of peaceful conditions and incitements of unrest. Nixon promised to quash these trends; his campaign language was effective and resulted in his presidential election. His strategy bears fruit even now, but the 1970s and 1980s were its heydays. Between 1968 and 1988, the Republican Party gradually and summarily adopted ideological conservativism.

BLACKS, EVANGELICALS, AND THE DEMOCRATIC PARTY

I grew up in the South in black Christianized communities. My observation is that black people tend to be moral conservatives. Conversations with the generations that precede mine will almost always include vehement criticisms of the same social ills (i.e., marriage, abortion, gender roles, etc.) against which ideological conservatives stand. So why would they choose, for the most part, to disassociate with a party that espouses these shared values?

Black and white people know two different Americas. So, on the whole, black voters do not limit their partisan decisions to the short list of conservative issues. They share historical occurrences but experience them in notably different ways. They have divergent hermeneutics (see chapter 3). For instance, William F. Buckley Jr. grew up wealthy and privileged in the American South. Therefore, he could thoughtlessly and sincerely contend that segregation was not inhumane (which is an example of the inexperienced assuming better understanding than the experienced; see chapter 3), and the South should receive adequate time to resolve racial problems; the federal government should not intervene. In contrast, black people recognized that federal intervention was necessary for the abolition of slavery, the outlawing of Black Codes and Jim Crow, and the provision of voting rights. When left to their own devices, local governments withheld these rights. Federal intervention was a godsend. The two groups share a past, but they have divergent historical narratives.

In the twentieth century, low expectations of conservatism shaded the whole discussion. When black people consider conservatism, they wrestle with the possibility that the marginalizing eras of the past could receive new life. White conservatives look to the past and long for what was lost.[20] Black people look to the past and rejoice over what they've overcome. Both perspectives shape political tribalism.

THE PROBLEM OF POLITICAL IDOLIZING

In 2018, Pastor Timothy Keller wrote a *New York Times* article entitled "How Do Christians Fit into the Two-Party System? They Don't." His take is not an assault against political activity or voting. It is, however, a well-considered critique of blind party affiliation among believers. It also defends kingdom-mindedness.

In the article, Keller maintains that whole-cloth fidelity to a political party is impossible for a devout believer. He argues that it unduly adds to the essential Christian identity, writing:

"It gives those considering the Christian faith the strong impression that to be converted, they need not only to believe in Jesus but also to become members of the (fill in the blank) party. It confirms what many skeptics want to believe about religion—that it is merely one more voting bloc aiming for power."[21] Adding political affiliation to the Christian identity can be misleading and obscure essential characteristics of our faith. Neglecting the careful distinction between political and theological values can lead to political obligations masked in theological rhetoric.

Keller also argues that political affiliation might cloud one's ethical commitments. What does one do when the chosen political party espouses a position that opposes a moral imperative derived from the Bible or the believer's conscience? This conflict is inevitable as no political party is wholly Christian in its values. Keller writes, "Christians these days cannot allow the church to be fully identified with any particular party [because] of what the British ethicist James Mumford calls 'package-deal ethics.' Increasingly, political parties insist that you cannot work on one issue with them if you don't embrace all of their approved positions."[22] Keller observes that the present political landscape divides the parties along politically "liberal" and politically "conservative" lines. He argues that this division does not overlap with evangelicalism because some biblical standards are considered liberal while others are considered conservative. The evangelical commitment to "racial justice and the poor" appeases one of the two tribes, but "understanding that sex is only for marriage and for nurturing family" aligns with the other tribe. Neither major political camp will perfectly square with evangelical Christian values. Treating either as wholly Christian is a disservice to the Christian identity.

KINGDOM LOYALTY

I affirm Keller's take. Whole-cloth political fealty undermines the evangelical's kingdom identity. The political and societal swings of the last century alone indicate the unstable nature of political parties. They adjust according to popular notions, so seasonal values dictate ethical views. The church, which is supposed to set culture, only follows their chosen party's cultural trends and cult personalities.

Identifying one party as the party of Christianity amounts to attaching ourselves to a sick horse. If evangelicalism is a wagon hitched to a dithering nag, inevitably, we are drawn in whichever direction it goes. Temporal and human-made standards determine our capacity to represent the kingdom. Such a decision ultimately violates our responsibility to lead, set culture, and proliferate the kingdom. Social brokenness can occur on our watch because some social ills are not on our political party's radar.

Also, if a sick horse powers us, then its death is our death. Presently, American evangelicalism is in decline. I maintain that it is on life support. There is more than one cause of this condition, and many of our wounds are self-inflicted. Indiscreetly aligning ourselves with political tribes has been an ongoing assault against the church's integrity. In the eyes of a watching world, the ethical failings of our chosen political tribe are our failings. As the tribe dies, we die.

Political action is commendable but should never exist in place of heavenly ambassadorship. When Christ entered the world, he made us citizens of a kingdom to which all earthly loyalties must submit. Instead, American evangelicalism has adopted a gospel message that fixates on a future kingdom and overlooks the inauguration of Christ's reign. This has led to an ethical void and self-inflicted powerlessness when confronting societal conditions. American evangelicalism has adopted political association as a strategy to fill the void. It is an attempt to change the world via politics. We've abandoned the strategy of the king for something much less powerful. Despite access to history, we are replicating the error of the Roman Church, which sought to expand the church by adopting the policies and practices of the Roman Empire. We are setting aside the divine power afforded us by God to employ human ingenuity. We are pulled along by political tribalism—a horse.

Radical political loyalty is a tactic that stems inevitably from a truncated gospel—the false assumption that we are not already citizens of an eternal kingdom that sets our ethics. Erroneously, political tribes are the Band-Aids utilized to hold us over as we await Christ's return. Attempting to provoke change via legislation is shortsighted behavior modification at the expense of real kingdom change. Without a king, we have no basis for ethics, justice, or sacrificial service. So we pretend we are something while we impotently await Christ's return. But, to my mind, it makes much more sense for us to embody the kingdom that we already have.

Chapter Nine

DO WE HAVE A WHOLE GOSPEL?

*In and through its evangelistic mission to the world,
the church is to enunciate and implement the revealed
principles that God addresses to the human race by
exemplary Christian leadership to the whole realm
of public affairs. Social justice is not, moreover,
simply an appendage to the evangelical message; it
is an intrinsic part of the whole, without which the
preaching of the gospel itself is truncated. Theology
devoid of social justice is a deforming weakness
of much present-day evangelical witness.*

—CARL F. H. HENRY[1]

I LIVE IN A COMMUNITY WITH A HOME OWNERS' ASSOCIATION (HOA). THEY enforce a covenant that requires, among other things, two trees in front of each house. In compliance, I have an oak near the curb and a smaller tree, of which I am rather fond, in the center of the yard. When we purchased the house, the smaller tree was little more than a sapling. I watched it grow into a unique piece on our street. Annually, it erupts into a bouquet of short-lived aromatic white blooms that proudly declare the arrival of spring. That tree is my house's *flagship* ornament.

A few years ago, I came home to find tree trimmers standing on my lawn—tools in hand. They'd already assaulted the oak, and their eyes betrayed unholy intentions as they examined the flagship. Almost as if rescuing one of my children, I sprung from my vehicle and insisted they explain their intrusion. As it turns out, the HOA, believing they were serving the residents, hired trimmers to "shape" the trees in our community. In no uncertain terms, I made it clear that I requested no such service and that "any attempts to trim my tree would be problematic." My annoyance turned to curiosity when they told me the HOA declared fruit trees off-limits, so the flagship was safe.

I didn't know it was a fruit tree. I've lived in the house for years, and the tree has yielded no fruit. The crew leader told me the blooms mark where the fruit would be, but "it is a *domesticated* pear tree." Botanists extracted its ability to bear fruit. Intrigued, I asked, "Why would someone do that?" He answered my question with questions, asking, "Why do you like the tree?" I replied, "It's the perfect size; it provides shade; it's aesthetically pleasing; I'm a fan of its blooms. . . " He interrupted to ask, "Do you want pears in your yard?" I replied, "No, now that you've mentioned it, I don't." Grateful for the ease with which I allowed him to demonstrate his point, he smiled and said, "Domesticating the tree gives you everything you want without the bothersome fruit."

THE DOMESTICATED GOSPEL

The evangelical message, the gospel, articulates what we are about and encapsulates our mission. It diagnoses creation's condition and is the sole means of redemption (Acts 4:12; Eph. 2:1–22). When a message is essential to a movement, understanding it is vital. We should ask, "What is the gospel?" Asking only once in a generation can be irresponsible because, if history holds, mission drift is inevitable. Usually, drift is the product of radical culturalization and the biases of a dominant people group. Unfortunately, we've defaulted to a partial message; it is not heretical per se but incomplete. We have willfully extracted critical aspects and domesticated the gospel, freeing us to have the parts we want without many of its bothersome fruits.

Quizzing the typical evangelical on the gospel produces a consistent refrain: the gospel eternally saves us from our sinful condition. We've managed to whittle the message down to a few key points. We usually package them as a cherished stump speech to get people "saved."

THE STUMP SPEECH

When presenting the gospel stump speech, most evangelicals use a longstanding script. Adam was humanity's federal head—chosen to represent us in the garden of Eden. He rebelled and fell; those he represented fell with him and are now at enmity with God. Adam's rebellion introduced death and sin to creation (Gen. 3; Rom. 5:12–21). We willingly walk according to our death, and no one is an exception to the sinful condition (Rom. 3:23; Eph. 2:1–3). Innate hopelessness stems from our inability to deliver ourselves. Any efforts to placate God's wrath are futile and contaminated by our sinfulness (Isa. 64:6; Eph. 2:8–10). God cannot glibly overlook rebellion; he is holy and must judge sin according to its treasonous nature. Death—eternal separation from God—is the appropriate penalty (Eph. 2:3). But he is also loving and merciful, so he desires to offer reconciliation to humanity. His plan to *justify* sinful humanity cannot conflict with his *just* and holy nature (Rom. 3:26).

Because the "wages of sin is death" (Rom. 6:23), God's inviolate plan to be the *just justifier* hinged on a willing and qualified substitute who would die on behalf of humanity. Enter Jesus the Christ, the eternal Son of God—the *logos*—who added humanity to his deity (John 1:1–14). Since the incarnation, he is at all times fully human and fully God. Our king is the incomparable God-man. In that role, he acts as our savior, bearing our sins in his body on the cross (1 Pet. 2:24). God the Father endorsed the Son's sacrifice by raising him on the third day after his death (Acts 10:40–41). Christ did the heavy lifting. Those who accept his excellent sacrifice are saved by grace, through faith, apart from works (Rom. 3:28; Eph. 2:8–9). We anticipate his return when he will consummate his kingdom, reap the whole fruits of his sacrifice, and judge the living and the dead (Acts 10:42).[2]

I embraced this message on the day of my conversion. To this moment, I assent to it; it fuels my evangelistic fervor. However, *it is a partial gospel.* We preach only part of the comprehensive message. With self-serving and shortsighted motives, we've domesticated the good news, excised some of its fruits. This, I assert, is why American evangelicalism can neglect the gospel's pertinence to the American racial rift. As a movement, we scarcely recognize interethnic harmony as innate to the gospel.

THE GOSPEL AND THE KINGDOM

The domesticated message overlooks an essential aspect of Jesus's work. He did not only die and resurrect; he *ascended*! We tend to fixate on the remission of our sin and the reserving of a celestial mansion, but that fixation can overlook that he is also seated at the right hand of God the Father, where he presently and endlessly reigns (Acts 7:55; Rom. 8:34; Col. 3:1; Heb. 1:3; 8:1; 10:12; 1 Pet. 3:22). His actions go beyond delivering us from the penalties of sin; they afford us kingdom citizenship. Christ launched his ministry by proclaiming, "Repent, for the kingdom of heaven *has come* near" (Matt. 4:17, italics mine). He then fulfilled all that was required to *inaugurate* his kingdom (Matt. 28:18–19). The upshot is that we are not anticipating a king; we have one. Matthew Bates lands this point commendably, writing:

> The gospel and our faith response must not be reduced to the cross, or even to the cross and resurrection. The gospel is bigger than that. Why does our gospel need to change? Because the climax of the biblical gospel is not the cross but something frequently not considered part of the gospel at all: the enthronement of Jesus. And when we see this, we might begin to see why saving faith in the Bible intends not just belief or interior trust in God's promises but bodily allegiance to a king. Seeing this compels us to rethink how faith, grace, and works fit together.[3]

Disregarding his present reign is a disservice to our comprehensive message.[4] Innate to Jesus's proclamation of "the good news of God" is the certainty that "the time *is fulfilled*, and the kingdom of God has come near" (Mark 1:14–15 NRSV, italics mine) While Christ was not announcing the consummation of his kingdom, he inextricably linked the gospel and the kingdom's arrival. Professed kingdom citizens are therefore compelled to "repent" and live in light of his reign (Mark 1:15). We contribute to the progressive embodiment of his inaugurated kingdom, which he will consummate upon his return. His future reign is not our license to remain idle in the interim. While we cannot fully accomplish the task, we are driven by his inauguration until the day of his consummation; ours is a mission of kingdom expansion. We make Christ famous throughout all creation—not only as savior but as king.[5]

THE KINGDOM'S KING

Christ is the ultimate monarch, and he announced it without subtlety, proclaiming, "*All authority* in *heaven and on earth* has been *given to me*" (Matt. 28:18, italics mine). His word choice is deliberate. "Authority" (ἐξουσία) is more than mere freedom to act. A robber with a gun can wield control over a victim, but Christ's supremacy is an ordained and legitimate authority. He has "official . . . power."[6] The Father bestowed upon the God-man the authority to reign in two domains: "in heaven *and* on earth" (Matt. 28:18, italics mine). Abraham Kuyper famously asserts, "There is not a square inch in the whole domain of our human existence over which Christ, who is Sovereign over all, does not cry, 'Mine!'" Kuyper's incongruous racism notwithstanding, I can imagine no better descriptor of the present and unbridled reign of Christ, our king![7]

Christ speaks of his kingly inauguration as an event that has already occurred. The authority "*has been* given" (italics mine). In other words, he did not speak in anticipation of the day he would be king; he asserted that the Father had already crowned him. The resurrection was a public recognition of his coronation.[8] On the day of the Great Commission, he spoke as the enthroned one. Speaking as king, Christ dispatched his disciples to make more disciples and shape cultures that reflect the new kingdom. He deputized them to fulfill his "Kingdom Agenda."[9] To this point, Rodney Reeves, commenting on Matthew's summation of the Great Commission (Matt. 28:16–20), writes:

> The way of the kingdom, the way disciples are made, the way we follow Jesus is to obey him. We obey not only the

instruction he gave in his sermons and parables but also the way he taught us about 'the way' of the kingdom by the way he lived as our king. And since he is our king and we are his brothers and sisters (v. 10), to be a disciple is to follow Jesus in word and deed. That's what disciples are supposed to do, and that's how disciples make disciples. *Ironically, when we do that, the way of the kingdom of heaven comes to earth. The reign of Christ our king—his resurrection power found in the cross—is evident on earth.*[10]

Any theory of discipleship or ethics that does not centralize the present proliferation of the heavenly kingdom's culture is an abdication of our earthly calling—an outright disregard of the Great Commission.

THE KING'S COMMISSION

After his resurrection, Christ issued an imperative that we've long called "The Great Commission." It is a charge to "go," and, *as we go*, we are to make disciples—"Baptizing" and "teaching" them (Matt. 28:16–20). It is an apostolic charge to increase a people and culture. Empowered by the Spirit of God, we add to the kingdom's citizenry and publish the king's reign. We function apostolically, laying claim to that which is already his.

The disciples' identity in Christ determines the ethical trajectory of their lives. Our actions should align with our affiliation to the king. A list of moral duties can be beneficial, and such lists appear in the Bible; the Ten Commandments come to mind. But awareness of one's identity and kingdom citizenship is much more thorough. It will never contradict the Bible's ethical lists and speaks unabashedly on matters where the Bible is silent. Christ did not merely tell his disciples what to do. He, speaking as our king, told them of their place in the kingdom. He then challenged them to live accordingly. We are his emissaries, representatives of his culture and values. The apostle Paul's use of the term *ambassadors* is not glib (2 Cor. 5:20). If you are a believer, you are a heavenly officer. God's mission is now yours.

Toward clarifying whom the disciples are, Christ identifies himself (Matt. 28:18). His identity is a point often overlooked, but it is essential to honoring the Great Commission because Christ's distinctiveness determines ours. He contrasts himself with Adam, whose rebellion in the garden of Eden plagued humanity with deadly sin. In contradistinction, Christ is one in whom the Father is well pleased (Matt. 3:17). Christ summarily confronted our sinful nature on the cross, and his excellence is now ours by adoption. In his resurrection, Christ conquered death. In his ascension, he reigns over creation. He is the new and excellent federal head of humanity; or, to borrow language from the apostle Paul, Christ is the "second" or "last Adam" (1 Cor. 15:45–49). Where Adam failed, Christ conquered. Daily we participate in his victory by making much of his kingdom (Rom. 8).

A PERILOUS TRUNCATION

The exclusion of Christ's ascension and reign has dire consequences, especially regarding ethics. The truncated gospel recognizes our hopeful future but overlooks the gospel's implications on the fallen world in which we presently live. I cannot count the many uniform rebukes: "Brandon, instead of focusing on *that social justice stuff*, you should just preach the gospel." But, from where I sit, the rebukes are self-refuting. It is impossible to preach a comprehensive gospel without regard for the "social justice stuff." The pursuit of Christ's kingdom culture is innate to the good news. Preaching a message that disregards temporal wholeness overlooks the present implications of our commission. Justice is indicative of his domain; it is, therefore, a firm responsibility among those who claim to embody his reign.

THE GOSPEL AND HUMAN SOCIETY

In a 2018 interview, Pastor John MacArthur avowed that his mandate is "to preach the gospel to the ends of the earth."[11] Such a mandate is biblical. However, he narrowly defines "the gospel," limiting it to "eternal issues." More to the point, he asserts that "reordering human society" is beyond the scope of our assignment. Christ's mission, according to MacArthur, is "to prevent us from going to hell forever by bearing our sins in his body on the cross," and that is the message we are to preach.

MacArthur argues for this definition of the gospel by citing the earthly ministry of Christ. He rightly believes that God cannot fail. Armed with this information, he infers that Christ achieved all he intended. His argument, in a nutshell, is that Jesus successfully confronted sin, proving it was his objective. But Jesus did not successfully reorient society, which, following MacArthur's logic, demonstrates it was not in the plan.

Knowing MacArthur's theological starting point is vital to understanding his take on the gospel. He assumes the gradual unfolding of a divine plan that occurs gradually and in phases. The earthly ministry of Christ launched a phase (MacArthur would probably call it a "dispensation") in which Jesus offers humanity the opportunity to be saved from the penalty of sin. For MacArthur, that was Jesus's plan, and he fulfilled it. MacArthur resists adding social change to the agenda, believing it falls beyond Jesus's goals for the gospel. To this point, he says:

> Keep this in mind. There were probably seventy million slaves in the Roman Empire during the life of Jesus; Jesus never tried to abolish slavery. If Jesus came to abolish slavery, he failed. If the Apostle Paul came to abolish slavery, he failed. If the rest of the apostles' agenda was to change the culture, knock off Caesar, and wipe out slavery, they failed. If that's true, then Jesus went to the cross and said "it is finished," but it wasn't.[12]

We must avoid a straw man argument here. Misrepresenting MacArthur's view benefits no one. In his interview, he did *not* say that Jesus would never accomplish social change. Instead, he asserts that Jesus never sought such change during his first advent. In MacArthur's view, Christ charged the church to preach a message of salvation and future restoration. At Christ's return, justice will be normative, and sinful institutions like slavery will cease.

MacArthur awaits the future triumph of Christ's kingdom, which will bring the king's values to fruition. Though better articulated, MacArthur's view is not unlike eighteenth- and nineteenth-century theologians who taught that slavery was part of God's providential plan for their lives.[13] They should anticipate his heavenly deliverance, but, until then, they should endure. I'm troubled by MacArthur's take on the gospel and its accomplishments. Dare I say it? It is myopic and, therefore, a deficient message preached from an influential platform.

MacArthur treats the doctrine of justification as the gospel's essential agenda. This is troubling because ignoring the inextricable link between the kingdom and Christ's presently inaugurated reign may occur at the expense of broader ethics.

The kingdom is a present reality and should result in the joyful compulsion to live according to our kingdom citizenship. Justice is innate to the kingdom so, as ambassadors, seeking justice is an imperative of our identity and heavenly office.

ALREADY, BUT NOT YET

When my wife was pregnant with my daughter, we decided we did not want to know the child's gender until the day of delivery. This created complexities around language since we reject the notion that an unborn child is not a person. 3D ultrasounds and prenatal jostling in my wife's womb only strengthened our resolve. Medical professionals, attempting to honor our decision to wait, referred to our child as "it." Never had I been so troubled by a pronoun; we spoke of a person, not a thing. We solved the problem by choosing a temporary gender-neutral moniker for our unborn child that we always used in place of "it," and our medical team followed suit.

We held firm to this conviction because our child was not becoming a person; she was a person. We anxiously awaited the day of delivery—a glorious day that was still in our future. But childbirth was not a new event; it was the culmination of the existing event. We lived and spoke as though we had a child during the pregnancy because we did have a child. Childbirth was the moment when a scarcely seen reality was visible and undeniable to everyone. The kingdom of God is no different. It is an existing reality, and we are to live accordingly. Will the day come when the kingdom will be visible and undeniable? Yes! But it is confirmed now—inaugurated in anticipation of inevitable consummation. Theologians refer to this as "already, but not yet" kingdom theology.[14] Adroitly, theologian Jeremy Treat avows that Christ's second coming "is the consummation of his atoning victorious work on the cross, *not* a further step beyond it."[15]

JESUS AND ISAIAH 61

MacArthur's theology runs headlong into some biblical texts. For instance, Jesus initiated his earthly ministry by announcing his long-awaited arrival and the inauguration of a new regime. According to Luke 4:16–19, Jesus entered the synagogue in Nazareth and read aloud from Isaiah 61, "The Spirit of the Lord is on me, because he has anointed me to proclaim good news to the poor. He has sent me to proclaim freedom for the prisoners and recovery of sight for the blind, to set the oppressed free, to proclaim the year of the Lord's favor."

Christ proclaimed a new and present era. According to Luke, after Jesus read the passage, "he rolled up the scroll, gave it back to the attendant and sat down. The eyes of everyone in the synagogue were fastened on him. He began by saying to them, '*Today*, this scripture *is fulfilled* in your hearing'" (Luke 4:20–21, emphasis mine). Jesus identified himself as the subject and the fulfillment of the text. He embodied (somewhat literally) the kingdom. I concede that Christ was not announcing the *consummation* of his kingdom; that will occur when he returns. But he proclaimed the *inauguration* of his reign, and we are to live accordingly.

THE KING'S MINISTRY IS OURS

Downplaying the *inauguration* of his kingdom only reduces the church's temporal mission and excuses a muted indifference toward our activistic mission in the fallen world. MacArthur correctly asserts that Christ did not complete social change during his earthly ministry. But he seems to overlook that Christ summarily established the means of deliverance, then he graciously handed the mission and its execution over to us—the church (Matt. 28:16–20, 25:31–46; 2 Cor. 5:16–21). Ignoring our ongoing role in his mission overlooks the comprehensive gospel's temporal worth. We are the deployed disciples. Our commissioning was an essential accomplishment of Christ's earthly ministry. We are ordained and Spirit-empowered messengers of Christ's values. We are charged with voicing, embodying, and increasing the kingdom in the interim between inauguration and consummation (Acts 1:8). Christ empowered us and gave us the mission of societal change.

Dr. Darrell Bock, a premier scholar on Luke-Acts, addresses Luke 4:16–21 in spectacular fashion. He prudently contextualizes Jesus's words and their relevance:

> The Old Testament background of the passage is significant, as is the history of the interpretation of Isa. 61. . . . The figure of Isa. 61 brings a messenger of God's deliverance to exiles. The deliverance imagery parallels the description of the Jubilee year (Lev. 25:8–17), when debts were canceled and slaves were freed every fiftieth year. It is a picture of forgiveness and spiritual liberation, which is at the center of Jesus's message.
>
> Isaiah 58 contains a prophetic rebuke of the nation for not exhibiting justice toward those in their nation who are in need. God declares in Isa. 58 that the fast he prefers is one that treats one's neighbor properly. Isaiah 61 proclaims a time like that envisioned but not carried out by the nation in Isa. 58. The two passages belong together because the release pictured in Isa. 58 has Jubilee overtones and also describes release in Sabbath terms, an event much like the year of Jubilee. When Jesus applies the passage to himself, he is saying that the *present time* is like the message of comfort that Isaiah brought to the nation. In fact, *the totality of the deliverance that Isaiah described is now put into motion with Jesus' coming.* He *is* the Servant par excellence.[16]

Jesus's message indeed assures future wholeness. But it also announces the induction of the new era.[17] The fallen world is blessed when the church progressively manifests Christ's inaugurated kingdom. It is our joyful compulsion to do so until the day of his return, when he will consummate his reign.

When Spirit-led and gospel-wielding, we are fully equipped for the task. To sit idly by and observe injustice and brokenness in the world is an abdication of our commissioning and empowerment. While we will not fully accomplish societal change, the charge to make kingdom disciples will bear culture-shaping fruit in a debased world. Redacting the ascension and reign of our king has made us impotent and complacent. Telling the marginalized to endure injustice while possessing the power and means to nurture kingdom culture is the most incredible hubris, especially when it comes from someone who does not have to endure.[18]

THE KING JESUS GOSPEL

Reducing the gospel to the means of eternal salvation commits an error known as *theological reductionism*; it reduces a whole idea to only one of its parts and treats the part as the whole. We radically emphasize the salvation afforded us by Christ's sacrifice on the cross; we now treat it as the whole message! We've made an idol of a good thing.

I vividly recall the moment I realized that we'd truncated the gospel. As part of a seminary assignment, I read *The King Jesus Gospel* by Dr. Scot McKnight and was distracted from the assignment as the book provoked prompt repentance. I realized that I had, for years, preached "salvation," but not a whole gospel. The gospel includes, but is not limited to, salvation. Fixation on salvation is reductionism, preaching part of the message as though it is the whole. To this point, McKnight writes,

> Evangelicalism is known for at least two words: *gospel* and (personal) *salvation*. Behind the word *gospel* is the Greek word *euangelion* and *evangel*, from which we get evangelicalism and evangelism. Now to our second word. Behind *salvation* is the Greek word *soteria*. I want to now make a stinging accusation. . . . We evangelicals (as a whole) are not really "evangelical" in the sense of the apostolic gospel, but instead we are *soterians* . . . we evangelicals (mistakenly) equate the word gospel with the word salvation. Hence, we are really "salvationists." When we evangelicals see the word gospel, our instinct is to think (personal) "salvation." We are wired this way.[19]

I once espoused MacArthur's understanding of the gospel. I preached it for years, believing it was the evangelical message. Only after a deep dive into the ascension of Christ did I appreciate the implications of having a present king. Christ broke into history and established a monarchy that confronts our brokenness. His sacrifice was effectual and bore timely fruit. Christ's kingdom, while not yet consummated, has been inaugurated, and, as believers, we are his ambassadors.

The comprehensive gospel message is not limited to the eternal destiny of human beings. Our message includes eternal salvation but should never be limited to it. The comprehensive (or "apostolic") gospel has irresistible implications on the temporal world in which we live. We exist to put the gospel on full display. A culture that honors the supremacy ideology undermines the kingdom and decreases the gospel—a quintessential example of theological reductionism.

THE POTENT MESSAGE THAT WE WIELD

Ephesians 2:1–10 was the passage used by the pastor who led me to Christ. It is a concise articulation of salvation. The format is clear—bad news followed by good news. The passage identifies me as dead, sinful, rebellious, surrendered to an unworthy master, and deserving of divine wrath (Eph. 2:1–3). Then Paul unambiguously identifies God's inbreaking as the means of my deliverance. God snatched me from death and made me alive in Christ (Eph. 2:4–8). This is the message of my salvation that I will stand by for as long as I live. Unfortunately, the second half of the chapter gets overlooked.

In Ephesians 2:11–22, Paul follows the same format as the first ten verses: he provides bad news followed by reorienting good news. The human rift between Jews and Gentiles is the bad news. The social and tribal chasm was a bold divide that defied human wisdom and prowess (Eph. 2:11–12). God intervened in verse 13, so "now in Christ Jesus you who once were far away have been brought near by the blood of Christ." The kingdom message reconciled humanity to God (Eph. 2:1–10), *and* it reconciled humanity to humanity (Eph. 2:11–22). The comprehensive gospel confronted both rifts.

For Paul, human conciliation and wholeness are products of Christ's work. The second half of Ephesians 2 obligates us to strive toward inconvenient human wholeness—the "one new humanity" (Eph. 2:15).[20] The reunion between God and humanity in verse 4 and the human union in verse 13 are deliberate fruits of the life, death, resurrection, and ascension of Christ. But we have domesticated the message to extract the fruits of human conciliation. We've been preaching a message fixated on a savior who is yet to be king. But it is the king who saved us toward the expansion of his kingdom.

Awaiting the arrival of a king who has already come insults his throne and disregards his claims as our sovereign. We are not anticipating a heavenly monarch; we have one, and there is no facet of creation beyond his "kingdom agenda."[21] As his representatives, the gospel empowers and commands us to exemplify his reign (2 Cor. 5:11–21; Col. 1:15–20)! We have a comprehensive message that brings wholeness to every area of creation, including present-day injustice, social rifts, and the hardships of the downtrodden (Matt. 23:23). We do not merely possess the capacity to pursue this wholeness; we live under the joyful compulsion to do so.

Part Four

REPENTANCE AND RESURGENCE

CAN THE MOVEMENT RECOVER BY ABANDONING ITS THEOLOGICALLY LOPSIDED and culturally myopic worldview? American evangelicalism is known for its emphasis on *orthodoxy* (right ideas), but have we neglected the equally important call to *orthopraxy* (right actions)? Theology, like a blade, is an inanimate tool. In deliberate hands, it is a scalpel—an instrument of healing. But when wielded by the culturally and socially oblivious, it is a mugger's knife—a weapon of injury. Without a balanced theological scheme that stands upon a comprehensive gospel message, we are off mission. Fortunately, evangelicalism had historical champions who stood firm on a kingdom-minded message. Part IV considers the comprehensive gospel message and pays homage to a sampling of Christian thinkers who embodied it.

Chapter Ten

IS CHRISTIANITY A WHITE MAN'S RELIGION?

The whitewashing of Christianity and its Eurocentric focus has led to growing sentiments among people of African descent, as well as people across the globe, that Christianity is a Western-created, European-influenced, white-owned religion of oppression. While this is historically inaccurate, there are legitimate reasons that many people have adopted this assertion.
—JEROME GAY JR.[1]

DURING MY YEARS AS A NATION OF ISLAM (NOI) SYMPATHIZER, THE WHITENESS of Christianity was a constant refrain. I couldn't count the times I heard, "Christianity is a white man's religion, weaponized by enslavers to make American slaves docile." While the NOI's assessment is erroneous, we shouldn't dismiss it too quickly. Unwittingly, they're observing a culturalized misrepresentation of the historic Christian faith. The NOI perpetuates a scandalous Christian caricature, and they are not alone.

Soon after my conversion, I met *a black* seminarian whose ideas of African Christians troubled me. Though he did not characterize Christianity as a weapon, he believed slavery was "an act of grace." He maintained it "allowed black people to come to America" and delivered us from Africa's "backwardness and paganism." "The trade-off," he believed, "was reasonable." He characterized Christianity as Europe's blessing to Africa, the intellectual foundation necessary to understand Christian doctrine was woefully lacking in Africa and carefully forged in Europe.

Imagine my bewilderment. I'd disavowed racist NOI doctrine only to now hear a seminarian and future pastor spew the Christianized version of the same drivel. I was exacerbated by his ethnic self-loathing. Hoping to redeem the conversation, I asked, "You've studied African civilizations?" "I know enough," he quipped. Then, he made an inadvertently brilliant suggestion: "You should examine what history and Scripture reveal about Africa. Then *you'll* know."

AFRICA, CIVILIZATION, AND CHRISTIANITY

The seminarian was uncouth and too sure of himself, but his advice was sound. Starting with *Beyond Roots II* by Williams Dwight McKissic and Tony Evans, I boned up on the African presence in early Christianity.[2] After additional reading, I surmised that the NOI and the twentieth-century American church share a misleading idea: both believe that Christianity is white. But the insightful and life-changing work of McKissic and Evans, "two African American evangelical[s]," introduced me to Africa's role in the blossoming church.[3]

AFRICAN PEOPLES

Westerners tend to perpetuate two enduring myths regarding Africa. First, we treat Africa as monocultural. In reality, it is home to various societies.[4] Europeans established the borders of African nations without regard for the varied indigenous peoples who occupied the land. According to journalist Max Fisher, "When Europeans left [Africa], the borders stayed (that's part of the African Union's mandate), forcing [culturally] different groups into the same national boxes."[5] So, vastly diverse peoples exist within foisted national borders, and their distinctiveness is treated as immaterial. Hence, we consider Africa a *culturally homogenous country* when it is an *expansive, varied continent.*

Second, we behave as though Africa is an uncharted mystery. But Europeans were aware of Africa's diversity and cultural advancements. When convenient, they ignored them. For instance, Portugal had trade treaties with African nations *before* enslaving them. African kings enforced the treaties and upheld their indigenous cultural values, insisting that Portugal behave accordingly. Historian John Thornton provides a pertinent anecdote, noting that African naval power

allowed Africans to conduct trade with Europeans on their own terms, collecting customs and other duties as they liked. For example, Afonso I [Mvemba a Nzinga], king of Kongo, seized a French ship and its crew in 1525 because it was trading illegally on his coast. It was perhaps because of incidents like this that João Afonso, a Portuguese sailor in French service, writing at about the same time, advised potential travelers from France to the Kongo to take care to conduct trade properly, explaining that when a ship enters the Zaire, it should wait until the officials on shore send one of their boats and do nothing without permission from the King of the Kongo.[6]

João Afonso knew of Kongo's unhidden civility and advised European sailors to honor the people of Kongo and their values.

Despite the well-known advancements of many African peoples, Portugal ultimately debased and enslaved them. Alemayehu Mekonnen, a missiologist, responds to this peculiar behavior with appropriate questions. He writes,

> It was this diplomatic relationship with African states that turned to a slave trade and colonialism with all kinds of exploitation involved including the human body. Does breaking treaties, betraying the Africans' trust and hospitality, make Portugal more civilized? If the African states had no system of governance, organized bureaucracy, or political and economic system, how could they have had a diplomatic relationship with Portugal? Can 'half-animals' be asked political treaties, unless the one who asks has wrong and unsubstantiated truth about Africans?[7]

Mekonnen's questions are valid. When Portugal labeled Africans "savage," they knew the accusation was false because "there were similarities between Europe and Africa, not only in civilization and development, but also in worldview and religion. . . . Africans were as civilized—perhaps even more advanced—than some European countries at the start of their contact with them."[8]

The West has long parodied Africa as a place rife with cultural backwardness and intellectual bankruptcy. But much of the philosophical and theological work attributed to Europe developed in Africa. Theologian Thomas Oden avers:

It is seldom mentioned in philosophical literature that the earliest advocates of Neoplatonism did *not* reside either in Greece or Rome, but in Africa. It is surprising to Hellenistic chauvinists to be reminded that Philo, Ammonias, Saccas and Plotinus—the central players in Neoplatonism—were all Africans. . . . Modern Intellectual historians have become too accustomed to the easy premise that whatever Africa learned, it learned from Europe. In the case of seminal Neoplatonism, however, its trajectory from Africa to Europe (a south-to-north movement) is textually clear. But why is it so easy to forget or dismiss this trajectory?[9]

Many African peoples had philosophical and religious practices indicative of their humanity, civility, and cognitive abilities. Revising their story is dishonoring. It occurs at the expense of good church history and our Christian legacy.

POPULAR EUROPEAN CHRISTIANITY

To be sure, pagan practices like witchcraft and magic occurred among African peoples. These habits are unbiblical but predictable on a culturally diverse continent, which explains why similar paganism existed in Europe, where Christianity mingled with folk religions and cultural superstitions.[10] According to historian Elizabeth Isichei, "The majority of the inhabitants of medieval Europe were sunk in animist worship of trees, stones and springs. . . . Christianity was the thinnest of veneers on top of this."[11] In his book *Europe: Was It Ever Really Christian?* Anton Wessels maintains that Europeans generally observed "the old pagan religions" masked by a "Christian veneer." There were Christians in Europe; it would be irresponsible to assert otherwise. Still, it is equally reckless to identify Europe as characteristically Christian. According to

Wessels, many Europeans did not adopt Christianity until the sixteenth-century Reformation.[12]

On the whole, those who colonized Africa were not upright theologians or missionaries; they were conquerors who espoused Europe's fusion of Christianity, paganism, and cultural values. So when Europeans set out to "civilize" or "Christianize" Africa, most were only imposing Europe's mingled cultural norms.

CHRISTIANITY IN AFRICA

The church emerged at the nexus of Europe, Asia, and Africa; it promptly expanded from Jerusalem and became a tricontinental faith (Acts 2).[13] Africa was home to early Christian churches.[14] They established traditions that they recorded using sophisticated written language.[15]

The longstanding association between Europe and Christianity is partly a product of Muslim conquests. Christianity thrived in Africa but ran into Islam in the seventh century.[16] Historian Philip Jenkins observes that "much of what we today call the Islamic world was once Christian."[17] Europe had no such opposition, so while the church was under assault in Africa, it existed relatively unabated in Europe. Ignoring these contexts can be disorienting. When we study church history, we tend to emphasize the second millennium, especially the sixteenth-century Reformation. We've obscured several centuries of theological development, an error that overlooks Africa's prominence in the early church.

Africans invested generations of scholarship to Christianity. Even after Islam's conquests, a sizable remnant of African Christians remained. We assume Europe was the champion of early Christianity. But according to Thomas Oden,

Africa played a decisive role in the formation of Christian culture. Decisive intellectual achievements of Christianity were explored and understood first in Africa before they were recognized in Europe, and a millennium before they found their way to North America. *Christianity has a much longer history than its Western or European expressions. The profound ways African teachers have shaped world Christianity have never been adequately studied or acknowledged.*[18]

Oden concludes, "Christianity would not have its present vitality in the Two-Thirds World without the intellectual understanding that developed in Africa between 50 and 500 C.E."[19] Asserting that Christianity is a product of Europe's purportedly high culture is an egregious example of historical revisionism.

THE WHITEWASHING OF CHRISTIANITY

Westerners did not just cancel African theologians; they sometimes "whitewashed" them.[20] J. Daniel Hays calls this "cultural pre-understanding," which is the tendency to "project much of our culture into the setting and into our understanding of the characters."[21] Cultural preunderstanding led many Christian scholars, wittingly and unwittingly, to categorize black Christian leaders of history as nonblack.[22] McKissic and Evans observe this tendency and note that, historically, "white" commentators adopted a definition of "white" that "includes people who otherwise would be thought of as Blacks or people of color."[23] This trend resulted in the flawed perception that Christian history has little or "no Black African involvement."[24]

In reality, Augustine of Hippo, Cyril of Alexandria, Athanasius (known as "the black dwarf"), Origen of Alexandria, Cyprian of Carthage, Tertullian of Carthage, and copious African Christian voices pondered and formulated essential Christian doctrines.[25] Their work shaped the blossoming church.[26] They were not merely along for the ride; they increased theological understanding.

Honoring Africa's role is paramount because her cultural norms were essential to codifying many Christian doctrines we now take for granted. Erasing their context disembodies our theological ideas and clouds our comprehension. We've kept many of Africa's theological terms but sacked their cultural nuance. American evangelicalism is Christianized, but is it evangelical when it willingly disassociates from its predecessors' cultural settings?

TERTULLIAN AND AFRICAN COMMUNAL CULTURE

A. Okechukwu Ogbonnaya avers, "The apparent assumption is that every good that occurred in Africa was the result of Roman or European influence."[27] My personal experience affirms Ogbonnaya's observation. Western Christians reflexively treat Christianity as a gift *from* Europe *to* Africa. But *many theological notions took shape in Africa and were, therefore, African contributions to Europe.*[28] I maintain that honoring Africa's theological donations would mean reincorporating many early Christian traits and reshaping American evangelicalism.[29]

CHRISTIAN DOCTRINE

As with all theologians, cultural contexts influenced African Christians. This is pertinent because several African civilizations have cultural norms that resemble the first-century Palestinian setting in which Jesus lived.[30] The similarities contribute to good biblical interpretation and theology. For example, in the second and third centuries, Tertullian, a black African theologian credited with coining the term *Trinity*, observed that the Bible identifies God as singular and plural. Many of his contemporaries and predecessors pondered the paradox, and some fell to erroneous explanations.[31] Tertullian observed no contradiction.[32]

It is imprudent to overlook indigenous African cultures and their contribution to Christian orthodoxy.[33] Tertullian's African communal values shaped his comprehension of the Trinity. He concluded that just as *one* community is comprised of many humans, the Triune community is one and many. Highlighting this point, Ogbonnaya writes:

> In [Tertullian's] thought, the African penchant for holding the One and the Many in balance through communal connectedness shows forth. . . . The work of Tertullian restates and replies to the question of the One and the Many, which Africans have been dealing with from the ancient times to the present. The concept of the One and the Many affects the way the African worships, the question of wholeness, and the relationship of the person to the community.[34]

In a communal culture, the notion of "the one and the many" is intuitive. So, seeing the Trinity as *an eternal harmonious community* is a short leap. Even now, we depend on Tertullian's theological groundwork. His African setting contributed to his notions; we cannot strike it from church history!

CHRISTIAN ETHICS

Tertullian's doctrine of the Trinity bears on Christian social ethics. Seeing God as a triune community provides instruction for human societies.[35] Following Tertullian's lead, thinkers like Jürgen Moltmann, a twentieth-century theologian, treated the "social" Trinity as our moral reference. He rejected many Western notions of God as inadequate because they shed no light on human societies.[36] The communal harmony exemplified by the three members of the Trinity should be the goal of all human communities.

The African emphasis on community aligns with biblical norms and ethics. According to E. Randolph Richards and Brandon J. O'Brien, "In a collectivist culture, *the most important entity is the community*—the family, the tribe, or the country—and *not* the individual. *Preserving the harmony of the community is everyone's primary goal*, and is perceived as much more important than self-expression or self-fulfillment of the individual."[37] In a collective, individuals are essential to the whole; injury to one person affects the community. The image of a human body illustrates the point. Many parts make up a body, but they exist as one. If I break my leg, it is not only my leg's concern; the fracture hampers my whole body. If I stub my smallest toe on a bedpost, my entire being reacts, and both hands come immediately to my toe's aid. Similarly, individuals in a community are one. An injury to one member hampers the collective. This understanding of communal harmony determines the societal response to anyone suffering injustice, hunger, or illness; the collective empathizes and renders relief.

These values were forgone conclusions among many African peoples and were boldly reminiscent of biblical imperatives to feed the hungry, quench the thirsty, welcome the stranger, clothe the naked, tend to the sick, and visit the imprisoned (Matt. 25:34–36). When Christ says, "Love your neighbor as yourself" (Mark 12:31), he advocates for communal harmony. His imperative requires societal empathy—oneness between "your neighbor" and "yourself." It is the same kind of harmony Christ experiences as a member of the eternal Trinity.

He expects human societies to reflect the triune community. Such a view of social harmony bans selfishness or radical individualism.

American evangelicalism has, in many ways, abandoned or revised the communal values that shape biblical Christian ethics. We've steered toward individualism—a fruit of our beloved Western culture. But our theological genealogy includes non-Western thinkers—many of them African—who codified the Christian worldview. Erasing or whitewashing their contributions destabilizes our missional footing by disconnecting us from our theological history and a communal legacy that commissions us against injustice and the suffering of individuals.

CUSH: A BLACK AFRICAN KINGDOM

After spending time in church history, I turned to the African presence in the Bible. I was not surprised to find that the seminarian was wrong, but I was fascinated by the extent of his error. Scripture esteems African peoples; it's not even subtle. For instance, noteworthy women are in the genealogy of Christ: Tamar, Bathsheba, Rahab, and Ruth (Matt. 1:1–17). They descend from Noah's son Ham, whose progeny settled in Africa after the worldwide flood (Gen. 10:6–20).[38] So four of the five women recorded in Matthew's genealogy of Jesus are of African descent![39]

And then there are the Cushites—decedents of Ham's son, Cush. They were a black African kingdom that God identified as a mighty nation.[40] The prophet Isaiah foretells their vital role in God's final plan (Isa. 11:11–12).[41] According to Hays,

They were clearly black people with 'Negroid' features. There are two lines of evidence for this conclusion. First,

the Cushites are presented this way in the ancient art of
the Egyptians, and, later in history, in that of the Greeks
and Romans. Second, numerous ancient literary texts
refer, directly and indirectly, to black skin color and other
'Negroid' features of the Cushites.[42]

At least one Egyptian Pharoah, Shebitku, was a Cushite
because Cush conquered Egypt. Hezekiah, king of Judah,
allied with Shebitku, the king of Cush and Pharoah of
Egypt.[43] Shebitku sent an army led by his brother, Tirhakah,
to aid Judah during their war with the Assyrians.[44] The Old
Testament twice records their role in protecting Jerusalem and
mentions Tirhakah by name (2 Kings 19:9; Isa. 37:9). Under
the leadership of Shebitku and Tirhakah, the Cushites were
loyal sacrificial allies of Judah, God's covenant people.

ACTS AND AFRICANS

Space does not allow for a comprehensive study of Africans
in the Bible. But considering the church is central to this discussion, I'd be remiss if I neglected the conspicuous presence
of black Africans in the book of Acts. Their role in the church
summarily negates those who downplay African Christianity.
Two passages come to mind.

THE ETHIOPIAN EUNUCH (ACTS 8:26-40)
The use of the term *Ethiopian* can be misleading. In Greek
culture, the word meant "the burnt faces." It was not limited to
the modern-day African country with the same name; Greeks
used it of black peoples south of Egypt.[45] As treasurer, the
Ethiopian eunuch was a ranking official under Queen Candace,
a vast black kingdom, and his chariot indicated his standing.[46]

The Ethiopian was a convert to Judaism who was in Jerusalem to observe religious feasts, so he was privy to the events of Pentecost (Acts 2). He was aware that the promised messiah had arrived, which explains why he reads the prophet Isaiah as his chariot "lumber[s] slowly homeward."[47] God directs Philip to approach the chariot, and upon hearing the Ethiopian read Isaiah 53, Philip segues into the gospel.

Eunuchs were not allowed to worship in the temple (Deut. 23:1), so, though the Ethiopian worshiped the God of the Old Testament, he was denied full initiation.[48] This probably prompted his inquiry after his Christian conversion. Upon receiving Christ and seeing a body of water, the Ethiopian asks, "What prevents me from being baptized?" (8:36 ESV). The question is deliberately worded. He is not simply asking for permission; he wonders if there are prohibitions against his full initiation into Christianity. There are none! Christ destroys physical barriers and racial chasms. So Phillip inducts a black eunuch into the eternal Christian household. Philip and the Ethiopian were siblings, not inequitable representatives of a racial hierarchy.[49] This passage affirms the early presence of African Christians and disproves the accusation of Africa's sweeping cultural backwardness. Moreover, it does not lend itself to the supremacy ideology which was espoused by prominent evangelical voices since America's founding.

While perhaps the Ethiopian did not start a massive Christian movement upon returning home, he almost certainly shared the details of his experience. At the very least, he was a seed planter. And it is noteworthy that the Ethiopian church is among the oldest Christian movements in church history.[50] According to Donald Fairbairn, a scholar of the church's patristic era, "In the earliest centuries, the African coast of the Mediterranean would be a great hotbed of Christianity."[51] *Africans themselves were the early purveyors of African Christianity!*

THE CHURCH IN ANTIOCH (ACTS 11:19-26; 13:1)

In Antioch, none of the better-known leaders (e.g., Peter, Paul, or Barnabas) were present during the church's founding. Luke ascribes Antioch's success to "the hand of the Lord." As the church thrived, conversions mounted, and they needed qualified leadership. In response, the church in Jerusalem sent Barnabas to provide direction. But upon arriving, Barnabas realized he would need help, so he reached out to Paul, who relocated from Tarsus to Antioch and joined the pastoral team.

There are two pertinent observations regarding the church in Antioch. First, they contextualized the gospel. Instead of enforcing a single culture, they presented the message according to the diverse peoples before them. We can contextualize the gospel without violating it. This contextualization led to a culturally varied congregation that reflected the demographics of the surrounding city while maintaining theological soundness (Acts 11:20). According to Craig Keener, "The Jesus movement shifts from a predominantly rural movement in Galilee to an urban movement in Jerusalem to a cosmopolitan movement in Antioch. Such a rapid transition is virtually unparalleled in antiquity and indicates considerable *social flexibility*."[52] The rapid spread of the gospel in Antioch discloses the church's socially savvy missiology. They engaged the city with the unchanging message, and they did so while acknowledging that the gospel is compatible with an array of civilizations. Universalizing one culture insults God's mosaic aspirations for the church.

Second, a church's leaders tend to indicate the body's ethnic and cultural makeup, and Antioch's elders were an ethnic spectrum. "Saul [Paul] was a Tarsian Roman citizen and Barnabas a Cypriote Levite."[53] They were Hellenized Jews—conversant in Greek culture and knowledgeable of the Old Testament Scriptures. Simeon was North African, likely a descendant of African converts to Judaism. His nickname, "Niger," Latin for "black," was undoubtedly a nonpejorative reference to his skin color. Lucius was "of Cyrene," which is in North Africa. He, like Simeon, was presumably a descendent of African proselytes. Manaen was a childhood companion of Herod Antipas, the son of Herod the Great. He was probably an aristocrat reared amid Rome's Latin cultural norms.[54] The leadership team represented many cultures, social standings, and socioeconomic classes.[55]

Antioch's leaders *indirectly* reflected the city's racial variety but *directly* reflected the church's diversity. They did not segregate into racial factions but gathered around the unifying gospel. Antioch was so diverse that the church, or "the Way" (Acts 9:2; 19:9), could no longer be considered a Jewish sect. Observers named them "Christians" (Acts 11:26), a word which was indicative of the church's cross-culturalism and devotion to Christ as king.[56] African people were not merely present in Antioch; they were leaders and pivotal to the budding church.

"LOUD AND UNINFORMED"

Non-Western cultures—many of them African—helped conceptualize Christian theology and ethics. But American evangelicalism is willfully Western, so our ethics are virtually anti-communal. We've adopted individualism and isolation at the expense of altruistically advocating for the marginalized, surrendering values that date back to the church's inception. Our choice has taken us off mission, especially regarding social justice. It is a shortcoming of racialized evangelicalism and snubbing of our non-Western heritage. We must repent of cultural snobbery and reclaim a rich theological legacy.

I have a continuing relationship with the seminary student who challenged me to "examine what history and the Bible reveal about Africa." He is now a pastor. While writing this book, I brought the fruits of my research to his attention, submitting a twenty-year-old assignment. To my delight, he'd taken his own advice, so he knew of Africa's estimable place in Christian history. He confessed, "I *honestly* believed a quick review of church history would prove Africa's backwardness. Consciously and unconsciously, seminary taught me that Christianity is a white man's religion. I just took it for granted." Then he said, tongue-in-cheek, "I was *loud* and *uninformed*." I assured him I've often regretted moments of outspoken ignorance. Then we prayed that American evangelicalism, realizing what is at stake, would recognize the need for similar repentance. May God be the force behind such a prayer.

Chapter Eleven

ARE THERE EXAMPLES OF ORTHO-BALANCE?

Christian biography, well chosen, combines all sorts of things pastors need but have so little time to pursue. Good biography is history and guards us against chronological snobbery (as C. S. Lewis calls it). It is also theology— the most powerful kind—because it burst forth from the lives of people like us. It is also adventure and suspense, for which we have a natural hunger. It is psychology and personal experience, which deepen our understanding of human nature (especially ourselves). Good biographies of great Christians make for remarkably efficient reading.

—JOHN PIPER[1]

DESPITE MY DISPARAGEMENT OF SOME PRACTITIONERS, I BELIEVE EVAN-gelical theology is sound, defensible, and viable. But, as a movement, American evangelicalism is better dubbed "Christian fundamentalism" or "Christian nationalism." Because of poorly chosen priorities, its role in the ethnic rift has occasions of obtuse behavior, if not outright complicity.

Still, I'd argue that this wing of the movement, though substantial, is an aberration.

Blessedly, many evangelicals—past and present—embody authentic evangelicalism. Christianity was essential to the abolition of American slavery in the nineteenth century and the civil rights progress that began in the twentieth century. While I stand firm on my assertion that American evangelicals played an essential role in the proliferation of the supremacy ideology, I am just as sure of pivotal leaders who staunchly upheld biblical ethics.

This chapter briefly lauds Christian stalwarts who acted on evangelical theology. These people and institutions model a characteristic that I call *ortho-balance*. Their stories display respect for orthodoxy (right beliefs) and orthopraxy (right actions); they avoided the error of choosing one at the expense of the other. We cannot allow their stories to go untold, especially since they often stood against American evangelicalism (fundamentalism) as it went astray. They serve as reference points, examples of faithfulness.

JARENA LEE

Jarena Lee (1783–18??) was born in Cape May, New Jersey, the child of a free black family. She served in the home of a white family while she was still a preadolescent. During childhood, she grappled with the gravity of her sin, but she came to saving faith in Christ as a twenty-year-old.

Lee attended St. Paul Episcopal Church but never made a covenant commitment to the congregation. She spoke of them as "distant." She observed a chasm between her and the community that deprived her of comfort, so she never recognized

St. Paul as a church home. Historians believe her rhetoric was a poetic attempt to describe the congregation's segregation. Eric Washington writes, "It appears that Lee used euphemistic language to describe either racial segregation or discrimination at the Episcopal church, a claim corroborated by historian Carol George's notes that the congregation segregated seating and that the service targeted the social elite rather than formerly enslaved or less educated persons."[2] In the early nineteenth century, the ethnic divide was brazen. But Lee spoke of the ethnic rift in eternal terms. Segregation undermined the potential for inter-ethnic communion. She observed the church's peculiar willingness to prepare for integrated heaven while deliberately segregating on earth. And they did it all in heaven's name. She could not ignore the contradiction.

Lee ultimately found fellowship in the African Methodist Episcopal Church (AME). She'd long felt compelled to preach the gospel, and the AME community affirmed her. I am awestruck by her assertion of God's divine call on her life. It was countercultural for a woman, much less a black woman, to take on such a task.

Lee was transparent when discussing her stints with sin, temptation, depression, and even bouts with suicidal thoughts. She wrestled with these strongholds throughout her life, desiring that her Christian identity would overtake them. For her, the gospel was both eternally and temporally relevant. It was her chosen means to earthly healing—her message for the world. She is an overlooked voice of America's Second Great Awakening. In that role, she shaped culture and confronted unholy values. While other itinerant preachers of the age affirmed slavery, she was an African American woman who stood firm on the gospel's deliverance.[3] Jarena Lee was an embodiment of authentic evangelicalism.

RICHARD ALLEN AND THE AME CHURCH

Richard Allen (1760–1831) was born into slavery. As a young man, he converted to Methodism and began preaching soon thereafter. His enslaver "allowed" him to "purchase his own freedom" in 1783.[4] Allen relocated to Philadelphia, where he joined St. George Methodist Church. Though he'd escaped the South, a land of de jure slavery, the racial caste system was no less entrenched in the North.[5] Black Codes and segregation were de facto cultural norms.

As a denomination, the Methodists affirmed inter-ethnic congregations. Still, many local churches segregated under one roof—white people occupying the main floor, black people restricted to the balcony. Allen occasionally preached on Sunday mornings, but his audience was limited to black people, and there was a cap on the number that could attend.[6]

St. George's racial discrimination came to a head when church officials forcefully removed black worshipers from the sanctuary as they knelt in prayer. In response, Allen led an exodus and, in cooperation with Absalom Jones, a formerly enslaved man, launched the AME Church in 1816. It was America's first independent black-led denomination.[7]

Allen served as the first presiding bishop of the AME Church and disseminated a timely gospel message mindful of the unjust caste system. During American slavery, Southern values confined the AME Church to nonslave states in the Northeast and Midwest. But, after the Civil War, the denomination became a refuge in the South among newly freed African Americans. During the Reconstruction era, it was a hub of social organization. The AME Church was a prototype that foreshadowed the social role played by the black church during the civil rights movement.[8]

Allen's message was relevant to the marginalized. In an age

when black people did not have titles or leadership roles, the AME Church was a place of self-worth and an opportunity to embody spiritual gifts. Even after Allen's death, the denomination was a voice of wholeness for black people. Theirs was a message fixated on the dignity of kingdom citizens.

CHARLES HADDON SPURGEON

Charles Haddon Spurgeon (1834–1892) was a British Baptist pastor known as the "prince of preachers." Spurgeon battled chronic physical pain and debilitating depression. These life experiences contributed to his emphasis on divine sovereignty—God's role in every detail of human life.[9] It also nurtured in him a heart for anyone who is suffering.

Spurgeon's messages assumed unashamed activism. It is not enough for the believer to possess Christian understanding. Genuine faith provokes the Christian to act (James 2:14–26). He and the Metropolitan Tabernacle, the London church where he served as pastor, were unremitting in their efforts toward the poor and orphaned (James 1:27). Moreover, Spurgeon was unambiguous when rebuking American enslavers. He called slavery "a crime of crimes, a soul destroying sin, and an iniquity that cries out for vengeance."[10] Never one to mince words, he wrote,

> I do from my inmost soul detest slavery anywhere and everywhere, and although I commune at the Lord's table with men of all creeds, yet with a slave-holder, I have no fellowship of any sort or kind. Whenever one has called upon me, I have considered it my duty to express my detestation of his wickedness, and I would as soon think of receiving a murderer into my church . . . as a man stealer.[11]

Spurgeon's public statements provoked the ire of many American clergy members. According to biographer Arnold Dallimore, Spurgeon's rhetoric

> drew a storm of protests, especially in the southern states. . . . His American publishers suspended the printing of his sermons, and various papers urged readers to destroy any they might possess and to forgo all purchases of his publications in the future. . . . But being so strongly moved against slavery he could do nothing else, and he willingly suffered this financial loss.[12]

Despite ostracism from evangelicals who once claimed him as a brother, Spurgeon was unmoved. He recognized that they prioritized carnal values over eternal ethics, and his kingdom-mindedness kept him from joining them. Regarding human equity, he was implacable, once avowing that "whenever topics which touch upon the rights of men, righteousness, and so on, come in my way, I endeavor to speak as emphatically as I can on the right side. It's part of my religion to *desire justice and freedom for all.*"[13] He preached of humanity's eternal destiny, but his faith also compelled him to pursue a holy society on earth. He valued right doctrine and rights actions equally.

CARL F. H. HENRY

Carl F. H. Henry (1913–2003) was an American Baptist theologian and one of the spearheads of the neo-evangelical movement. He hoped to nurture good theological dialogues with the nonbelieving world, including intellectuals. To that end, he cofounded institutions like Fuller Theological Seminary and *Christianity Today.*

He directly critiqued fundamentalists, challenging them to recognize the gospel's temporal worth and societal implications. This is the agenda of his book *The Uneasy Conscience of Modern Fundamentalists*.[14]

Henry's magnum opus is the six-volume *God, Revelation, and Authority*, of which historian Carl Trueman writes,

> [It] must be understood as an attempt to restate conservative Protestant theology in a manner which takes seriously the epistemological concerns of the Enlightenment without surrendering the content and truth-claims of orthodox Christianity. In doing so, Henry defined himself over against theological traditions on both the left and right of the spectrum.[15]

Trueman's description rightly places Henry in the middle of two theological extremes. He fought to preserve historical Christian doctrines while addressing legitimate worldly concerns. He embodied good Christian theology *and* social relevance.

Henry maintained that members of the redeemed family have a message for the world, and abdicating that message is an insult to the king who provided it. Forthrightly, he writes,

> In and through its evangelistic mission to the world, the church is to enunciate and implement the revealed principles that God addresses to the human race by exemplary Christian leadership to the whole realm of public affairs. Social justice is not, moreover, simply an appendage to the evangelical message; it is an intrinsic part of the whole, without which the preaching of the gospel itself is truncated. Theology devoid of social justice is a deforming weakness of much present-day evangelical witness.[16]

Henry stood for a comprehensive gospel as the only effectual means of confronting social ills. He was frustrated by the fundamentalist strategies of isolation and theological reductionism. Repeatedly, he reminded the church that we've inherited a whole and pertinent message. Ignoring its vital parts takes us off our mission.

STANLEY J. GRENZ AND WOLFHART PANNENBERG

Stanley J. Grenz (1950–2005) was an American Baptist systematic theologian, ethicist, and pastor.[17] Grenz was a top-shelf scholar, and his academic prowess may have overshadowed his pastoral tendencies. But I believe his penchant for shepherding informed his ethical theories. For him, evangelical notions were more than fodder for ivory-tower discussions and think tanks. Theology that is irrelevant to our lives is of little worth.

Wolfhart Pannenberg (1928–2014) was a German Lutheran theologian and ethicist. Upon completing his doctoral studies, he taught at the University of Munich for the duration of his academic career, retiring in 1993. For Pannenberg, good theology is God's balm for real-world suffering.[18]

The lives of these men intersected while Grenz was a doctoral student under Pannenberg's supervision at the University of Munich. Grenz inherited an ortho-balanced approach to systematic theology from his teacher. I delight in their iteration of Christian theology. They are a one-two punch that shapes my understanding.

First, Pannenberg sustained a "theology of hope,"[19] a product of God's deliberate revelation. God is knowable and his promises are sure, so we can justifiably anticipate eternal "fellowship with God."[20] The upshot is that our hope is not blind; it hinges on God's promised kingdom, which Christ will fully disclose when he returns. Our guaranteed future—eternal citizenship—is our social bedrock and determines how we live in the present. We are kingdom ambassadors, which sets our ethics. Summarizing Pannenberg's theology, Grenz writes,

> The biblical message of the kingdom . . . is eschatological in orientation, for this message proclaims the final lordship of God over creation, *which has already broken into history in the appearance of Jesus*. En route to the *eschaton* the Christian community lives in hopeful expectation of the final consummation of God's rule over the entire world.[21]

Since we have a king, awaiting a coronation is inappropriate. Christ reigns, and we exist to embody his character and values. In his name, we stand against antikingdom norms like division and injustice. Idleness embarrasses his name.

Second, Grenz recognized community as the basis for ethics. Our God is a "social trinity," the prototype for healthy societies.[22] God lives as an eternally harmonious community (triunity), and through the gospel, we participate in it. The gospel provides more than a shield from sin; it affords us participation in God's eternal society. That community has already come to humanity through Christ! The church embodies and advocates for this society in a fallen world. So we can never bifurcate the gospel from social action. Whenever necessary, we take a stand against discord and injustice.

We are in the world to embody the harmony innate to the Trinity. It is a gospel act. To this point, Grenz writes,

> *The biblical gospel . . . is explicitly social.* It focuses on reconciliation with God, of course. But reconciliation is a social reality, for we are in right standing with God only as

we are likewise being brought into right relationship with others. Consequently, the gospel is also essentially social in application. It demands that reconciliation with God be embodied in social relationships, even in earthly social institutions such as family, business, and government. The gospel is the announcement of the presence of God's reign, which establishes community. *The community God is creating is a reconciled people who are concerned about compassion, justice, righteousness, and above all, love.*[23]

Ours is an innately communal message. Abdication of our social responsibilities diminishes the Great Commission.

Pannenberg asserts that God has afforded us hope in this world, and Grenz avows that the divine community sets our ethical course. So, what would occur if American evangelicalism embodied trinitarian unity and, fueled by hope, brought the gospel to bear on our ethnic rift? Our willful disregard for this question occurs at the expense of our mission.

JONATHAN BLANCHARD AND WHEATON COLLEGE

Jonathan Blanchard (1811–1892) was an American pastor, educator, abolitionist, and newspaper publisher. He was ordained as a Presbyterian but eventually disavowed the denomination because of its ambivalent views on slavery. His abolitionist stance was an ongoing theme of his publications and sermons. Slavery was the prominent social defect of his day, and ignoring it heaped sin upon sin.[24] As an educator, his approach to Christian learning incorporated an uncompromising call to effect social change. For Blanchard, theological insight without societal engagement was a wasted education.

Wheaton College (est. 1853) is an evangelical liberal arts school founded by antislavery Wesleyan Methodists. Blanchard served as the school's first president. Under his leadership, Wheaton adopted an evangelical identity and highlighted abolitionism as one of the school's essential values. In the preamble years of the Civil War, the founders of Wheaton took an unwavering stand against racialized bondage.[25]

Recently discovered manuscripts may verify a long-believed facet of Wheaton's story. Historians are investigating Wheaton's participation in the Underground Railroad—a series of secret rest stops that harbored Northern-bound escapees from slavery. The claim appears viable because the school was a known haven. Ezra Cook, a student at the time, referred to Wheaton as an "abolition school in an abolition town." He recalls "fugitive slaves walking openly, interacting with students, and attending chapel services." His wife, Maria Blanchard Cook, President Cook's daughter, referred to the Wheaton stop on the Underground Railroad as "above ground." Students and faculty were unashamed of their antislavery activity.[26] If escapees could find their way to campus, the school offered sanctuary. A building now known as "Blanchard Hall" was a place of refuge. Under President Blanchard, the school underlined good theological notions and corresponding social activism.[27]

One cannot necessarily evaluate a school by its graduates. Still, I note that alumni like Carl F. H. Henry, Jim Elliot, Elisabeth Elliot, Nate Saint, C. Herbert Oliver, and Billy Graham—active evangelicals all—spent formative years at Wheaton College. The school's fuller story includes moments of succumbing to politicized tribalism during the civil rights era, when some students and faculty waffled during the social and racialized divisions of the day.[28] But when they carefully hearkened back to the school's founding principles of kingdom theology and social engagement, course correction ensued. Remembering their story keeps them on track.

VERNON C. GROUNDS

Vernon C. Grounds (1914–2010) was an evangelical theologian and educator who served as president and chancellor of Denver Seminary. He had a pivotal hand in shaping the school's values. I had the privilege of walking with him, literally.

I had an early class during the spring of my first seminary year that tested my resolve to stay awake. Midway through the lecture, the professor gave us a ten-minute break, and I'd step into the Denver chill to shock myself toward alertness. During such a break, I noticed a small older man gingerly exiting the passenger side of a car. I kept an eye on him as he stepped onto a deposit of unforgiving snow. In one hand, he had two books; in the other, he held a black lunch pail like a coal miner might carry on his way to work. He noticed me observing him and gestured for me to come closer. He handed the books to me and took my free hand. He did not grab my wrist but took my hand as my wife would. Then, as if our meeting was prearranged, he started toward the library with me in tow. I imagined the conversations we provoked—the young, large black man and the elderly, diminutive white man strolling across a snowy campus hand in hand.

Each Monday, during the class break, I rushed to the drop-off point, hoping no one had beaten me to him. I knew his name but little else about him. He'd ask how classes were going and follow up with words of advice. It was organic mentoring. He once asked a question I did not expect. "How is it being a black student at a white evangelical school?" His matter-of-fact inquiry caught me off guard. I do not remember my answer, but as I recall, it was bumbling. He listened patiently, then summarized my emoting in a single sentence, "Most everyone here shares culture and language, but you must translate, and no one notices it." He said it far better than I could. He wrapped our time, saying, "I know that is happening. Yours is the generation that will change it." He then turned and walked into the library, behaving as though we'd been discussing something benign, like the weather. He never broached the subject again. He didn't have to.

The man with the coal miner's pail was Vernon C. Grounds. Our walks occurred in the spring of 2004, only months before his ninetieth birthday. That diminutive man was a giant who, for more than six decades, fought for a God-honoring evangelical movement. Dr. Grounds stood firm on the biblical call to social action when it was distinctly unpopular, believing it was an evangelical imperative.[29]

In 1950, during the height of Jim Crow segregation, Dr. Grounds, a consummate educator, put pen to pad. He published an article that asked matter-of-factly, "Is Love in the Fundamentalist Creed?"[30] He observed the emptying of the gospel, which stripped it of social worth. In a later essay entitled "Evangelicalism and Social Responsibility," he asserts that "the evidence of a right relationship with God is a right relationship with one's neighbor—and this implies a willingness to struggle for his rights."[31] He criticizes American evangelical sects that showed disregard for "this-worldly" concerns.[32] Many fundamentalists disassociated from him, but he was implacable.[33]

Dr. Grounds's written works merely supplemented his preached messages and a life of action. The man was an evangelical champion. For him, the gospel is eternally and temporally relevant. As wielders of the message, we do not have the privilege of sitting idle. Years after meeting him, I read a biography of Dr. Grounds aptly titled *Transformed by Love*.[34] It unmasked the champion, revealing a laudable life that never came up during our strolls. Instead of citing his resume, he remained anonymous and spoke only of our shared mission.

Upon graduating from Denver Seminary, I received an award named in honor of Dr. Grounds. In my office, it has a place of prominence beyond even my diploma. Nearly all who decided on the award were unaware that he and I shared snowy walks, during which he assured me that mine is the generation that will see change. I take his words as the passing of a prophetic mantle (1 Kings 19:19–21). The work is unfinished; it is ours to continue. So the "Vernon C. Grounds Award" is an Ebenezer, a reminder of my mission. We share a message, and I strive to embody it. He was an authentic evangelical, unashamed of the gospel and its impact on a racially divided world. I refuse to surrender the house that he and those like him built!

"PEOPLE OF THEIR TIME"

When I critique evangelical heroes like Jonathan Edwards, George Whitefield, and Robert Dabney, all of whom advocated for a racial hierarchy and consequent slavery, the response is almost always the same. "They were men of their time. Judging them by today's standards is unfair." I've heard this argument more times than I care to count. My responses are unchanged.

First, regarding American slavery, referring to a Christian enslaver as someone "of their time" does them no favors. It may only indicate their unexamined culturalized priorities. As ambassadors of Christ's timeless kingdom, it is inappropriate for us to be shaped irresistibly by the ethics of an era.

God commissioned us to influence culture, so we should never blindly impersonate it.

Moreover, the "of their time" argument ignores the reality that many evangelical leaders contributed to the horrible circumstances. Lauded theologians attempted to use the Bible when justifying racialized bondage. They were often not just mimics but trailblazers of sin. Whitefield was the most famous preacher in the world. Edwards was a world-class theologian and a spearhead of the Great Awakening. Dabney's theology had a bearing on Presbyterian camps for over a century. And they all advocated for chattel slavery, citing God as their cosigner. They were not men shaped by their time; they were the shapers of their time. Imagine their kingdom impact had they set biblical racial ethics instead of adopting the world's racial perversions.

Second, citing the norms of "their time" as mitigating factors discounts evangelical leaders like those mentioned earlier in this chapter. Racialized slavery was a norm despite its barefaced sinfulness. Many of slavery's perpetrators were aware of their atrocities in real time. Even Thomas Jefferson, who enslaved hundreds, called it "moral depravity."[35] Opponents of slavery spoke on firm evangelical footing. But their stance opposed national preferences, so they did not win the day.

Christian leaders like John Newton, John Wesley, William Wilberforce, Charles Finney, and Harriet Beecher Stowe were unsubtle in their campaigns to abolish racialized slavery. Christian movements like the Wesleyan Methodists and the Quakers openly opposed slavery and often purchased freedom for the enslaved. Last but not least, millions of black people— enslaved and free—took a stand from the societal margins.[36] They organized rebellions, devised escape plans, and, upon acquiring freedom, published their testimonies. Frederick Douglass, Sojourner Truth, Phyllis Wheatley, and Olaudah

Equiano were eloquent and convincing while identifying slavery as grossly ungodly.[37] There was no dearth of antislavery voices. But their appeals did not align with the corporate assumption of a racial hierarchy, so their voices were unheeded. Treating racialized slavery as an incidental byproduct "of their time" only revises history and flouts millions of antislavery appeals.

A PERTINENT QUESTION

Spotlighting the duplicity of professing Christians who endorse the supremacy ideology, Equiano writes, "O ye nominal Christians! Might not an African ask you, learned you this from your God? Who says unto you, Do unto all men as you would men should do unto you?"[38] Upon Equiano's conversion, evangelicalism was relatively new. He did not identify the budding Christian movement as a culprit of his bondage. Instead, he rhetorically asked if an ethnic caste system was from God. His irony is subtle but outward enough to reveal the inferable answer: "No!"

Equiano refused to have Christianity's uprightness blemished by interlopers who claimed Jesus but held him loosely, often subordinating him to their racialized preferences. He considered them marginal believers—trespassers cloaked as devout saints. Regarding ethnicity, they misrepresented evangelical theology. Their misrepresentation traversed well into the twentieth century. If Equiano's notion is correct, borderline Christians were the problem, not evangelicalism. It begs a pertinent question: Can the movement return to kingdom form if we repent of nominal Christian values?

Chapter Twelve

IS RIGHT BELIEF ENOUGH?

*But God fiercely rebukes his hypocritical people who
imagine that ritualistic worship and theological discussion
are acceptable substitutes for social justice! God himself
defines acceptable worship in terms of specific acts of
charity and justice. . . . Unquestionably, therefore, the
Old Testament insists on social justice. Passionately it
affirms that the evidence of a right relationship with
God is a right relationship with one's neighbor—and
this implies a willingness to struggle for his rights.*

—VERNON GROUNDS[1]

I DIDN'T HEAR THE TERM *EVANGELICAL* UNTIL MORE THAN A YEAR AFTER MY conversion. I was a college student, but I was on the campus of a prominent seminary that I hoped to attend one day; their library was my preferred study location. During a break, I walked to the student center for lunch and found a small group pondering "a good definition of evangelicalism." They had the same textbook, and its title implied I was hearing spillover from a church history class. They seemed knowledgeable. I struggled to follow their streams of thought. In retrospect, they were exaggerating their grasp of the subject. One of them seemed too self-assured, speaking with more confidence and conviction than the rest. He estimated, "It's simple. The term defines itself. An evangelical is someone who values the gospel *and* evangelism." His unsophisticated definition was indicative of his confidence.

In the late 1990s, the church dealt with an aberrant theological quake known as the "prosperity gospel." The movement averred that those who live by faith inherit compulsory health and wealth. It had a large following but ran headlong into the Bible and much of church history. One of the seminarians chided the confident one, saying, "Using your definition, those prosperity heretics are evangelicals." Refusing bastardization of his idea, the confident one added, "Evangelicals have good Christian theology." Then, a lightbulb lit up over the group. They'd accidentally stumbled upon their definition, "An evangelical is someone who is an evangelist and has solid Christian theology." They were pleased with themselves and took a moment to celebrate their accomplishment—hi-fives all around. When the celebration calmed, the confident one, true to form, snagged the last word, saying, "Evangelicals have good theology. *Right belief is all we need.*" It made sense to me. I didn't know enough to think otherwise. In retrospect, they were not necessarily wrong, but their definition was unfinished and uncomplicated. It begged questions. What is "evangelism?" What is "solid Christian theology?" Is right belief "all we need"?

That group of seminary students has come to mind often over the last twenty-five years. I wonder how much life has shaped them. Do they look back at that conversation and chuckle, embarrassed for the naïve youngsters they once were? I do. When I was their age, I enjoyed the uncomplicated. I took pride in my ability to reduce nuanced issues to manageable pieces. That tendency allowed me to appear bright and aware. Then two decades of pastoral ministry and theological study took hold. Life's complexities are nagging, tending to assert themselves and remind us that simple is not always an option.

Here's what I know now. An evangelical is not merely a person who preaches a message of future salvation. The gospel has temporal relevance. I use "evangelical" when speaking of representatives of the eternal king and his heavenly kingdom. Christ is the *evangel*. He is the initial messenger *and* the message. His kingdom is present and unveiled, pertinent for today. Christ gave us a message that hinges on his inaugurated reign and the consummation that will occur on the day of his return. The king's message provides eternal hope and is relevant to our current condition. So, borrowing language from Michael Bird that is as good as I've ever seen, evangelicalism "is a *historic* and *global* phenomenon that seeks to achieve renewal in Christian churches by bringing the church into conformity to the gospel and by *making the promotion of the gospel the chief mission of the church*."[2]

In my estimation, evangelicalism has done well in attending to Christian orthodoxy (right belief). While efforts were imperfect, a review of church history shows that orthodoxy has long been a value. Laudable responses to heretical views produced creeds that, to this day, shape the church and its ideas. That is a good thing. Still, good ideas can be useless when they are void of relevant actions (James 2:14–26). For us, orthodoxy is an idol vaunted above orthopraxy. Our guilt is not merely one of indifference; in the case of the American ethnic rift, some of our most revered leaders have been complicit. Christian "belief" was weaponized against human dignity and gave rise to corrupt actions. This book is my unabashed appeal to American evangelicalism: Repent and embody the message of our king. Let us not merely have a comprehensive gospel, let us live it!

AN HONEST ASSESSMENT

Christianity is thriving in the Global South.[3] Insightfully, these regions see America and Europe as mission fields. Evangelical churches and denominations in Asia, Africa, and South America send gospel preachers to Western nations, hoping for repentance. Their presence will bear measurable fruit, so we will always have evangelicals.

However, as a movement, American evangelicalism may be dying by its own hand. We enjoyed centuries of influence. North America benefited from Jonathan Edwards, George Whitefield, and John Wesley as voices of ethics and values. Their ministries bore fruit, and evangelical influence carried into the twentieth century, such as when Billy Graham had the opportunity to advise an unbroken series of US presidents, starting with Harry S. Truman.[4] Nevertheless, as modernity took hold and America gradually followed Europe toward secularistic worldviews, that influence waned. In reaction, fundamentalist evangelicalism aligned with ideological tribes throughout the twentieth century in an effort to retain influence. Unabashed political power has replaced gospel influence as our strategy for social change.

My observation is not an absolute renunciation. As godly citizens, Christians should participate in their nation's political structures so long as they do it well (Rom. 13). But our pursuit of seats at political tables can sometimes subsume our kingdom devotion. In lieu of societal influence, we settled for partisan sway. The strategy is brazen during election seasons. When we summarily align with tribalized political parties, our witness is in the hands of ideologues who, too often, misrepresent kingdom values. Adopting the rhetoric of a political camp can be pragmatic but not always virtuous. When tribes set our course, the Great Commission might be abandoned or redefined beyond recognition.

Consider the implications of the Roman Church submitting to the tenets and values of the Roman Empire. Within a few fleeting generations, the two were nearly in lockstep. They shaped one another, so the church adopted much of Rome's perception. Christian monarchs adopted Rome's colonial guidelines and deployed them in Christ's name. The alignment improperly swayed the Christian mission, so the church authorized the devastation and enslavement of indigenous peoples in Africa and the Americas.

The pragmatic desire to survive and even thrive was met. The Roman Church became one of the most influential institutions in Europe—even monarchs consulted popes on international policies. But at what cost? Bartolomé de Las Casas, a Catholic priest, called the colonial conquests "evil" and "tyrannical." He called the policies "libelous" embarrassments to "the sweet name of Christ" and deduced that they are the cause of "infinite new blasphemies against the true God and the Christian religion."[5] His language was deliberate because popes sanctioned many of these conquests. In short, the church adopted unholy notions and approved profane practices in Christ's name. The Christian witness was under attack from within. *The house was on fire.*

Before being roused to anger against Roman Catholicism for being complicit in self-serving genocide and land acquisition, we should pause to recognize the unbroken thread between the Roman Church and American evangelicalism. We've made a similar strategic arrangement, and we reap its consequences. Our witness is devastated because we are too often an Americanized political tribe superficially stamped with Jesus's name. As the tribe trundles toward a cliff, we blindly follow to our demise.

THE FUNDAMENTALIST HIJACKING

The imperative from the king is to make disciples. It is possible to espouse such language without recognizing its implications. A gospel message that is too narrow will sound the same as a kingdom-minded message, but it will not look the same. Fixation on well-produced worship gatherings makes for first-rate holy huddles. But how well have we attended to engaging the world with a whole gospel message? In response to the present mass exodus, we critique disenchanted "*ex*vangelicals." Some critiques have merit; the world willingly turns toward secularism (Rom. 1:21–32), but how often do we carefully weigh our role in their disillusionment?

I maintain that, on the whole, American evangelicalism adopted a tribalized political identity and reduced the Christian message to honor the tribe. This decision has exposed us. Our truncated talking points allow the world to see us as we are, and what they see does not resemble the kingdom we claim. The truncation occurs at the expense of credibility. In no uncertain terms, Vernon Grounds blames American evangelicalism (fundamentalism) for its own precipitous descent. He writes,

> According to the Scripture neighbor-love is the royal law, a duty which should reign supreme in Christian behavior. Yet, strangely enough, this supreme fundamental has been grossly ignored. And perhaps that neglect explains to a large degree why fundamentalism has in many quarters degenerated into legalistic Phariseeism, hard, frigid, ineffective,

unethical and loveless. And because of this, it is high time
we rehabilitate the forgotten fundamental of neighbor-love.[6]

Grounds observes that fundamentalists neglect, ironically,
"neighbor-love," the "supreme fundamental," and replace it
with "legalistic Phariseeism." Overall, American evangelicalism characterizes itself by a set of reactionary policies shaped
by ideological attempts to revitalize the values of former times.
This strategy put prominent Christian leaders on the wrong
side of endeavors like the civil rights movement. Instead of
moving toward the steady embodiment of the biblical kingdom,
American evangelicalism looked back to a time they preferred
and decided the "good ol' days" were kingdom enough.

Usually, longing for former times occurs at the expense of
lower groups in the American caste system. That should have
given the movement pause, and for many, it did. For authentic evangelicals like Grounds, Carl F. H. Henry, and Harold
Ockenga, God tailored the Christian faith to confront social
ills, not just eternal destiny. It rejects segregation and all other
relics of a racial hierarchy, deeming them antithetical to the
gospel. We are empowered to lead, even when relegated to
the margins. Our message is potent. I cannot improve on the
words of Dennis Edwards: "The dominant culture frequently
overlooks the power of marginalized people. Even so, we who
have been in the shadows can reshape American Christianity.
Part of reshaping Christianity is telling the truth about how
we understand and perform the gospel of Jesus Christ."[7]
Grounds, Henry, and Ockenga advocated for the marginalized with a sound message. They performed the gospel of
Jesus Christ, expecting social fruit, including justice. But from
where I sit, these leaders, and those like them, lost a cold war
with fundamentalism. Fundamentalism inherited evangelicalism's seat and name. Though they are different, the American

populace perceives them as one and the same.[8] Historical rejection of our essential message divided the church and contributed to America's racial rift. American evangelicalism is on life support, and fundamentalist mutineers inflicted the mortal wound.

WHERE WE WENT WRONG

Ignoring prophetic appeals from leaders like Grounds, Henry, and Ockenga, not to mention the black church and civil rights movement, contributed to our theological reductionism and ethical complacency. American evangelicalism tends to limit the gospel to heaven-bound salvation.[9] We've long deemed future deliverance the sole fruit of the cross, which belittles the gospel.[10] We treat the church's calling as a mission to rescue passengers from a sinking ship: get as many people saved as possible before the fated world sinks.[11] But the cross has both eternal and temporal implications. Emphasizing the former at the latter's expense undermines our history, mission, and message.

Under organizations like the Southern Christian Leadership Conference (SCLC), the civil rights movement was a gospel act.[12] But their work occurred amid the church's debate over conservatism and progressivism. Unnecessarily, we choose between two binary ideological tribes that are often irreconcilable. And the needless choice obscures the church's nuanced mission. The language of the civil rights movement had the tenor of progress, so fundamentalists, holding to conservatism, stood in opposition. Tribalized politics—not good evangelical theology—shaped this choice. But it occurred in Christ's name, so evangelicalism took the public-relations hit.

THE FALLOUT OF TRIBALIZED CHRISTIANITY

Consider for a moment the implications of being the object of a message that deems you *other.* Now add that Christianity is cited as the basis of the message. Essentially, God considers you *other* and desires racial separation. It may be hard to imagine such a message, but it occurred. Jerry Falwell Sr. openly criticized the 1954 *Brown v. Board* decision as an insult against the Christian segregationist God. He asserted that those who disagree do not know "God's word." He said,

> We have left God out of decisions altogether. If Chief Justice Warren and his associates had known God's word and had desired to do the Lord's will, I am quite confident that the 1954 decision would never have been made. . . . The facilities should be separate. When God has drawn a line of distinction, we should not attempt to cross that line.[13]

Falwell believed these notions were so evident that even black people would affirm them, saying, "The true Negro does not want integration. . . . He realizes his potential is far better among his own race."[14]

Having read these words, now consider their implications on the Christian witness. Falwell did not package his message as personal opinion, he presented it as objective fact—a revelation from God himself. He then went on to be one of the most influential Christian voices in the country, spearheading a tribal movement. From that seat, Falwell sought policies indicative of his ideology. He did so under the Christian banner during the civil rights movement. Frankly, the black church in America is a miraculous display of God's providential hand. The fact that so many maintained loyalty to evangelicalism is an act of magnificent grace. Many who left did so because Falwell and his fundamentalist kin preached a message that cracked the church into factions. To be sure, he rescinded some of his divisive notions toward his life's end, but with only a fraction of his segregationist zeal. Deep wounds do not mend quickly, and our past haunts our present.

EVANGELICALISM IN A GLOBAL CONTEXT

American evangelicalism is all but conjoined to Western civilization. Both proponents and detractors of the movement tend to see American evangelicalism as a religion conceived and shaped by European and American minds.[15] This is historically inaccurate, a sad disregard for non-Western voices that contributed to the church's formation.

Moreover, in the postmodern era, Western Christianity is in noticeable decline. In Europe, especially among proudly secular countries like France, the church is moved, sometimes forcefully, toward relic status. Historic Christian facilities are on the verge of becoming religious museums. In America, detachment and self-imposed irrelevance are the popular assessment of the Christian worldview. Historical sins and uncareful attention to social concerns, particularly regarding race, contribute to our muzzling. American evangelicalism has lost much of the influence it once enjoyed, so we settle for tribalized politics. I cannot deny that Christianity bears fruit in the West. But it is equally evident that in America evangelicalism does not thrive. It is disconcerting, and, by global standards, it is peculiar.[16]

In *The Next Christendom*, Philip Jenkins notes the decline of the "Euro-American" or Western church. But he highlights the swell of Christianity in the Global South and East.

These regions rise toward being the representation of sound Christianity.[17] Michael Bird notes:

> Evangelicalism is slowly becoming shaped by voices beyond Anglo-American networks. The last quarter of the twentieth century saw a steady decline in Christianity and a simultaneous surge in evangelical and Pentecostal Christianity in Asia, Africa, and South America. The international composition of the World Evangelical Alliance and the Lausanne Movement show evangelicalism is now a global phenomenon. *The future of evangelicalism in the world is nonwhite.*[18]

Missiologists, statisticians, and common sense sustain Bird's projections.[19] This should give us pause because assessments of the accomplishments in other global regions may be a diagnosis of our condition. I suspect the Global South and East have values that we, on the whole, lack in the West. American evangelicalism and global Christianity are, for the most part, theologically aligned but ethically divided—shared orthodoxy, divergent orthopraxy. Our deficiencies in orthopraxy perhaps contribute to our descent.

THEOLOGICAL RETRIEVAL AND INTEGRATION

I maintain that the solutions are obvious but taxing, saddled with unwelcome complexity. We can experience revival, which is innate to evangelical DNA. But we must first esteem and return to values embodied by nascent church leaders like Tertullian, early evangelicals like John Wesley, and twentieth-century stalwarts like Carl F. H. Henry. They all championed a message that sustained communal values and had temporal relevance. They saw the kingdom gospel as authentic and applicable to the current world, so the imperative to "love your neighbor as yourself" (Mark 12:31) was formative, a marker of the Christian faith.

In this book's first chapter, I identified integration as essential to American evangelicalism's redemption. The language of diversity and integration is troubling on two fronts. First, integration can be fabricated. A diverse worship gathering may falsely represent cultural assortment and mutual submission. A snapshot of such a room can mislead distant onlookers. But more often than we'd care to admit, such an image is little more than an array of people who exist under one cultural norm. The dominant group sets the narrative, and their perspective is compulsory. Minority groups must code switch to be present. This is not integration but disingenuous assimilation (see chapter 1).[20] The language of integration must be clear to avoid dishonest snapshots.

Second, when I use "integration," many assume I refer to a mingling of varied racialized American cultures. While that assumption is often accurate, in this work, it is not. Instead, I am appealing for the incorporation of *global* Christian perspectives. Willingness to separate from the worldwide Christian community is American evangelicalism's chief hindrance. Our hubris has been our downfall. As we embraced Westernization and individualism, many of the communal values of non-Western Christian communities, which accurately embody New Testament values, are lost. American evangelicalism's desire to set its own course can be stubborn and myopic. Ironically, our hubris has taken us off course. Incorporating values typical of many non-Western civilizations would amend our orthopraxy—specifically, our approach to race, culture, and social empathy. Injustice, racism, classism, sexism, and a list of systemic sins are weaknesses, and as the church, we must bring the gospel to bear on them all.

In the scheme of church history, the assertion that Christ never planned to "reorder human society" is peculiar.[21] It is foreign to the global Christian community and the notions of many early Christian theologians.[22] I maintain it is a somewhat new notion influenced by America's isolated variety of Christianity.[23] God charged us with authoritatively shaping society. He will summarily complete the process upon his return. Until then, we, the church, are empowered and equipped to trudge toward kingdom-consciousness. While we await his return, we declare victory already "fulfilled" and pertinent. We "proclaim good news to the poor . . . freedom for the prisoners . . . and recovery of sight for the blind," and we act "to set the oppressed free" (Luke 4:17–21). Because of Christ's sacrifice, the mission is practicable now.

A ROUTE TO RECOVERY

Benefiting from cultural norms that thrive in the Global South and East will require a measure of surrender from the church in the West. It is not merely a surrender to what I believe is God's plan for us; it is more than that. It will require a willingness to submit to the discipleship of non-Western Christian leaders. The American church, which often touts itself as the fount of sound theology and missiology, will have to recognize the need for theological formation and sit at the feet of African, Asian, and Latin American Christian leaders.

There is hope for such a venture because it is not new. It is a return to our roots. Jenkins notes that, in church history, most Christian cities were Eastern. Rome was the sole exception![24] Christianity existed in non-Western civilizations alongside Buddhism in India and China.[25] Even amid Islamic opposition, any sincere historical study concludes that Christianity had a historical foothold in Eastern civilizations.[26] Understanding them will shape our theological notions. Christianity has always existed in non-Western settings. Reengaging these Christian leaders is not the devolution of the church but a resurgence of values that were norms in the age of nascent Christianity. Incorporating the values of non-Western Christianity results in at least four boons for American evangelicalism.

GLOBAL COOPERATION

Theology occurs in a specific cultural context; it is never a set of sterile ideas independent of influence. This is not necessarily a bad thing. However, if we are not careful, we will treat our culturally shaped theology as *the* God-sanctioned set of ideas. Long ago, I recognized that American evangelicalism appointed itself the ordained arbiter of good Christian ideas. This is not true of every evangelical in America, but it is a mission generally adopted by the movement's weightier voices. American evangelicalism (or fundamentalism) sits atop an ivory tower and, from hubris, evaluates *everyone*. But is American evangelicalism open to similar examination?

Without Christian voices outside our Western cultural circles, the movement is hamstrung by theological myopia. Without external accountability, it is nearly impossible to properly appraise ideas and be sure we are teaching what is right. Cooperation between American evangelicalism and non-Western church communities is mutually beneficial, resulting in a better perspective on Christian theology. For instance, I assure you that African Christian theologians had credible arguments against slavery and segregation. During apartheid, South African sages like Bishop Desmond Tutu were voices of reconning. Their ideas were thoroughly relevant to Jim Crow America, but they received little to no deference as unscrupulous arguments for racial caste systems mounted. It requires humility and repentance. Cooperation and mutual submission among global Christian communities are the best guards against such transgressions.

THEOLOGICAL RETRIEVAL

While in seminary, I had a professor warn against "novel theology." He said, "Honestly examine all ideas as they come, but after two thousand years, we can be suspicious of theological notions that are entirely 'new under the sun' (Eccl. 1:9)." The professor was advocating for *theological retrieval*. He advised we consult theologians of previous generations who almost certainly pondered Christian values and recorded the fruits of their findings. Our ideas are best when filtered through two millennia of good Christian theologians.

The resurgence of the Christian mission needs continuous input from godly predecessors. They serve as reference points that keep the church on mission. For some it is counterintuitive, but eyes toward the past are essential to our present and future. Instead of inventing something new, we may need to retrieve and reimplement older abandoned ideas. David Buschart and Kent Eilers regard "retrieval" a proper "mode of theological discernment."[27] And Gavin Ortlund avers,

> Sometimes the best way to go forward is, paradoxically, to go backward. This is true in solving math problems, executing military operations, navigating relational conflict, and . . . doing theology. That is to say contemporary evangelical theology can be enriched and strengthened in her current task by going back to retrieve classic theological resources.[28]

American evangelicalism's overall strategy of isolation is not just geographical but chronological. In addition to a lack of global cooperation, we are casual regarding previous eras, which selectively hushes historical Christian voices.

During Jim Crow, American evangelicals (fundamentalists) blazed a racial path that was askew of the early church. American evangelicalism independently cultivated its own theological notions of race. For instance, the supremacy ideology and the theory of black inferiority run headlong into the first millennium's non-Western church leaders, many of them African theologians who helped codify Christian values. A lax or self-serving view of Christian predecessors is a sure way of deviating from the Christian mission. In contradistinction, willful attention to historical minds can bring clarity to matters addressed long ago. Theological retrieval—a look backward and a return to foundational values—is essential to the resuscitation of American evangelicalism.

NON-WESTERN COMMUNAL PERSPECTIVE

About three years ago, I was among a group of pastors invited to lunch with the president of an American evangelical university. Two faculty members—Old Testament and New Testament professors—joined us for the meal. The school was seeking a relationship with Christian leaders, and, to their credit, they identified their mission as supplemental to the local church.

Introducing us to the school's "strategic priorities" was on the meeting's agenda. We received information packets that included a list of the school's values. One of them leaped from the page as an homage to "Western civilization." I am no poker player, so I'm sure my facial expression revealed my assessment. When we finished, I met briefly with the New Testament professor. During our meeting, I asked, "Is the Bible Western?" He replied, "Ah, I knew that caught your attention." I told him, "If Western civilization is the school's 'strategic priority,' then you are not making disciples; you're recruiting students to a politicized tribe."

The Bible was written in non-Western, communal settings. The context is essential to appreciating many of its ethical imperatives. For instance, the West values individualism. The emphasis on "pulling yourself up by your own bootstraps" is an example of this value. But the biblical authors were mindful of people who do not have boots, and Christ identifies with them. He says, "Truly I tell you, whatever you did for one of the least of these brothers and sisters of mine, you did for me" (Matt. 25:40). Christ read the scenario through the lens of non-Western communal values, and they determined his ethical expectations. The Euro-American tendency to Westernize Christianity has occurred at the expense of many essential Christian norms.

The pitfalls of centralizing Western civilization will be apparent if we cooperate with global Christians and use retrieval as a means of theological discernment. An eye toward the past looks back to a time before Western civilization shaped Christian values. We must reembrace the Bible's emphasis on community. Recognizing ourselves as advocates of communal health allows us to emphasize biblical values like justice and cross-cultural harmony. Otherwise, we are imposing our ideas on God's Word.

KINGDOM CITIZENSHIP OVER TRIBAL AFFILIATION

As human beings, we tend to despise complexity. The person or group who can simplify ideas will draw a crowd, especially if they package it well. A co-sign from God is, by far, the most attractive packaging. So it stands to reason that an ideological or politicized tribe endorsed by esteemed Christian leaders will receive quite the following. But what if that occurs at the expense of kingdom citizenship?

For the most part, America has split into two binary camps: conservative and progressive (liberal). American evangelicalism has chosen one of the two, and premier Christian leaders have identified loyalty to the camp as a test of Christian devotion.[29] This is unfortunate for several reasons. First, despite our desire for simplicity, some things are complex. Each of the camps possesses values that align with Christianity, while both maintain values that are demonstrably non-Christian. Choosing one to the exclusion of the other only puts devotees in conflict with some biblical values. Second, the binary nature of the camps only contributed to our division. My conservative friends accuse me of being liberal, and my liberal friends mourn my conservativism. Because I cannot, with a clear conscience, choose either tribe, each of them assigns me to the enemy camp. It would be hilarious if it were not so sad.

For me, the solution is paradoxically simple. Align with the eternal unifying kingdom, and eschew divisive temporal tribes. Where the tribes are weak, the kingdom is solid. And the king does not force me to side occasionally against kingdom values. For instance, Christ charges me to advocate for the unborn, and he compels me to confront the senseless death of Trayvon Martin. As image bearers, Trayvon and the unborn share the image of God (Gen. 1:27). The kingdom would never allow for chattel slavery, Jim Crow, or disenfranchisement. These practices had premier Christian advocates and were even ascribed to God. We still battle the consequences of this error. It is the downfall of following the lead of a human-made tribe when we have an eternal kingdom as our reference point. My hope may be delusional, but I appeal for repentance. Turning from tribalism is essential to the resurgence of American evangelicalism.

PRIORITIZE THE COMPREHENSIVE GOSPEL

Coming from people who call themselves "evangelical," truncating the gospel is peculiar. We've reduced our message to the means of our eternal deliverance when it is much more. Our diminished agenda frees us to sit idly when injustice and disharmony persist. It's not necessarily indifference, but it amounts to saying, "Be patient, one day Christ will come back and fix it." Such a message stands condemned by the Great Commission and the imperatives of Christ (Matt. 25:31–46; 28:16–20). We do not await the future launch of his kingdom; we are presently ambassadors (2 Cor. 5:21–22). So while we wait, we make headway, small as it may be, toward his divine culture. A message that ignores this imperative relishes in having a king without serving him. The truncation of the gospel is our foundational error. A deliberate and public 180-degree turn is essential to restoring American evangelicalism.

HAVE WE LOST SIGHT OF OUR GOOD THEOLOGY?

In 2016 I had a challenging conversation with a good friend who'd embraced a Black Religious Identity Cult (BRIC).[30] I'd noticed that BRICs enjoyed a surge in our community, but that is not uncommon; like the tide, their flow usually gives way to a predictable ebb. However, during this tidal flood, I noticed that the number of BRICs was expanding, and they had a tighter hold. The Nation of Islam (NOI) usually reaps a harvest from those who leave the church. Their historical prominence in the black community is not accidental. They have no good answers and atrocious theology, but their message acknowledges the racial problem. So when the church either ignores the rift or confronts it poorly, the NOI is there with open arms. Malcolm X mentioned this deliberate act of "fishing" in his autobiography. In 2016, the NOI was not the only receptive sect. Black Hebrew Israelites, the Five-Percent

Nation, and various shades of Kemeticism were enjoying a foothold. Several new fishermen now had lines in the water.

I prepared for the conversation with my friend by studying his BRIC of choice. I boned up on their theology and called on a colleague who clarified the sect's ideas and deficiencies. But when I sat with my friend, theology was secondary. His struggle regarded American evangelicalism's social inaction and, worse still, segregationist complicity throughout history. He didn't stumble over Christian orthodoxy; he was put off by American evangelical orthopraxy. He believes our ideas and actions are misaligned. Citing a sermon by a megachurch pastor in Dallas—an unabashed tribute to Christian nationalism—he rapped his knuckles on the table between us and said, *"If he is evangelical, then I am not."*

I concluded the conversation by sharing the comprehensive gospel (see chapter 9). I did all I could to bring our discussion back to the Christ of the Bible. Moreover, when his assessments of American evangelicalism were accurate, I affirmed his concerns. He was taken aback by my willingness to admit that some of his critiques had merit. I acknowledged the supremacy ideology, whitewashing, defenses of racialized slavery, a racial hierarchy, and sexism—sins espoused by some prominent Christian leaders whom I mentioned by name. But I also reminded him of the leaders who took a kingdom stand. I specified Vernon Grounds, who, seventy years ago amid Jim Crow, penned similar scathing critiques of Christian fundamentalists. *He was genuinely evangelical, so I am.*

I stand firm on the assertion that no other worldview is as capable of explaining the human condition while providing hope for redemption. Sound evangelicalism values and moves toward Christ's kingdom while fighting for its present embodiment. But American evangelicalism tends to fulfill the Christian mission using human temporal means. Strategic shortcuts and truncation of our message ignore the reality that God is mindful of our present well-being, not just our eternal destination.

Our bad reputation is not *because* of who we are; it results from *falling short* of who we are. The solution is taxing but uncomplicated: repent and return to the love we had at first (Rev. 2:4). We do not need novel ideas; we need only embrace the ones we always had. There is nothing wrong with evangelical theology, but we've neglected it, so it is in disrepair. Reorienting ourselves toward the king and his kingdom is our sole hope.

ACKNOWLEDGMENTS

THERE IS DANGER IN COMPILING A LIST OF NAMES BECAUSE I WILL SURELY omit worthy people. Please chalk omissions up to my limited competence and the confines of writing space.

Rarely is an author the sole person sacrificing for a book; family serves the dual role of encouragement and accountability. My wife, *Cheri*, created margin, allowing me to bury myself in my study and press toward the mark. She saw this opportunity years before I ever dreamed it likely, so when it arrived, she was ready. I see you, lady. My accomplishments are yours. My children, *Reese and Ellis*, my father, *Edward*, and my brother, *Edmond*, were cheerleaders who made research and deadlines bearable. Resting on my laurels was no option. You all reminded me of a task needing completion. My late mother, *Patricia*, anticipated this moment when I was still a child. In 1987, as part of an elementary school project, I "wrote" a "book" entitled *The Appalling Alligator*. I still have it. Inside the front cover, she penned a farsighted note to her eleven-year-old son, "Brandon, one day you will be an author; this is only your first book." Mothers always know.

Pastor Derrick Kelsey, you deemed this book an act of spiritual warfare and insisted I get it done. You are my sounding board, teammate, and friend—the Bird to my Dizzy. I could not have done this without you.

Dozens of pastors have influenced me, but five were paramount. *Rev. Freddie B. Moore Sr.*, you introduced me to the gospel—a message that is relevant to time and eternity. *Pastor Leroy R. Armstrong Jr.*, you were the first pastor to affirm my call to think publicly. As I prepared for seminary, I told you of my peculiar aspirations, and you replied, "Yeah, that sounds about right. Now, go get it done." *Dr. Felix Gilbert*, you were the visionary who challenged me to stay on task. You gave me a platform and insisted others listen. God called you home before I was ready, but we have the resurrection—until then, *mon frère. Dr. Eric Mason*, I've known you since the year of my conversion, and the entire time you've been a valued friend, brother, and mentor. Yours is a prophetic voice fixed on God's Word. You opened doors that made this book possible, and your selflessness did not go unnoticed. I would be remiss if I did not acknowledge the contributions of Maurice Pugh, Ikki Soma, James Womack, Bob Fomer, Robert Gelinas, Paul Flannery, Keita Andrews, and Ray Cook. In diverse ways, you all affirmed me and sought to invest towards my spiritual formation. Finally, *Dr. Anthony T. Evans Sr.*, you oriented me toward the "kingdom agenda." For years, I sat on a pew engrossed as you passionately proclaimed the kingdom's relevance to "every area of our lives." Your words found their mark. None of the ideas in this book are novel; they are merely the repackaging of notions you have been preaching for decades. You are a spiritual father to many, and I count myself among them.

My time at Fellowship Associates was among the most formative seasons of my Christian life. I was shaped by Bill Wellons, Steve Snider, Mike Boschetti, and every team member—*all of you*—who made the world's greatest church planting residency possible. Even now, I am refreshed at the sound of that Little Rock, Arkansas accent. It reminds me of good times and the joy of seeing kingdom citizens on mission.

Denver Seminary introduced me to what I call "thoughtful thinking." *Dr. Don J. Payne*, you rest at the hallowed intersection of shepherd and scholar, and I've never seen anyone do it so well. Because of you, I value method and nuance. You did not teach me merely what to know; you taught me how to know, and you stressed the real-world worth of theology. *Dr. M. Daniel Carroll Rodas*, you taught me that social concern is fundamental to the gospel—a value that will not expire. God used you to shape my lenses. With conviction, I assert that YHWH relishes in "justice" and "righteousness" (Amos 5:24). *Dr. Craig Blomberg*, you taught me that the gospel is much more than a ticket to a celestial mansion. Our message is a comprehensive balm for a fallen world. The book of Acts is a snapshot of our mission, and Acts 1:8 charts our course. *Dr. Dieumème Noelliste*, you fostered my affinity for theological ethics. When the world and even the church go astray, kingdom consciousness compels me to stand firm. *Dr. W. David Buschart*, I was under your tutelage while coping with my love-hate relationship with American evangelicalism. You spoke into the dysfunction by stressing the merits of theological retrieval. *Dr. Scott Wenig*, in the first hour of the first day of the first semester of church history class, you said, "You cannot be a good theologian without being a good historian." It was a formative moment. *Dr. Reginald Moore*, you tended incessantly to my mental health as I recovered from the heartache that prompted this book. During a trying time, you were implacable. *Dr. Mark Young* and *Dr. Randy MacFarland*, you were God's instruments of conciliation. You know what you did.

Finally, and chiefly, I offer my gratitude to the triune God— the Father who chose, the Son who redeems, and the Spirit who seals (Eph. 1:1–14). May the content of this book and the "meditation of my heart be pleasing in your sight, Lord, my Rock and my Redeemer" (Ps. 19:14). I pray my words will spotlight the *evangel*: Christ has come, and he reigns (Mark 1:15).

BRANDON WASHINGTON
January 1, 2023

NOTES

INTRODUCTION

1. Bruce Shelley, *Transformed by Love: The Vernon Grounds Story* (Grand Rapids: Discovery House, 2002), 99.
2. Martyn Whittock, "The Strange Decline of U.S. Evangelicalism," *Christian Today*, July 28, 2021, https://www.christiantoday.com/article/the.strange.decline.of.us.evangelicalism/137169.htm.
3. Robert Wald Sussman, *The Myth of Race: The Troubling Persistence of an Unscientific Idea* (Cambridge: Harvard University Press, 2014), 1–6, 11–42.
4. Jarvis Williams, "Biblical Steps toward Removing the Stain of Racism," in *Removing the Stain of Racism from the Southern Baptist Convention: Diverse African American and White Perspectives* (Nashville: B&H, 2017), 21; italics original.
5. "Frederick Douglass," *New York Times*, February 23, 1895, 3–4; Randall Kennedy, *Say It Loud! On Race, Law, History, and Culture* (New York: Pantheon, 2021), 234. Douglass's father was an unidentified white man. Douglass was never certain of his father's identity. It appears that he suspected Aaron Anthony, his mother's enslaver—making Douglass's mother a victim of bondage-rape. See David W. Blight, *Frederick Douglass: Prophet of Freedom* (New York: Simon & Schuster, 2018), 13–16.

6. Thomas averred that "negro intelligence is both superficial and delusive," and black people are, thus, disinclined "to make any valuable deductions." He concludes that the negro "lives wholly in his passions, and is never so happy as when enveloped in the glitter and gloss of shams." William Hannibal Thomas, *The American Negro: What He Was, What He Is, and What He May Become; A Critical and Practical Discussion* (New York: Macmillan, 1901), 106, 111; Kennedy, *Say It Loud!*, 140–53.

7. Sussman, *The Myth of Race*, 1–6.

8. Benjamin Isaac, *The Invention of Racism in Classical Antiquity* (Princeton: Princeton University Press, 2004), 23.

9. Ta-Nehisi Coates, *Between the World and Me* (New York: One World, 2015), 7.

10. Ta-Nehisi Coates, "What This Cruel War Was Over," *The Atlantic*, June 22, 2015, https://www.theatlantic.com/politics /archive/2015/06/what-this-cruel-war-was-over/396482/.

11. Teresa J. Guess, "The Social Construction of Whiteness: Racism by Intent, Racism by Consequence," *Critical Sociology* 32 no. 4 (2006): 660.

12. James M. McPherson, *Battle Cry of Freedom: The Civil War Era* (New York: Oxford University Press, 1988), 241, 234–75; Edward E. Baptist, *The Half Has Never Been Told: Slavery and the Making of American Capitalism* (New York: Basic Books, 2016), 390.

13. Lerone Bennett Jr., *Before the Mayflower: A History of the Negro in America, 1619–1962* (Eastford: Martino Fine, 2018).

14. W. E. B. Du Bois, *Black Reconstruction in America: 1860– 1880* (New York: Free Press, 1935, 1992), 700–701.

15. Ella Myers, "Beyond the Psychological Wage: Du Bois on White Dominion," *Political Theory* 47 (2019): 7.

16. Karen E. Fields and Barbara J. Fields, *Racecraft: The Soul of Inequality in American Life* (London: Verso, 2014), 18–20.

17. Italians and the Irish were considered racially ambiguous or "inconclusive." They weren't nonwhite, but they were a lesser

white. Matthew Frye Jacobson, *Whiteness of a Different Color: European Immigrants and the Alchemy of Race* (London: Harvard University Press, 1998), 4–6; Michael O. Emerson and Christian Smith, *Divided by Faith: Evangelical Religion and the Problem of Race in America* (Oxford: Oxford University Press, 2000), 7.

18. Jacobson, *Whiteness of a Different Color*, 3–6.
19. Brent Staples, "How Italians Became 'White,'" *New York Times*, October 12, 2019, https://www.nytimes.com/interactive/2019/10/12/opinion/columbus-day-italian-american-racism.html.
20. Jacobson, *Whiteness of a Different Color*, 56–59; Staples, "How Italians Became 'White.'"
21. Emerson and Smith, *Divided by Faith*, 7.
22. Trevin Wax, "Trevor Wax Interview with N. T. Wright," *The Gospel Coalition*, November 19, 2007, https://www.thegospelcoalition.org/blogs/trevin-wax/trevin-wax-interview-with-nt-wright-full-transcript/.
23. Mark A. Noll, *American Evangelical Christianity: An Introduction* (Oxford: Blackwell, 2001), 13.
24. W. David Buschart and Kent Eilers, *Theology as Retrieval: Receiving the Past, Renewing the Church* (Downers Grove, IL: IVP Academic, 2015), 15.
25. Gavin Ortlund, *Theological Retrieval for Evangelicals: Why We Need Our Past to Have a Future* (Wheaton, IL: Crossway, 2019), 13.
26. Thomas C. Oden, *A Change of Heart: A Personal and Theological Memoir* (Downers Grove, IL: IVP Academic, 2014), 138–39.

CHAPTER 1: FRATERNAL TWINS BUT ALOOF STRANGERS

1. Tony Evans, *Oneness Embraced: A Kingdom Race Theology for Reconciliation, Unity, and Justice* (Chicago: Moody, 2022), 112.
2. Brandon Washington, "Black and Evangelical: Why I Keep the

Label," *Christianity Today*, March 28, 2019, www.christianity
today.com/ct/2019/march-web-only/black-and-evangelical-why
-i-keep-label.html.

3. Carl F. H. Henry, *God, Revelation and Authority: God Who
Speaks and Shows*, vol. 4 (Wheaton, IL: Crossway, 1999), 551.

4. Russell Moore, "Losing Our Religion," *RussellMoore.com*,
April 15, 2021, www.russellmoore.com/2021/04/15/losing-our
-religion/.

5. With caveats, I use racial rhetoric in this book. For an explanation, see "Introduction."

6. Jarvis J. Williams, *Redemptive Kingdom Diversity: A Biblical
Theology of the People of God* (Grand Rapids: Baker Academic,
2021), 2–3.

7. Williams, *Redemptive Kingdom Diversity*, 108.

8. Vince Bantu, *A Multitude of All Peoples: Engaging Ancient
Christianity's Global Identity* (Downers Grove, IL: Inter-
Varsity, 2020), 1, 219–25; J. Daniel Hays, *From Every People
and Nation: A Biblical Theology of Race* (Downers Grove, IL:
InterVarsity, 2003), 181–200.

9. Scot McKnight, *Reading Romans Backwards: A Gospel of
Peace in the Midst of Empire* (Waco: Baylor University Press,
2019), 19.

10. Kate Shellnutt, "Two Prominent Pastors Break with SBC after
Critical Race Theory Statement," *Christianity Today*, December
18, 2020, www.christianitytoday.com/news/2020/december
/charlie-dates-ralph-west-southern-baptist-sbc-crt.html.

11. Michael O. Emerson and Christian Smith, *Divided by Faith:
Evangelical Religion and the Problem of Race in America*
(Oxford: Oxford University Press, 2000), 45–48.

12. Emerson and Smith, *Divided by Faith*.

13. Soong-Chan Rah, "Evangelical Futures," in *Still Evangelical?
Insiders Reconsider Political, Social, and Theological
Meaning*, ed. Mark Labberton (Downers Grove, IL:
InterVarsity, 2018), 92.

14. Evans, *Oneness Embraced*, 205.

15. Veli-Matti Kärkkäinen, *Trinity and Revelation* (Grand Rapids: Eerdmans, 2014), 3–5; Kenneth L. Archer, *A Pentecostal Hermeneutic: Spirit, Scripture, and Community* (Cleveland: CPT, 2005), 173.

16. Kärkkäinen, *Trinity and Revelation*, 3–5; Evans, *Oneness Embraced*, 89–119; Michael F. Bird, "Some Parts of Evangelicalism Do Not Need to Be Deconstructed . . . They Need to Be Destroyed! A Response to John Leeman," *Word from the Bird*, November 20, 2021, https://michaelfbird .substack.com/p/some-parts-of-evangelicalism-do-not?fbclid=I wAR0PA5BpoLL6bTQ7D9FoL7mx3jXmSXy4gKn9F4nUIMo QSu2PQvcX4L_Nkeo.

17. Michel-Rolph Trouillot, *Silencing the Past: Power and the Production of History* (Boston: Beacon, 2015), 1–30; Edward E. Baptist, *The Half Has Never Been Told: Slavery and the Making of American Capitalism* (New York: Basic Books, 2016), xviii–xxix.

18. Esau McCaulley, *Reading While Black: African American Biblical Interpretation as an Exercise in Hope* (Downers Grove, IL: InterVarsity, 2020); Carl Ellis, *Free at Last? The Gospel in the African American Experience* (Downers Grove, IL: InterVarsity, 1996).

19. Dennis R. Edwards, *Might from the Margins: The Gospel's Power to Turn the Tables on Injustice* (Harrisonburg, VA: Herald, 2020).

20. McCaulley, *Reading While Black*, 71–95; Ellis, *Free At Last?*, 84–91.

21. Drew G. I. Hart, *Who Will Be a Witness? Igniting Activism for God's Justice, Love, and Deliverance* (Harrisonburg, VA: Herald, 2020).

22. Imani Perry, *Prophets of the Word: Politics and Poetics in Hip Hop* (Durham: Duke University Press, 2004), 23, 60, 67, 107, 117, 148, 152–53.

23. Malcolm X with Alex Haley, *The Autobiography of Malcolm X* (New York: Ballantine, 1999).

24. Damon Richardson, "Nation of Islam," in *Urban Apologetics: Restoring Black Dignity with the Gospel*, ed. Eric Mason (Grand Rapids: Zondervan, 2021), 67–91; Elijah Muhammad, *Message to the Blackman in America* (Chicago: Muhammad's Temple No. 2, 1965), 100–122.

25. Brandon Washington, "Philosophy and Worldviews," in *Urban Apologetics: Restoring Black Dignity with the Gospel*, ed. Eric Mason (Grand Rapids: Zondervan, 2021), 189–203.

26. Hans-Georg Gadamer, *Truth and Method*, 2nd ed., trans. J. Weinsherimer and D. G. Marshall (London: Continuum, 2004), 17.

27. Nicholas O. Wolterstorff, "Empiricism" in *The Cambridge Dictionary of Philosophy*, ed. Robert Audi (Cambridge: Cambridge University Press, 1995), 224–25; Alan Lacey, "Empiricism" in *The Oxford Companion to Philosophy*, ed. Ted Honderich (Oxford: Oxford University Press, 1995), 226–29.

28. Emerson and Smith, *Divided by Faith*, 80–91.

29. Jemar Tisby, *The Color of Compromise: The Truth about the American Church's Complicity in Racism* (Grand Rapids: Zondervan, 2019), 15–17; Emerson and Smith, *Divided by Faith*, 14–17.

30. David Winston Swanson, *Rediscipling the White Church: From Cheap Diversity to True Solidarity* (Downers Grove, IL: InterVarsity, 2020), 30–35.

31. Campbell Robertson, "A Quiet Exodus: Why Black Worshipers Are Leaving White Evangelical Churches," *New York Times*, March 9, 2018, www.nytimes.com/2018/03/09/us/blacks -evangelical-churches.html.

32. CNN Editorial Research, "Trayvon Martin Shooting Fast Facts," *CNN*, February 17, 2021, www.cnn.com/2013/06/05 /us/trayvon-martin-shooting-fast-facts.

33. Voddie T. Baucham Jr., *Fault Lines: The Social Justice Movement and Evangelicalism's Looming Catastrophe* (Washington, DC: Salem, 2021), 113–30.

34. W. E. B. Du Bois masterfully delineates this sense of *otherness* or *differentness* as being "shutout from the [white] world by a vast veil." He asks, "Why did God make me an outcast and a stranger in my own house?" W. E. B. Du Bois, *The Souls of Black Folk* (New York: Dover, 1903, 1994), 1–2.

35. Henry, *God, Revelation and Authority*, 4:551.

36. Archer, *A Pentecostal Hermeneutic*, 173; Jürgen Moltmann, ed., *How I Have Changed: Reflections on Thirty Years of Theology* (Harrisburg, PA: Trinity Press International, 1997), 20.

37. E. Randolph Richards and Brandon J. O'Brien, *Misreading Scripture with Western Eyes: Removing Cultural Blinders to Better Understand the Bible* (Downers Grove, IL: InterVarsity, 2012), 9–27, 95–112.

38. Richards and O'Brien, *Misreading Scripture with Western Eyes*, 95–112; E. Randolph Richards and Richard James, *Misreading Scripture with Individualist Eyes: Patronage, Honor, and Shame in the Biblical World* (Downers Grove, IL: IVP Academic, 2020).

39. Harry Belafonte with Michael Shnayerson, *My Song: A Memoir* (New York: Alfred A. Knopf, 2011), 328–29; James Baldwin, *The Fire Next Time* (New York: Vintage International, 1993), 94.

40. Isabel Wilkerson, *The Warmth of Other Suns: The Epic Story of America's Great Migration* (New York: Random House, 2010), 36–42.

41. Andree K. Franklin, "King in 1967: My Dream Has 'Turned Into a Nightmare,'" *NBC News*, August 27, 2013, https://www.nbcnews.com/nightly-news/king-1967-my-dream-has-turned-nightmare-flna8c11013179.

42. Tisby, *The Color of Compromise*, 144–51.

43. Isabel Wilkerson, *Caste: The Origins of Our Discontents* (New York: Random House, 2020), 21–25, 29, 42, 64–68, 70–72, 74–75, 78–88, 101–8.

44. James M. Washington, ed., *A Testament of Hope: The Essential*

Writings and Speeches of Martin Luther King Jr. (San Francisco: HarperCollins, 1991), 123; Ellis, *Free At Last?*, 88–89.

45. Anders Walker, *The Ghost of Jim Crow: How Southern Moderates Used* Brown v. Board of Education *to Stall Civil Rights* (Oxford: Oxford University Press, 2009), 56–62.

46. J. Russell Hawkins, *The Bible Told Them So: How Southern Evangelicals Fought to Preserve White Supremacy* (New York: Oxford University Press, 2021), 14–42.

47. W. E. B. Du Bois, *Black Reconstruction in America: 1860–1880* (New York: Free Press, 1935, 1998).

48. Jarvis Williams, *Galatians* (Eugene, OR: Cascade, 2020), 61.

49. Jarvis Williams, *One New Man: The Cross and Racial Reconciliation in Pauline Theology* (Nashville: B&H Academic, 2010), 62–100, 140–41.

50. Evans, *Oneness Embraced*, 12–13, 17–18.

51. Ida Harris, "Code Switching Is Not Trying to Fit In to White Culture, It's Surviving It," *Yes Magazine!*, December 17, 2019, www.yesmagazine.org/opinion/2019/12/17/culture-code-switching/.

52. Swanson, *Rediscipling the White Church*, 37.

53. Jerome Gay, *The Whitewashing of Christianity: A Hidden Past, A Hurtful Present, and a Hopeful Future* (Chicago: 13th & Joan, 2021), 9–26; Bantu, *A Multitude of All Peoples*, 219–25.

54. Belafonte with Shnayerson, *My Song*, 329.

CHAPTER 2: THE EVANGELICAL MARKERS

1. Michael F. Bird, *Evangelicalism Theology: A Biblical and Systematic Introduction*, 2nd ed. (Grand Rapids: Zondervan Academic, 2020), xxv.

2. Mark Young, "Recapturing Evangelical Identity and Mission" in *Still Evangelical? Insiders Reconsider Political, Social, and Theological Meaning*, ed. Mark Labberton (Downers Grove, IL: InterVarsity, 2018), 55.

3. Mark A. Noll, *American Evangelical Christianity: An Introduction* (Oxford: Blackwell, 2001), 14–15.

4. Ronald J. Sider, *The Scandal of Evangelical Politics: Why Are Christians Missing the Chance to Really Change the World?* (Grand Rapids: Baker, 2008), 15–23.

5. Noll, *American Evangelical Christianity*, 15.

6. There are other categories, but we seem most obsessed with these. John S. Dickerson, *The Great Evangelical Recession: 6 Factors That Will Crash the American Church . . . and How to Prepare* (Grand Rapids: Baker, 2013), 21–35.

7. Dickerson, *Great Evangelical Recession*, 25–26.

8. Ed Stetzer, "Defining Evangelicals in Research," *Evangelicals Magazine*, Winter 2017/18, www.nae.net/defining-evangelicals-research/.

9. C. S. Lewis, *The Screwtape Letters* (New York: Simon & Shuster, 1961, 1996), 38–39.

10. John Fea, *Was America Founded as a Christian Nation? A Historical Introduction*, 2nd ed. (Louisville: Westminster John Knox, 2016); Mark David Hall, *Did America Have a Christian Founding? Separating Modern Myth from Historical Truth* (Nashville: Nelson, 2019), 1.

11. Thomas S. Kidd, *Who Is an Evangelical? The History of a Movement in Crisis* (New Haven: Yale University Press, 2019), 144–56.

12. Dickerson, *Great Evangelical Recession*, 24.

13. William Wilberforce, *Real Christianity* (Bloomington, MN: Bethany House, 2006), 19–25.

14. Lewis, *Screwtape Letters*, 39.

15. Andrew L. Whitehead and Samuel L. Perry, *Taking America Back for God: Christian Nationalism in the United States* (New York: Oxford University Press, 2020).

16. Bird, *Evangelicalism Theology*, 9.

17. Eric Mason, ed., *Urban Apologetics: Restoring Black Dignity with the Gospel* (Grand Rapids: Zondervan, 2021).

18. See John Thornhill, *Modernity: Christianity's Estranged Child Reconstructed* (Grand Rapids: Eerdmans, 2000).

19. Soong-Chan Rah, *The Next Evangelicalism: Releasing the*

Church from Western Cultural Captivity (Downers Grove, IL: InterVarsity, 2009), 41–43.

20. Adam Higginbotham, "The Inkjet Counterfeiter," *Wired Magazine*, May 10, 2009, https://www.wired.co.uk/article/the -inkjet-counterfeiter.

21. Higginbotham, "The Inkjet Counterfeiter."

22. Higginbotham, "The Inkjet Counterfeiter."

23. Carl F. H. Henry, *Architect of Evangelicalism: Essential Essays of Carl F. H. Henry* (Bellis, 2019), 11–16.

24. Henry, *Architect of Evangelicalism*, 11.

25. Mark Noll, "One Word but Three Crises," in *Evangelicals: Who They Have Been, Are Now, and Could Be*, ed. Mark Noll, David W. Bebbington, and George M. Marsden (Grand Rapids: Eerdmans, 2019), 1–9.

26. David W. Bebbington, *Evangelicalism in Modern Britain: A History from the 1730s to the 1980s* (London: Routledge, 2002), 1–2.

27. Noll, *American Evangelical Christianity*, 185.

28. Timothy Larsen, "Defining and Locating Evangelicalism," in *The Cambridge Companion to Evangelical Theology* (Cambridge: Cambridge University Press, 2007), 2.

29. Scot McKnight, *The King Jesus Gospel: The Original Good News Revisited* (Grand Rapids: Zondervan, 2011), 28–33.

30. Mark A. Noll, David W. Bebbington, and George A. Rawlyk, eds., "Introduction," in *Evangelicalism: Comparative Studies of Popular Protestantism in North America, The British Isles, and Beyond, 1700–1900* (New York: Oxford University Press, 1994), 6; italics mine.

31. David Bebbington, "The Nature of Evangelical Religion," in *Evangelicals: Who They Have Been, Are Now, and Could Be* (Grand Rapids: Eerdmans, 2019), 48.

32. Bebbington, "The Nature of Evangelical Religion," 48.

33. Bebbington, "The Nature of Evangelical Religion," 48.

34. E. Randolph Richards and Brandon J. O'Brien, *Misreading Scripture with Western Eyes: Removing Cultural Blinders to*

Better Understand the Bible (Downers Grove, IL: InterVarsity, 2012), 95–112.

35. Young, "Recapturing Evangelical Identity and Mission," 53–55.

36. Bruce L. Shelley, *Church History in Plain Language*, 5th ed., ed. Marshall Shelley (Grand Rapids: Zondervan Academic, 2020), 403–6, 504–5, 511–12.

37. Lisa Sharon Harper, "Will Evangelicalism Surrender?" in *Still Evangelical? Insiders Reconsider Political, Social, and Theological Meaning*, ed. Mark Labberton (Downers Grove, IL: InterVarsity, 2018), 20–21.

38. Larsen, "Defining and Locating Evangelicalism," 1.

39. Larsen, "Defining and Locating Evangelicalism," 1.

40. Larsen, "Defining and Locating Evangelicalism," 12.

41. Scot McKnight, "John MacArthur's Accusation against N. T. Wright," *Patheos*, July 10, 2017, https://www.patheos.com/blogs/jesuscreed/2017/07/10/john-macarthurs-accusations-nt-wright/.

42. Voddie Baucham Jr., *Fault Lines: The Social Justice Movement and Evangelicalism's Looming Catastrophe* (Washington, DC: Salem, 2021), 113–30; John MacArthur, "Foreword," in *Christianity and Wokeness: How the Social Justice Movement Is Hijacking the Gospel—and the Way to Stop It*, by Owen Strachan (Washington, DC: Salem, 2021), xix–xxi.

43. Moisés Silva, *New International Dictionary of New Testament Theology and Exegesis*, vol. 2, 2nd ed. (Grand Rapids: Zondervan, 2014), 306–13.

44. Stanley J. Grenz, *Revisioning Evangelical Theology: A Fresh Agenda for the 21st Century* (Downers Grove, IL: InterVarsity, 1993), 21–22; Jarvis Williams, "Biblical Steps toward Removing the Stain of Racism from the Southern Baptist Convention," in *Removing the Stain of Racism from the Southern Baptist Convention: Diverse African American and White Perspectives* (Nashville: B&H Academic, 2017), 31–39.

45. Bird, *Evangelical Theology*, xxv–xxx.

46. Jeremy R. Treat, *The Crucified King: Atonement and*

Kingdom in Biblical and Systematic Theology (Grand Rapids: Zondervan, 2014), 112–14; McKnight, *The King Jesus Gospel*, 92–100.

47. Treat, *The Crucified King*, 112–14; 214–17.
48. Tony Evans, *The Kingdom Agenda: Life Under God* (Chicago: Moody, 2013), 27–76.
49. Gavin Ortlund, *Theological Retrieval for Evangelicals: Why We Need Our Past to Have a Future* (Wheaton, IL: Crossway, 2019), 45.
50. Alister McGrath, *Evangelicalism and the Future of Christianity* (Downers Grove, IL: InterVarsity, 1949), 22.
51. Bebbington, "The Nature of Evangelical Religion," 31–55; Larsen, "Defining and Locating Evangelicalism," 1.

CHAPTER 3: HISTORY HAUNTS THE PRESENT

1. James Baldwin, "The White Man's Guilt," *Ebony* 20, no. 10 (August 1965): 47.
2. Jake Silverstein, "Why We Published the 1619 Project," *New York Times Magazine*, December 20, 2019, https://www.nytimes.com/interactive/2019/12/20/magazine/1619-intro.html.
3. Nikole Hannah-Jones et al., "The 1619 Project," *New York Times Magazine*, August 18, 2019, 14–22.
4. Silverstein, "Why We Published the 1619 Project."
5. Nicole Gaudiano, "Trump Creates 1776 Commission to Promote 'Patriotic Education,'" *Politico*, November 2, 2020, https://www.politico.com/news/2020/11/02/trump-1776-commission-education-433885; Elana Lyn Gross, "Trump Signs Executive Order to Establish a 1776 Commission to Instill 'Patriotic Education,'" *Forbes*, November 2, 2020, https://www.forbes.com/sites/elanagross/2020/11/02/trump-signs-executive-order-to-establish-a-1776-commission-to-instill-patriotic-education/?sh=4567cbf6dc3a.
6. Jack Brewster, "Trump's 1776 Commission—Created to Challenge Controversial 1619 Project—Release Report on MLK Day," *Forbes*, January 18, 2021, https://www.forbes.com/sites

/jackbrewster/2021/01/18/trumps-1776-commission-created-to
-challenge-controversial-1619-project—releases-report-on-mlk
-day/?sh=99bbba456fc9.

7. The President's Advisory 1776 Commission, *The 1776
   Report* (Monee, IL, 2021), 8–12, 23; Danielle S. Allen, *Our
   Declaration: A Reading of the Declaration of Independence in
   Defense of Equality* (New York: Liveright, 2014), 27.

8. John Fea, *Why Study History? Reflecting on the Importance
   of the Past* (Grand Rapids: Baker Academic, 2013), 3.

9. Carl R. Trueman, *Histories and Fallacies: Problems Faced in the
   Writing of History* (Wheaton, IL: Crossway, 2010), 14, 27–28.

10. The "Five Cs" of historiography are Context, Change over
    Time, Causality, Contingency, and *Complexity*; Fea, *Why
    Study History?*, 7–15.

11. Amanda Ripley, "Complicating the Narratives," *Solutions
    Journalism*, June 27, 2018 [Updated January 11, 2019], https://
    thewholestory.solutionsjournalism.org/complicating-the
    -narratives-b91ea06ddf63. Italics added.

12. Fea, *Why Study History?*, 2–6.

13. Paul A. Cohen, *History in Three Keys: The Boxers as Event,
    Experience, and Myth* (New York: Columbia University Press,
    1997), 7.

14. Fea, *Why Study History?*, 3.

15. Thomas S. Kidd, *American History: 1492–1877*, vol. 1
    (Nashville: B&H Academic, 2019), 122.

16. Ron Chernow, *Washington: A Life* (New York: Penguin,
    2010), 657–60; David McCullough, *John Adams* (New York:
    Simon & Schuster, 2001), 444–45; Ron Chernow, *Alexander
    Hamilton* (New York: Penguin, 2004), 314–18.

17. The French Republic devolved into an authoritarian regime
    under Napoléon Bonaparte; Jeremy D. Popkin, *The History of
    the French Revolution: The New World Begins* (New York:
    Basic Books, 2019), 555.

18. Chernow, *Washington*, 657–58; Ron Chernow, *Alexander
    Hamilton* (New York: Penguin, 2004), 314–18.

19. Trueman, *Histories and Fallacies*, 15.

20. Fea, *Why Study History?*, 3.

21. Allen C. Guelzo, *Reconstruction: A Concise History* (New York: Oxford University Press, 2018), 124.

22. Cohen, *History in Three Keys*, 7.

23. William Grimes, "Mortimer Adler, 98, Dies; Helped Create Study of Classics," *New York Times*, June 29, 2001, https://www.nytimes.com/2001/06/29/nyregion/mortimer-adler-98-dies-helped-create-study-of-classics.html.

24. Mortimer Jerome Adler and Charles Van Doren, *How to Read a Book* (New York: Touchstone, 2014), 230–32; D. A. Carson, *The Gagging of God* (Grand Rapids: Zondervan, 2011), 25.

25. Craig S. Keener, *Acts* (Cambridge: Cambridge University Press, 2020), 16.

26. Cohen, *History in Three Keys*, 4.

27. Trueman, *Histories and Fallacies*, 27, 171.

28. Craig Blomberg, *Jesus and the Gospels: An Introduction and Survey* (Nashville: Broadman & Holman, 2009), 159–60; Craig Blomberg and Darlene Seal, *From Pentecost to Patmos: An Introduction to Acts through Revelation* (Nashville: B&H, 2021), 9.

29. Keener, *Acts*, 3–22.

30. Luke probably used Mark and a text dubbed by many scholars as "Q." Keener, *Acts*, 3.

31. Keener, *Acts*, 14; N. T. Wright and Michael F. Bird, *The New Testament in Its World: An Introduction to the History, Literature, and Theology of the First Christians* (Grand Rapids: Zondervan Academic, 2019), 605.

32. Anthony C. Thiselton, *The Hermeneutics of Doctrine* (Grand Rapids: Eerdmans, 2007), xvii; Bernard C. Lategan, "Hermeneutics" in *The Anchor Bible*, vol. 3 (New York: Doubleday, 1992), 149.

33. Jens Zimmerman, *Hermeneutics: A Very Short Introduction* (Oxford: Oxford University Press, 2015), 1; Thiselton, *Hermeneutics of Doctrine*, xvii.

34. Lategan, "Hermeneutics," 149.

35. Zimmerman, *Hermeneutics*, 2; italics mine.

36. Zimmerman, *Hermeneutics*, 2, 12–18.

37. David W. Blight, *Frederick Douglass: Prophet of Freedom* (New York: Simon & Schuster, 2018), 229; Susan Kelley, "July Fourth and Early Black Americans: It's Complicated," *Cornell Chronicle*, July 2, 2021, https://news.cornell.edu /stories/2021/07/july-fourth-and-early-black-americans-its -complicated.

38. Blight, *Frederick Douglass: Prophet of Freedom*, 229.

39. Frederick Douglass, *Narrative of the Life of Frederick Douglass and the Fourth of July Speech* (Orinda: SeaWolf, 2020), 112.

40. D. H. Dilbeck, *Frederick Douglass: America's Prophet* (Chapel Hill: University of North Carolina Press, 2018), 80–85.

41. Ta-Nehisi Coates, *We Were Eight Years in Power: An American Tragedy* (New York: One World, 2017), 248.

42. Frederick Douglass, "Narrative of the Life of Frederick Douglass," in *Douglass: Autobiographies* (New York: Library of America, 1994), 84–96; Blight, *Frederick Douglass*, 202.

43. Blight, *Frederick Douglass*, 234–36; Kidd, *American History*, 1:212, 217, 223, 262.

44. Douglass, *Narrative of the Life of Frederick Douglass and the Fourth of July Speech*, 112.

45. Michel-Rolph Trouillot, *Silencing the Past: Power and the Production of History* (Boston: Beacon, 2015), 14–15; Ana Lucia Araujo, *Slavery in the Age of Memory: Engaging the Past* (New York: Bloomsbury Academic, 2019).

46. David W. Blight, *Race and Reunion: The Civil War in American Memory* (Cambridge, MA: Belknap, 2001), 78.

47. Clint Smith, *How the Word is Passed: A Reckoning with the History of Slavery Across America* (New York: Little, Brown, 2021).

48. Thiselton, *Hermeneutics of Doctrine*, xvii.

49. Hans-Georg Gadamer, *Truth and Method*, 2nd ed., trans.

J. Weinsheimer and D. G. Marshall (London: Continuum, 2004), 17.

50. Thiselton, *Hermeneutics of Doctrine*, xvii.

51. Gadamer, *Truth and Method*, 19–30.

52. Janice Kelsey, *I Woke Up with My Mind on Freedom* (Pittsburgh: Urban, 2017), v-viii.

53. Kelsey, *I Woke Up*, vi.

54. *I Am Not Your Negro*, DVD, directed by Raoul Peck, New York, Magnolia Pictures, 2017.

55. Blight, *Race and Reunion*, 77–84.

56. Paul Cohen, *History and Popular Memory: The Power of Story in Moments of Crisis* (New York: Columbia University Press, 2014).

57. Gina Wisker, "Remembering and Disremembering *Beloved*: Lacunae and Hauntings," in *Reassessing the Twentieth Century Canon: From Joseph Conrad to Zadie Smith*, ed. Nicola Allen and David Simmons (New York: Palgrave Macmillan, 2014), 266–80.

58. Nikole Hannah-Jones, "The Resegregation of Jefferson County," *New York Times Magazine*, September 6, 2017, https://www.nytimes.com/2017/09/06/magazine/the-resegregation-of-jefferson-county.html.

59. Beth Barton Schweiger, "Seeing Things: Knowledge and Love in History," in *Confessing History: Explorations in Christian Faith and the Historian's Vocation* (Notre Dame, IN: University of Notre Dame Press, 2010), 62.

60. Arnn et al., *The 1776 Report*, 36–37.

61. Fea, *Why Study History?*, 6–15.

62. Trueman, *Histories and Fallacies*, 146–52.

63. Cohen, *History in Three Keys*, xiv, 59–68, 211, 290; italics mine.

64. Cohen, *History in Three Keys*, 213.

65. D. A. Carson, ed., *NIV Zondervan Study Bible* (Grand Rapids: Zondervan, 2015), 2200–2206.

66. Darrell Bock asserts that Luke's genealogy is through Mary,

and Matthew's is through Joseph. Craig Blomberg maintains that both are through Joseph, who descends from David via two sons. While both views affirm Jesus's legal right to the throne and federal headship, I believe Blomberg's assertion has merit. Both Matthew and Luke identify Joseph as genealogically pivotal (Matt. 1:16; Luke 3:23). Blomberg, *Jesus and the Gospels*, 148–51, 164, 70; Darrell Bock, *Luke: 1:1–9:50* (Grand Rapids: Baker, 2004), 350.

67. Miroslav Volf, *The End of Memory: Remembering Rightly in a Violent World* (Grand Rapids: Eerdmans, 2006), 65; Schweiger, "Seeing Things," 62.

68. Volf, *End of Memory*, 18.

CHAPTER 4: THE GESTATION PERIOD AND A SEMINAL IDEOLOGY

1. Eddie S. Glaude Jr., *Begin Again: James Baldwin's America and Its Urgent Lesson for Our Own* (New York: Crown, 2020), 186.

2. W. E. B. Du Bois, *Black Reconstruction in America: 1860–1880* (New York: Free Press, 1998), 711–29.

3. Mark Charles and Soong-Chan Rah, *Unsettling Truths: The Ongoing, Dehumanizing Legacy of the Doctrine of Discovery* (Downers Grove, IL: InterVarsity, 2019), 12, 20.

4. Washington Irving, *The Life and Voyages of Christopher Columbus* (London: Forgotten, 2015), 40–47; Brent Staples, "How Italians Became 'White,'" *New York Times*, October 12, 2019, https://www.nytimes.com/interactive/2019/10/12/opinion/columbus-day-italian-american-racism.html.

5. Roxanne Dunbar-Ortiz, *An Indigenous Peoples' History of the United States* (Boston: Beacon, 2014), 4.

6. Andrés Reséndez, *The Other Slavery: The Uncovered Story of Indian Enslavement in America* (Boston: Mariner, 2016), 3–4.

7. Paul Ricoeur, *Hermeneutics and the Human Sciences*, ed. and trans. John B. Thompson (Cambridge: Cambridge University Press, 1981), 39.

8. Peter Railton, "Ideology," in *The Oxford Companion to*

Philosophy, ed. Ted Honderich (Oxford: Oxford University Press, 1995), 392–93.

9. Simon Blackburn, *Oxford Dictionary of Philosophy* (Oxford: Oxford University Press, 2016), 235.

10. C. S. Lewis, *The Four Loves* (New York: Harper One, 1960), 77; C.S. Lewis, *The Abolition of Man* (San Francisco: Harper San Francisco, 1974), 18, 43–44.

11. Robert J. Miller, *Native America, Discovered and Conquered: Thomas Jefferson, Lewis and Clark, and Manifest Destiny* (Lincoln: University of Nebraska Press, 2008), 1, 10.

12. James Muldoon, ed., *The Expansion of Europe: The First Phase* (Philadelphia: University of Pennsylvania Press, 1977); Miller, *Native America*, 13.

13. Donald Fairbairn, *The Global Church: The First Eight Centuries* (Grand Rapids: Zondervan Academic, 2021), 263–82.

14. Justo L. González, *The Story of Christianity*, vol. 2, *The Reformation to the Present Day*, revised and updated ed. (New York: HarperCollins, 2010), 7–8.

15. Justo L. González, *The Story of Christianity*, vol. 1, *The Early Church to the Dawn of the Reformation*, revised and updated ed. (New York: HarperCollins, 2010), 331.

16. Antony Anghie, *Imperialism, Sovereignty, and the Making of International Law* (Cambridge: Cambridge University Press, 2007), 19; Francisco de Vitoria, *Political Writings*, ed. Anthony Pagden and Jeremy Lawrance (Cambridge: Cambridge University Press, 1991), 239–40.

17. Edgar Prestage, *The Portuguese Pioneers* (London: Black, 1933), ix, 3.

18. Martin Meredith, *The Fortunes of Africa: A 5000-Year History of Wealth, Greed, and Endeavour* (New York: Public Affairs, 2014), 95.

19. Bruce L. Shelley, *Church History in Plain Language* (Grand Rapids: Zondervan, 2020), 168–77.

20. Thomas Asbridge, *The First Crusade, A New History: The*

Roots of Conflict between Christianity and Islam (Oxford: Oxford University Press, 2004), 11.

21. Joseph E. Harris, *Africans and Their History*, 2nd ed. (New York: Meridian, 1998), 96.

22. Willie James Jennings, *The Christian Imagination: Theology and the Origin of Race* (New Haven, CT: Yale University Press, 2010), 29. Italics added.

23. John Dickson, *Bullies and Saints: An Honest Look at the Good and Evil of Christian History* (Grand Rapids: Zondervan Reflective, 2021), 4–7; Asbridge, *First Crusade*, 1–39.

24. Meredith, *The Fortunes of Africa*, 94, 98. Italics added.

25. Kidd, *American History*, 1:8–9.

26. Jennings, *Christian Imagination*, 16.

27. J. M. Cohen, ed. and trans., *The Four Voyages of Christopher Columbus* (Harmondsworth, UK: Penguin, 1969), 37; Prestage, *Portuguese Pioneers*, 237.

28. Miller, *Native America*, 14.

29. Prestage, *Portuguese Pioneers*, 233–35; Robert J. Miller, Jacinta Ruru, Larissa Behrendt, and Tracey Lindberg, *Discovering Indigenous Lands: The Doctrine of Discovery in the English Colonies* (Oxford: Oxford University Press, 2010), 11.

30. Cohen, *Four Voyages of Christopher Columbus*, 12, 38; Prestage, *Portuguese Pioneers*, 234.

31. Kathleen Kuiper, ed., *Indigenous Peoples of the Arctic, Subarctic, and Northwest Coast* (New York: Rosen Educational Services, 2012), xiv; Edmund S. Morgan, *American Slavery, American Freedom: The Ordeal of Colonial Virginia* (New York: Norton, 2003), 301; Kidd, *American History*, 1:10.

32. Meredith, *Fortunes of Africa*, 116.

33. Cohen, *Four Voyages of Christopher Columbus*, 37–76, 90–92.

34. *New Oxford American Dictionary*, 3rd ed. (Oxford: Oxford University Press, 2010), 369.

35. Kidd, *American History*, 1:11.

36. Steven T. Newcomb, *Pagans in the Promised Land: Decoding*

the Doctrine of Christian Discovery (Golden, CO: Fulcrum, 2008), 51–52.

37. Kidd, *American History*, 1:11; Miller, *Native America*, 14–15.

38. David Abulafia, *The Discovery of Mankind: Atlantic Encounters in the Age of Columbus* (New Haven, CT: Yale University Press, 2009), 203–4.

39. Bartolomé de Las Casas, *A Short Account of the Destruction of the Indies*, trans. Nigel Griffin (London: Penguin, 1992), 14–17.

40. Elmina Castle was the first European slave-trading post in sub-Saharan Africa—known for the infamous "Door of No Return," the exit through which enslaved Africans boarded ships bound for the Americas. Kidd, *American History*, 1:8.

41. Reséndez, *The Other Slavery*, 23–25.

42. Jake Page, *The Hands of the Great Spirit: The 20,000-Year History of American Indians* (New York: Free Press, 2003), 111–12.

43. Cohen, *Four Voyages of Christopher Columbus*, 90–92.

44. Las Casas, *A Short Account of the Destruction of the Indies*, 14–17; Abulafia, *Discovery of Mankind*, 203–04.

45. Reséndez, *The Other Slavery*, 24–25.

46. K. Russell Lohse, "Mexico and Central America," in *The Oxford Handbook of Slavery in the Americas* (Oxford: Oxford University Press, 2010), 50; Jared Diamond, *Guns, Germs, and Steel: The Fates of Human Societies* (New York: Norton, 2005), 197, 210–14.

47. Meredith, *Fortunes of Africa*, 116–17.

48. Dickson, *Bullies and Saints*, xxii–xxiii.

49. Justo L. González, *The Story of Christianity*, 1:149–55.

50. Will Durant, *The Story of Civilization*, vol. 3, *Caesar and Christ, A History of Roman Civilization and of Christianity from Their Beginnings to A.D. 325* (New York: Simon & Schuster, 1944), 618–19. Italics mine.

51. J. W. C. Wand, *A History of the Modern Church from 1500 to the Present Day* (London: Methuen, 1971), 3.

CHAPTER 5: COLONIALISM AND SLAVERY

1. Frederick Douglass, "Life and Times of Frederick Douglass" in *Douglass: Autobiographies* (New York: The Library of America, 1994), 912.

2. S. Jonathan Bass, *Blessed Are the Peacemakers: Martin Luther King Jr., Eight White Religious Leaders, and the "Letter from Birmingham Jail"* (Baton Rouge: Louisiana State University Press, 2021), 265.

3. Martin Luther King Jr., *Why We Can't Wait* (New York: Signet Classics, 2000), 86, 90–93.

4. Alex Haley, *Roots: The Saga of an American Family* (New York: Doubleday, 1976), 212–44.

5. Orlando Patterson, *Slavery and Social Death: A Comparative Study* (Cambridge: Harvard University Press, 1982), 54–55.

6. Mark Charles and Soong-Chan Rah, *Unsettling Truths: The Ongoing, Dehumanizing Legacy of the Doctrine of Discovery* (Downers Grove, IL: InterVarsity, 2019), 19–20.

7. Kris Manjapra, *Colonialism in Global Perspective* (Cambridge: Cambridge University Press, 2020), 3, 29.

8. Steven T. Newcomb, *Pagans in the Promised Land: Decoding the Doctrine of Christian Discovery* (Golden: Fulcrum, 2008), 94.

9. Bartolomé de Las Casas, "Thirty Very Juridical Propositions," in *Introduction to Contemporary Civilization in the West*, vol. 1, 3rd ed., ed. Staff at Columbia College, Columbia University (New York: Columbia University Press, 1961); italics mine. Perhaps swayed by the appeals of Las Casas, King Charles I of Spain implemented laws regulating slavery in the Americas, but it was too late; any of the natives of the Caribbean islands were extinct or numerically endangered. The laws were hardly enforced and eventually forgotten. See Justo L. González, *The Story of Christianity*, vol. 2, *The Reformation to the Present Day*, 2nd ed. (New York: HarperCollins, 2010), 452–54.

10. Charles and Rah, *Unsettling Truths*, 8–10; Miller, *Native*

America, 2–3, 142–43; Newcomb, *Pagans in the Promised Land*, 51–52.

11. Immanuel Kant, *To Perpetual Peace: A Philosophical Sketch*, trans. Ted Humphrey (Indianapolis: Hackett, 2003), 16; italics mine.

12. Bruce Shelley, *Church History in Plain Language*, 5th ed., ed. Marshall Shelley (Grand Rapids: Zondervan Academic, 2020), 286.

13. Eamon Duffy, *Saints and Sinners: A History of the Pope*, 4th ed. (New Haven: Yale University Press, 2014), 185–86; italics mine.

14. See chapter 4; Miller, *Native America*, 12.

15. Roland H. Bainton, *Here I Stand: A Life of Martin Luther* (Nashville: Abingdon, 1978), 189–202, 293–305.

16. Shelley, *Church History in Plain Language*, 281.

17. Kidd, *American History*, 1:20–24.

18. González, *The Story of Christianity*, 2:90, 94–99.

19. Kidd, *American History*, 1:24–27.

20. Miller, *Native America*, 17–21.

21. Kidd, *American History*, 1:24, 25. Recent excavations of Jamestown discovered knife and fork marks on human bones, which may substantiate the whispers.

22. Paul Johnson, *A History of the American People* (New York: HarperCollins, 1997), 26.

23. James Horn, *1619: Jamestown and the Forging of American Democracy* (New York: Basic Books, 2018), 200–201.

24. Johnson, *History of the American People*, 25–28.

25. Peter Kolchin, *American Slavery: 1629–1877* (New York: Hill and Wang, 1993), 8.

26. Kidd, *American History*, 1:23–26.

27. Kidd, *American History*, 1:24, 26.

28. Johnson, *History of the American People*, 27.

29. Lerone Bennet Jr., *Before the Mayflower: A History of the Negro in America 1619–1962* (Eastford, CT: Martino Fine, 2018), 29.

30. Johnson, *History of the American People*, 26–27.

31. Kidd, *American History*, 1:26.

32. In the eighteenth and nineteenth centuries, the Southern United States was an unsubtle expression of the feudalistic vestiges. Plantations had a "master" and "slaves"; the relationship was a throwback to former times. Thomas Jefferson's Monticello, for instance, was a relic of medieval social structure. See Robert Yusef Rabiee, *Medieval America: Feudalism and Liberalism in Nineteenth-Century U.S. Culture* (Athens: University of Georgia Press, 2020), 1–59.

33. Kolchin, *American Slavery*, 14–5.

34. Johnson, *History of the American People*, 13–4, 27–8.

35. Kolchin, *American Slavery*, 14.

36. Joseph E. Harris, *Africans and Their History*, 2nd ed. (New York: Meridian, 1998), 81. Italics added.

37. Lorenzo J. Greene, *The Negro in Colonial New England* (New York: Columbia University Press, 2016), 167–90.

38. Kidd, *American History*, 1:23–33, 55.

39. Kolchin, *American Slavery*, 7. Italics added.

40. Marcus Rediker, *The Slave Ship: A Human History* (New York: Penguin, 2007), 41–72.

41. Kidd, *American History*, 1:55. Italics added.

42. Elizabeth McKellar, "Transatlantic Architecture: Classism, Colonialism, and Race," in *Art, Commerce and Colonialism 1600–1800*, ed. Emma Barker (Manchester: Manchester University Press, 2017), 153–54.

43. Paul Gilroy, *The Black Atlantic: Modernity and Double-Consciousness* (Cambridge: Harvard University Press, 1993).

CHAPTER 6: REASON OVER THEOLOGY

1. Elizabeth Alexander, *The Trayvon Generation* (New York: Grand Central, 2022), 4.

2. Alexander, *The Trayvon Generation*, 101–04.

3. Alexander, *The Trayvon Generation*, 104.

4. Thomas S. Kidd, *American History: 1492–1877*, vol. 1 (Nashville: B&H Academic, 2019), 20–22.

5. Norman Hampson, *The Enlightenment: An Evaluation of Its Assumptions, Attitudes, and Values* (New York: Penguin, 1990), 16–17.

6. M. J. Inwood, "Enlightenment," in *The Oxford Companion to Philosophy*, ed. Ted Honderich (Oxford: Oxford University Press, 1995), 236; italics mine.

7. Edmund S. Morgan, "The Puritan Ethic and the American Revolution," in *The Challenge of the American Revolution* (New York: Norton, 1978), 93.

8. Thomas C. Oden, *A Change of Heart: A Personal and Theological Memoir* (Downers Grove, IL: IVP Academic, 2014), 160; The Enlightenment and Romanticism combined to produce modernity; see Harold Netland, *Encountering Religious Pluralism: The Challenge to Christian Faith and Mission* (Downers Grove, IL: InterVarsity, 2001), 65–74.

9. Tom Shachtman, *Gentlemen Scientists and Revolutionaries: The Founding Fathers in the Age of Enlightenment* (New York: Palgrave Macmillan, 2014), xii–xiv, 187.

10. John Locke, *An Essay Concerning Human Understanding*, ed. Peter H. Nidditch (Oxford: Oxford University Press, 1975), 687–88, 700–706.

11. Charles Hodge, *Systematic Theology*, vol. 1 (Peabody, MA: Hendrickson, 1999), 1–17.

12. Michael F. Bird, *Evangelical Theology: A Biblical and Systematic Introduction*, 2nd ed. (Grand Rapids: Zondervan Academic, 2020), 9–12; italics mine.

13. Bird, *Evangelical Theology*, 13; italics mine.

14. Mortimer J. Adler, "A Philosopher Religious Faith," in *Philosophers Who Believe*, ed. Kelly James Clark (Downers Grove, IL: InterVarsity, 1993), 214–15; Alvin Plantinga, *Warranted Christian Belief* (New York: Oxford University Press, 2000).

15. Hampson, *The Enlightenment*, 15–17.

16. Saint Thomas Aquinas, *Summa Contra Gentiles, Book One: God*, trans. Anton C. Pegis (Notre Dame, IN: University of Notre Dame Press, 2012), 59; italics mine.

17. Dorinda Outram, *The Enlightenment* (Cambridge: Cambridge University Press, 2013), 67.

18. Thomas Aquinas, *Commentary on Aristotle's Politics*, trans. Richard H. Regan (Indianapolis: Hackett, 2007), 38; italics mine.

19. John Locke, *Two Treatises of Government*, ed. Peter Laslett (Cambridge: Cambridge University Press, 2017); Thomas Hobbes, *Leviathan* (Indianapolis: Hackett, 1994).

20. Outram, *The Enlightenment*, 67–83; Ivan Hannaford, *Race: The History of an Idea in the West* (Baltimore: Johns Hopkins University Press, 1995), xii, 6.

21. Thomas S. Kidd, *Thomas Jefferson: A Biography of Spirit and Flesh* (New Haven, CT: Yale University Press, 2022), 55.

22. Edmund S. Morgan, *The Meaning of Independence: John Adams, George Washington, and Thomas Jefferson* (Charlottesville: University of Virginia Press, 1976), 64.

23. Thomas Jefferson, *The Papers of Thomas Jefferson*, ed. Julian P. Boyd (Princeton: Princeton University Press, 1958), 14:492–92.

24. Morgan, *The Meaning of Independence*, 64.

25. Thomas Jefferson, *Notes on the State of Virginia* (New York: Penguin, 1999), 146.

26. Jefferson, *Notes on the State of Virginia*, 145–47.

27. Hannaford, *Race*, 6.

28. *The Uncomfortable Truth*, directed by Loki Mulholland, New York, Taylor Street Films, 2017, https://www.amazon.com /Uncomfortable-Truth-Loki-Mulholland/dp/B0751191PZ/ref =sr_1_1?crid=JQBF5M8TWEQL&keywords=400+years+of +racism&qid=1652564561&s=instant-video&sprefix=400 +years+of+racism%2Cinstant-video%2C149&sr=1–1.

29. George M. Marsden, *Jonathan Edwards: A Life* (New Haven: Yale University Press, 2003), 255; Douglas A. Sweeney, *Jonathan Edwards and the Ministry of the Word: A Model of Faith and Thought* (Downers Grove, IL: IVP Academic, 2009), 66.

30. Kenneth P. Minkema, "Jonathan Edwards on Slavery and the Slave Trade," *The William and Mary Quarterly* 54, no. 4 (1997): 825.

31. Kidd, *American History*, 61.

32. Sweeney, *Jonathan Edwards and the Ministry of the Word*, 68; Minkema, "Jonathan Edwards on Slavery," 825.

33. Minkema, "Jonathan Edwards on Slavery," 825.

34. Minkema, "Jonathan Edwards on Slavery," 826.

35. Thomas S. Kidd, *George Whitefield: America's Spiritual Founding Father* (New Haven, CT: Yale University Press, 2014), 1–2.

36. Peter Y. Choi, *George Whitefield: Evangelist for God and Empire* (Grand Rapids: Eerdmans, 2018), 127–68; Kidd, *George Whitefield*, 106–29, 188–90.

37. Choi, *George Whitefield*, 161.

38. Choi, *George Whitefield*, 145–48.

39. Robert Lewis Dabney, *Discussion* (Richmond: Presbyterian Committee of Publication, 1890–1897), 4:44; Robert Lewis Dabney, *A Defense of Virginia* (New York: Hale, 1867), 206.

40. Dabney, *Discussion*, 2:201.

41. Sean Michael Lucas, *Robert Lewis Dabney: A Southern Presbyterian Life* (Phillipsburg, NJ: P&R, 2005), 148–49.

42. John MacArthur, "The Consequences of Non-expositional Preaching, Part 1," *Grace to You*, February 22, 2009, https://www.gty.org/library/sermons-library/90–372/the -consequences-of-nonexpositional-preaching-part-1; Douglas Wilson, *Black and Tan: Essays and Excursions on Slavery, Culture War, and Scripture in America* (Moscow: Canon, 2005), 79–94; Steve Wilkins and Douglas Wilson, *Southern Slavery As It Was* (Moscow: Canon, 1996). I have a half-dozen "friends" who commended Wilson's work to correct my understanding of slavery. Wilson's views disproportionately depend on Dabney's historical and theological methods; he imbues Dabney's racist ideas with perennial life.

43. Lucas, *Robert Lewis Dabney*, 180–81; italics mine.

44. Lucas, *Robert Lewis Dabney*, 30.

45. Lucas, *Robert Lewis Dabney*, 179–82.

46. R. Albert Mohler Jr., "Conceived in Sin, Called by the Gospel: The Root Cause of the Stain of Racism in the Southern Baptist Convention" in *Removing the Stain of Racism from the Southern Baptist Convention: Diverse African American and White Perspectives*, ed. Jarvis J. Williams and Kevin M. Jones (Nashville: B&H Academic, 2017), 2–3. Italics added.

47. The Southern Baptist Theological Seminary, *Report on Slavery and Racism in the History of the Southern Baptist Theological Seminary*, December 12, 2018, https://www.sbts.edu/southern-project/. Italics added.

48. The Southern Baptist Theological Seminary, *Report on Slavery and Racism in the History of the Southern Baptist Theological Seminary*. Italics added.

49. Sarah Eekhoff Zylstra, "Presbyterian Church in America Apologizes for Old and New Racism," *Christianity Today*, June 24, 2016, https://www.christianitytoday.com/news/2016/june/pca-apologizes-for-new-and-old-racism.html.

50. Eric Mason, *Woke Church: An Urgent Call For Christians in America to Confront Racial Injustice* (Chicago: Moody, 2018), 99.

CHAPTER 7: CHAMPIONS, MONSTERS, OR BOTH?

1. John Dickson, *Bullies and Saints: An Honest Look at the Good and Evil of Christian History* (Grand Rapids: Zondervan Reflective, 2021), 44.

2. Clarissa Guy, "Denver's 'Harlem of the West,'" *Rocky Mountain PBS*, May 13, 2020, https://www.rmpbs.org/blogs/rocky-mountain-pbs/denvers-harlem-of-the-west/.

3. Thomas S. Kidd, *American History: 1492–1877*, vol. 1 (Nashville: B&H Academic, 2019), 106.

4. Julia Floyd Smith, *Slavery and Rice Culture in Low Country Georgia* (Knoxville: University of Tennessee Press, 1986).

5. David Blight, "History 119: The Civil War and Reconstruction

Era, 1845–1877, 'A Southern World View: The Old South and Proslavery Ideology,'" *Open Yale Courses*, Spring 2008, https://oyc.yale.edu/history/hist-119/lecture-3. Blight allows for the lines to be debatable and concedes the existence of localized slavery, particularly in Africa and Asia. But, in Blight's estimation, the larger slave societies were: (1) ancient Greece, (2) ancient Rome, (3) eighteenth-century Brazil, (4) the Great West Indies under the colonial reign of the French, British, Dutch, and Spanish, and (5) the American South.

6. David Blight, "History 119: The Civil War and Reconstruction Era, 1845–1877, 'Southern Slavery, King Cotton, and Antebellum America's 'Peculiar' Region,'" *Open Yale Courses*, Spring 2008, https://oyc.yale.edu/history/hist-119/lecture-2.

7. Blight, "Southern Slavery, King Cotton, and Antebellum America's 'Peculiar' Region"; italics mine.

8. Blight, "Southern Slavery, King Cotton, and Antebellum America's 'Peculiar' Region."

9. Kidd, *American History*, 1:170.

10. James McPherson, *Battle Cry of Freedom: The Civil War Era* (New York: Oxford University Press, 1988), 99–100; see Edward E. Baptist, *The Half Has Never Been Told: Slavery and the Making of American Capitalism* (New York: Basic Books, 2016), 171–76.

11. Fred Bateman and Thomas Weiss, *A Deplorable Scarcity: The Failure of Industrialization in the Slave Economy* (Chapel Hill: University of North Carolina Press, 1981), 3–4; See also Robert William Fogel and Stanley L. Engerman, *Time on the Cross: The Economics of American Negro Slavery* (New York: Norton, 1995), 274.

12. Bruce Shelley, *Church History in Plain Language*, 5th ed. (Grand Rapids: Zondervan Academic, 2020), 505–10.

13. Shelley, *Church History in Plain Language*, 505–10.

14. Shelley, *Church History in Plain Language*, 508–10.

15. Shelley, *Church History in Plain Language*, 508–10.

16. Francis Fitzgerald, *The Evangelicals: The Struggle to Shape America* (New York: Simon and Schuster, 2017), 310.

17. The neo-evangelicals launched Fuller Seminary and *Christianity Today* magazine.

18. Gustave Niebuhr, "Interracial Dating Ban to End at Bob Jones University," March 4, 2000, https://archive.nytimes.com/www .nytimes.com/library/national/030400bobjones-edu.html ?Partner=iVillage&RefId=LmyyW=jEFnnnnNnwm.

CHAPTER 8: ARE WE HITCHED TO A SICK HORSE?

1. Tony Evans, *Kingdom Agenda: Life under God* (Chicago: Moody, 2013), 29.

2. Gunnar Myrdal, *An American Dilemma: The Negro Problem and Modern Democracy* (New York: Routledge, 1944, 1962), 431.

3. The Emancipation Proclamation did *not* free all of the enslaved. It did not apply to the four slave states (Missouri, Delaware, Kentucky, Maryland) that remained loyal to the Union. "Nor did it free [enslaved persons] in certain Southern territories already under Union control." See Randall Kennedy, *Say It Loud! On Race, Law, History, and Culture* (New York: Pantheon, 2021), 256.

4. Myrdal, *An American Dilemma*, 431.

5. See Rayford W. Logan, *The Betrayal of the Negro: From Rutherford B. Hayes to Woodrow Wilson* (New York: Da Capo, 1997).

6. Myrdal, *An American Dilemma*, 1:220–50.

7. Allen C. Geulzo, *Reconstruction: A Concise History* (New York: Oxford University Press, 2018), 124.

8. Paul Johnson, *A History of the American People* (New York: Harper Collins, 1997), 549; Brooks D. Simpson, "Introduction" in *Reconstruction: Voices From Americas First Great Struggle For Racial Equality* (New York: Library of America, 2018), xxiii–xxix; Roy Morris, Jr., *Fraud of the*

Century: Rutherford B. Hayes, Samuel Tilden and The Stolen Election of 1876 (New York: Simon and Schuster, 2003).

9. Elaine Frantz Parson, *Ku Klux: The Birth of the Klan During Reconstruction* (Chapel Hill: University of North Carolina Press, 2015), 6, 20, 25, 160; See Linda Gordon, *The Second Coming of the KKK: The Ku Klux Klan of the 1920s and the American Political Tradition* (New York: Norton, 2017).

10. Geulzo, *Reconstruction*, 20–21, 110–14, 124; Eric Foner, *Reconstruction: America's Unfinished Revolution 1863–1877* (New York: Harper Perennial, 2014), 557–60.

11. Logan, *The Betrayal of the Negro*, 52.

12. W. E. B. Du Bois, *Black Reconstruction in America: 1860–1880* (New York: Free Press, 1935, 1992), 671–710.

13. Du Bois, *Black Reconstruction in America*, 30.

14. See Isabel Wilkerson, *The Warmth of Other Suns: The Epic Story of America's Great Migration* (New York: Random House, 2010).

15. William F. Buckley, "Why The South Must Prevail," *National Review*, August 24, 1957, 148–49.

16. Nicholas Buccola, *The Fire Next Time: James Baldwin, William F. Buckley Jr., and the Debate over Race in America* (Princeton: Princeton University Press, 2019), 14.

17. Buccola, *The Fire Next Time*, 14.

18. Buckley, "Why The South Must Prevail," 148–49; italics mine.

19. William F. Buckley also argued that many white people should not have the right to vote. In a debate with James Baldwin, he famously asserted, "The problem is not that there are not enough black voters, it's that there are too many white voters." His take on voting was not only racist; it was elitist.

20. See Roland Martin with Leah Lakins, *White Fear: How the Browning of America Is Making White Folks Lose Their Minds* (Dallas: BenBella, 2022).

21. Tim Keller, "How Do Christians Fit into the Two-Party System? They Don't," *New York Times*, September 29, 2018, https://

www.nytimes.com/2018/09/29/opinion/sunday/christians
-politics-belief.html.

22. Tim Keller, "How Do Christians Fit into the Two-Party
System? They Don't."

CHAPTER 9: DO WE HAVE A WHOLE GOSPEL?

1. Carl F. H. Henry, *God, Revelation and Authority: God Who
Speaks and Shows,* vol. 4 (Wheaton, IL: Crossway, 1999), 551.

2. Greg Gilbert, *What Is the Gospel* (Wheaton, IL: Crossway,
2010), 15–36.

3. Matthew W. Bates, *Gospel Allegiance: What Faith in Jesus
Misses for Salvation in Christ* (Grand Rapids: Brazos,
2019), 18.

4. Scot McKnight, *The King Jesus Gospel: The Original Good
News Revisited* (Grand Rapids: Zondervan, 2011), 28–34.

5. Jeremy R. Treat, *The Crucified King: Atonement and
Kingdom in Biblical and Systematic Theology* (Grand Rapids:
Zondervan, 2014), 220; Craig L. Blomberg, *Jesus and the
Gospels: An Introduction and Survey,* 2nd ed. (Nashville:
B&H Academic, 2009), 448–49.

6. Louis A. Barbieri Jr., "Matthew," in *The Bible Knowledge
Commentary: An Exposition of the Scriptures by Dallas
Seminary Faculty,* ed. John F. Walvoord and Roy B. Zuck
(Wheaton, IL: Victor, 1983), 93.

7. Roger Henderson, "Kuyper's Inch," *Pro Rege* 35, no. 3 (2008):
13–14; Abraham Kuyper affirmed Christ's reign, but his
understanding was somewhat sullied by his anthropology,
which prompted his theory of white supremacy. Commenting
on colonialism and apartheid in South Africa, Kuyper cites
"the superiority of every white race" among the virtues that
qualifies England's colonizing ventures. See Abraham Kuyper,
The South African Crisis (London: Stop the War Committee,
1900), 71.

8. Rodney Reeves, *Matthew: The Story of God Bible*

Commentary, ed. Tremper Longman III and Scot McKnight (Grand Rapids: Zondervan, 2017), 568.

9. Tony Evans, *The Kingdom Agenda: Life under God* (Chicago: Moody, 2013), 27–46.

10. Reeves, *Matthew*, 568; italics mine.

11. Ben Shapiro, "Pastor John MacArthur," on *The Ben Shapiro Show*, produced by *The Daily Wire*, December 1, 2018, https://www.dailywire.com/episode/sunday%20special%20ep-29-pastor-john-macarthur.

12. Ben Shapiro, "Pastor John MacArthur," *The Ben Shapiro Show*.

13. Mark A. Noll, *The Civil War as a Theological Crisis* (Chapel Hill: University of North Carolina Press, 2006), 81–84.

14. Blomberg, *Jesus and the Gospels*, 449.

15. Treat, *The Crucified King*, 220; italics mine.

16. Darrell L. Bock, *Luke*, vol. 1, *1:1–9:50* (Grand Rapids: Baker, 1994), 405–06; italics mine.

17. Blomberg, *Jesus and the Gospels*, 286–87.

18. Martin Luther King Jr., *Why We Can't Wait* (New York: Signet Classics, 2000).

19. McKnight, *The King Jesus Gospel*, 29.

20. Jarvis J. Williams, *One New Man: The Cross and Racial Reconciliation in Pauline Theology* (Nashville: B&H Academic, 2010).

21. Tony Evans, *Kingdom Agenda: Living Life God's Way* (Nashville: LifeWay, 2013), 29–30.

CHAPTER 10: IS CHRISTIANITY A WHITE MAN'S RELIGION?

1. Jerome Gay, "All White Everything," in *Urban Apologetics: Restoring Black Dignity with the Gospel*, ed. Eric Mason (Grand Rapids: Zondervan, 2021), 15.

2. William Dwight McKissic and Anthony T. Evans, *Beyond Roots II: If Anybody Ask You Who I Am* (Wenonah, NJ: Renaissance, 1994),125–46.

3. McKissic and Evans, *Beyond Roots II*, 7.

4. Thomas C. Oden, *How Africa Shaped the Christian Mind: Rediscovering the African Seedbed of Western Christianity* (Downers Grove, IL: InterVarsity, 2007), 16; Albert J. Raboteau, *Canaan Land: A Religious History of African Americans* (Oxford: Oxford University Press, 2001), 7.

5. Max Fisher, "A Revealing Map of The World's Most and Least Ethnically Diverse Countries," *The Washington Post*, May 16, 2013, https://www.washingtonpost.com/news/worldviews/wp /2013/05/16/a-revealing-map-of-the-worlds-most-and-least -ethnically-diverse-countries/.

6. John Thornton, *Africa and Africans in the Making of the Atlantic, 1400–1800* (New York: Cambridge University Press, 1998), 39.

7. Alemayehu Mekonnen, *The West and China in Africa: Civilization without Justice* (Eugene, OR: Wipf & Stock, 2015), 71.

8. Mekonnen, *The West and China in Africa*, 71.

9. Oden, *How Africa Shaped the Christian Mind*, 55–56.

10. Mekonnen, *The West and China in Africa*, 71.

11. Elizabeth Isichei, *A History of Christianity in Africa: From Antiquity to Present* (Grand Rapids: Eerdmans, 1995), 54.

12. Anton Wessels, *Europe: Was It Ever Really Christian?* (London: SCM, 2012), 3–4.

13. Oden, *How Africa Shaped the Christian Mind*, 14–17; Philip Jenkins, *The Lost History of Christianity: The Thousand-Year Golden Age of the Church in the Middle East, Africa, and Asia—and How It Died* (New York: HarperOne, 2009), 4.

14. Oden, *How Africa Shaped the Christian Mind*, 15.

15. John Parker and Richard Rathbone, *African History: A Very Short Introduction* (Oxford: Oxford University Press, 2007), 51.

16. Donald Fairbairn, *The Global Church: The First Eight Centuries; From Pentecost through the Rise of Islam* (Grand Rapids: Zondervan Academic, 2021), xv.

17. Jenkins, *The Lost History of Christianity*, 4.
18. Oden, *How Africa Shaped the Christian Mind*, 9. Italics added.
19. Oden, *How Africa Shaped the Christian Mind*, 9.
20. See Jerome Gay, *The Whitewashing of Christianity: A Hidden Past, a Hurtful Present, and a Hopeful Future* (Chicago: 13th & Joan, 2021).
21. J. Daniel Hays, *From Every People and Nation: A Biblical Theology of Race* (Downers Grove, IL: InterVarsity, 2003), 25.
22. Hays, *From Every People and Nation*, 27.
23. McKissic and Evans, *Beyond Roots II*, 95.
24. Hays, *From Every People and Nation*, 27.
25. Gay, *The Whitewashing of Christianity*, 110–29; McKissic and Evans, *Beyond Roots II*, 125–46.
26. Oden, *How Africa Shaped the Christian Mind*, 9.
27. A. Okechukwu Ogbonnaya, *On Communitarian Divinity: An African Interpretation of the Trinity* (New York: Paragon House, 1994), 53.
28. Oden, *How Africa Shaped the Christian Mind*, 9.
29. Philip Jenkins, *The Next Christendom: The Coming of Global Christianity*, 3rd ed. (Oxford: Oxford University Press, 2011), 21–26.
30. See Ogbonnaya, *On Communitarian Divinity*.
31. Jürgen Moltmann, *The Trinity and The Kingdom* (Minneapolis: Fortress, 1993), 132–137.
32. Mark Edwards, "Exegesis and the Early Christian Doctrine of the Trinity," in *The Oxford Handbook of the Trinity*, ed. Gilles Emery, OP, and Matthew Levering (Oxford: Oxford University Press, 2014), 84–86.
33. Ogbonnaya, *On Communitarian Divinity*, 51–72.
34. Ogbonnaya, *On Communitarian Divinity*, 52–53.
35. Moltmann, *The Trinity and the Kingdom*, 137–39.
36. T. A. Nobel, *Holy Trinity: Holy People; The Theology of Christian Perfecting* (Eugene, OR: Cascade, 2013), 213–19; Moltmann, *The Trinity and the Kingdom*, 16–20.

37. E. Randolph Richards and Brandon J. O'Brien, *Misreading Scripture with Western Eyes: Removing Cultural Blinders to Better Understand the Bible* (Downers Grove, IL: InterVarsity, 2012), 97; italics mine.

38. Hays, *From Every People and Nation*, 40.

39. Gay, *The Whitewashing of Christianity*, 46–47.

40. Hays, *From Every People and Nation*, 26.

41. Hays, *From Every People and Nation*, 106.

42. Hays, *From Every People and Nation*, 36.

43. J. Daniel Hays, "The Cushites: A Black Nation in Ancient History," *Bibliotheca Sacra* 153 (1996): 409.

44. Hays, *From Every People and Nation*, 94–5.

45. Hays, *From Every People and Nation*, 35–36; Ben Witherington III, *The Acts of the Apostles: A Socio-Rhetorical Commentary* (Grand Rapids: Eerdmans, 1998), 295.

46. Witherington, *Acts of the Apostles*, 346.

47. John B. Polhill, *Acts* (Nashville: B&H, 1995), 224.

48. Craig S. Keener, *Acts: An Exegetical Commentary*, 4 vols. (Grand Rapids: Baker, 2013), 2:1566; Hays, *From Every People and Nation*, 172–74.

49. Polhill, *Acts*, 226.

50. Harold Dollar, *St. Luke's Missiology: A Cross-Cultural Challenge* (Pasadena, CA: William Carey Library, 2012), 22.

51. Fairbairn, *Global Church*, 40.

52. Craig Keener, *The IVP Bible Background: New Testament*, 2nd ed. (Downers Grove: IVP Academic, 2014), 346; italics mine.

53. Craig Keener, *Acts: New Cambridge Bible Commentary* (Cambridge: Cambridge University Press, 2020), 329.

54. Darrell L. Bock, *Acts* (Grand Rapids: Baker Academic, 2007), 439; Keener, *Acts: New Cambridge Bible Commentary*, 330; Jerome Crowe, *From Jerusalem to Antioch: The Gospel across Cultures* (Collegeville, MN: Liturgical, 1997), 92.

55. Keener, *Acts: New Cambridge Bible Commentary*, 329.

56. Bock, *Acts*, 416; Witherington, *Acts of the Apostles*, 371.

CHAPTER 11: ARE THERE EXAMPLES OF ORTHO-BALANCE?

1. John Piper, "Brothers, Read Good Biography," *Desiring God*, January 1, 1995, https://www.desiringgod.org/articles/brothers -read-christian-biography.

2. Eric Washington, "Jarena Lee: Trailblazing African American Preacher and 'Self-made' Woman," *Christianity Today*, May 23, 2017, https://www.christianitytoday.com/history/people /pastorsandpreachers/jarena-lee.html.

3. See Phebe Davidson, "Jarena Lee (1783–18??)," *Legacy* 10, no. 2 (1993), 135–141; National Museum of African American History & Culture, "Jarena Lee and the Early A.M.E. Church," *Smithsonian*, https://nmaahc.si.edu/explore/stories /jarena-lee-and-early-ame-church.

4. Thomas Kidd, *American History: 1429–1877*, vol. 1 (Nashville: B&H Academic, 2019), 121, 150.

5. Justo L. González, *The Story of Christianity: The Reformation to the Present Day*, vol. 2, 2nd ed. (New York: HarperCollins, 2010), 335.

6. Bruce Shelley, *Church History in Plain Language*, 5th ed., ed. Marshall Shelley (Grand Rapids: Zondervan Academic, 2020), 454.

7. Richard Allen, "Life Experiences and Gospel Labors," in *African American Religious History: A Documentary Witness*, 2nd ed., ed. Milton C. Sernett (Durham: Duke University Press, 1999), 139–154; Kidd, *American History*, 1:121.

8. González, *Story of Christianity*, 2:335.

9. See Matt Carter and Aaron Ivey, *Steal Away Home: Charles Spurgeon and Thomas Johnson, Unlikely Friends on the Passage to Freedom* (Nashville: B&H, 2017).

10. G. Holden Pike, *The Life and Work of Charles Haddon Spurgeon*, vol. 2 (London: Cassell, 1900), 331.

11. Pike, *Life and Work of Charles Haddon Spurgeon*, 331.

12. Arnold Dallimore, *Spurgeon: A New Biography* (Carlisle, PA: Banner of Truth, 1985), 96–97.

13. Charles Haddon Spurgeon, *Surgeon's Autobiography:*

Compiled from His Diary, Letters, and Records by His Wife and His Private Secretary, 1878–1892, vol. 4 (Philadelphia: American Baptist Publication Society), 132. Italics added.

14. See Carl F. H. Henry, *The Uneasy Conscience of Modern Fundamentalism* (Grand Rapids: Eerdmans, 1947, 2003).

15. See Carl Trueman, "Admiring the Sistine Chapel: Reflections on Carl F. H. Henry's God, Revelation and Authority," *Themelios* 25, no. 1 (2000).

16. Carl F. H. Henry, *God, Revelation and Authority: God Who Speaks and Shows*, vol. 4 (Wheaton, IL: Crossway, 1999), 551.

17. Stanley J. Grenz, "Biographical Information," *stanleygrenz.com*, https://www.stanleyjgrenz.com/bio/bio.html.

18. Wolfhart Pannenberg, *Theology and the Kingdom of God*, ed. Richard John Neuhaus (Louisville: Westminster John Knox, 1969).

19. Wolfhart Pannenberg, *Systematic Theology*, vol. 2 (Edinburgh: Eerdmans, 1994), 271–72.

20. Pannenberg, *Systematic Theology*, 2:271.

21. Stanley Grenz, *Reason for Hope: The Systematic Theology of Wolfhart Pannenberg* (New York: Oxford University Press, 1990), 9. Italics added.

22. Jason S. Sexton, *The Trinitarian Theology of Stanley Grenz* (London: Bloomsbury T&T Clark, 2013), 57–66, 87–120.

23. Stanley J. Grenz, *Theology for the Community of God* (Grand Rapids: Eerdmans, 2000), 508. Italics added.

24. W. Wyeth Willard, *Fire on the Prairie: The Story of Wheaton College* (Wheaton, IL: Van Kamoer, 1950), 25–34.

25. Willard, *Fire on the Prairie*, 20.

26. Jennifer Grant, "School's Past Comes to Light," *Chicago Tribune*, November 12, 2009, https://www.chicagotribune.com/news/ct-xpm-2009-11-13-0911110459-story.html.

27. Grant, "School's Past Comes to Light."

28. David B. Malone, "Passing Generations: Struggles for Equality at an Abolitionist School," *Wheaton Magazine* 21, no. 2 (Spring 2018).

29. See Vernon C. Grounds, *Evangelicalism and Social Responsibility* (Scottdale, PA: Herald, 1969, 1972).

30. Vernon Grounds, "Is Love in the Fundamentalist Creed," *Eternity* 5 No. 6 (1950).

31. Grounds, *Evangelicalism and Social Responsibility*, 16.

32. Grounds, *Evangelicalism and Social Responsibility*, 4.

33. Bruce L. Shelley, *Transformed by Love: The Vernon Grounds Story* (Grand Rapids: Discovery House, 2002), 85–102.

34. Shelley, *Transformed By Love*.

35. Thomas Jefferson, "Thomas Jefferson to Thomas Cooper, September 10, 1814," in *The Papers of Thomas Jefferson* (Princeton: Princeton University Press, 2004), 7:652.

36. Eric Washington, "Olaudah Equiano's Argument against Slavery Was His Life Experience," *Christianity Today*, May 14, 2019, https://www.christianitytoday.com/history/2019 /june/olaudah-equiano-slave-memoir-trade-interesting -narrative.html.

37. See Frederick Douglass, *Autobiographies: Narrative of the Life of Frederick Douglass, An American Slave / My Bondage and My Freedom / Life and Times of Frederick Douglass* (New York: Library of America, 1992); Sojourner Truth, *Narrative of Sojourner Truth* (New York: Penguin, 1998); Olaudah Equiano, "The Interesting Narrative of the Life of Olaudah Equiano or Gustavas Vassa, The African, Written by Himself," in *The Classic Slave Narratives*, ed. Henry Louis Gates Jr. (New York: Signet Classics, 2002), 1–215; Phyllis Wheatley, *Complete Writings* (New York: Penguin, 2001).

38. Equiano, "The Interesting Narrative," 60.

CHAPTER 12: IS RIGHT BELIEF ENOUGH?

1. Grounds, *Evangelicalism and Social Responsibility*, 14–16.

2. Michael F. Bird, *Evangelical Theology: A Biblical and Systematic Introduction*, 2nd ed. (Grand Rapids: Zondervan Academic, 2020), xxv. Italics added.

3. Philip Jenkins, *The Next Christendom: The Coming of Global Christianity* (Oxford: Oxford University Press, 2011).

4. Billy Graham, *Just as I Am: A Biography* (New York: Harper Collins, 1997), xvii–xviii.

5. Bartolomé de Las Casas, "Thirty Very Juridical Propositions," in *Introduction to Contemporary Civilization in the West*, vol. 1, 3rd ed., ed. Staff at Columbia College, Columbia University (New York: Columbia University Press, 1961).

6. Vernon Grounds, "Is Love in the Fundamentalist Creed? The Forgotten Fundamental of Neighbor-Love Must Be Restored to Its Supreme Place in Christian Behavior," *Eternity Magazine*, June 1954, 13–14, 41–42.

7. Dennis R. Edwards, *Might from the Margins: The Gospel's Power to Turn the Tables on Injustice* (Harrisonburg, VA: Herald, 2020), 15–16.

8. Bird, *Evangelical Theology*, xxvi.

9. Jarvis Williams, "Biblical Steps toward Removing the Stain of Racism," in *Removing the Stain of Racism from the Southern Baptist Convention: Diverse African American and White Perspectives* (Nashville: B&H, 2017), 28–31.

10. Jeremy R. Treat, *The Crucified King: Atonement and Kingdom in Biblical and Systematic Theology* (Grand Rapids: Zondervan, 2014), 49.

11. Bruce L. Shelley, *Church History in Plain Language*, 5th ed., ed. Marshall Shelley (Grand Rapids: Zondervan Academic, 2020), 504.

12. The Southern Christian Leadership Conference (SCLC), the Student Nonviolent Leadership Committee (SNCC), the Congress of Racial Equality (CORE), and the Council of Federated Organizations (COFO) all cited Christian convictions as motivation for their mission; Charles Marsh, *The Beloved Community: How Faith Shapes Social Justice, From the Civil Rights Movement to Today* (New York: Basic Books, 2005), 2–4.

13. "Segregation or Integration: Which?" presented by Jerry Falwell, Thomas Road Baptist Church, Lynchburg, VA, 1958.

14. "Segregation or Integration: Which?" presented by Jerry Falwell, Thomas Road Baptist Church, Lynchburg, VA, 1958.

15. Philip Jenkins, *The Next Christendom: The Coming of Global Christianity*, 3rd ed. (Oxford: Oxford University Press, 2011), xi.

16. Jenkins, *Next Christendom*, 1.

17. Jenkins, *Next Christendom*.

18. Bird, *Evangelical Theology*, xxvi.

19. Jenkins, *Next Christendom*, 1–6.

20. Michael O. Emerson and Christian Smith, *Divided by Faith: Evangelical Religion and the Problem of Race in America* (Oxford: Oxford University Press, 2000), 44–48.

21. Ben Shapiro and John MacArthur, "The Ben Shapiro Show Sunday Special," episode 29, *The Daily Wire*, December 1, 2018, https://www.dailywire.com/episode/sunday%20special%20ep-29-pastor-john-macarthur.

22. See St. Basil the Great, *On Social Justice* (Crestwood, NY: St. Vladimir's Seminary Press, 2009).

23. E. Randolph Richards and Brandon J. O'Brien, *Misreading Scripture with Western Eyes: Removing Cultural Blinders to Better Understand the Bible* (Downers Grove, IL: InterVarsity, 2012), 9–27, 95–112.

24. Jenkins, *Next Christendom*, 23.

25. Jenkins, *Next Christendom*, 29.

26. Jenkins, *Next Christendom*, 30–31.

27. W. David Buschart and Kent D. Eilers, *Theology of Retrieval: Receiving the Past, Renewing the Church* (Downers Grove: IVP Academic, 2015), 12–13.

28. Gavin Ortlund, *Theological Retrieval for Evangelicals: Why We Need Our Past to Have a Future* (Wheaton, IL: Crossway, 2019), 45.

29. Michael Foust, "'Any Real True Believer' Will Support Trump in November, John MacArthur Says," *Christian Headlines*,

August 25, 2020, https://www.christianheadlines.com
/contributors/michael-foust/any-real-true-believer-will-support
-trump-in-november-john-macarthur-says.html.

30. Zion McGregor, "Why the Black Church Must Be Relevant," in
Urban Apologetics: Restoring Black Dignity with the Gospel,
ed. Eric Mason (Grand Rapids: Zondervan, 2021), 55, 62.